# International Organizations

D0223410

What is the role of international organizations in the international political system?

The fourth edition of Clive Archer's widely used textbook continues to provide students with an introduction to international organizations, exploring their rise and development, and accounts for their significance in the modern international political system.

*International Organizations* fourth edition:

- has been fully updated to take into account the considerable developments in the field since the last edition was published in 2001.
- continues to offer a unique, concise yet comprehensive approach, providing students with an accessible and manageable introduction to this core part of international relations.
- offers an authoritative guide to the literature about international organizations and provides advice on further reading.

**Clive Archer** was, until 2009, Research Professor at Manchester Metropolitan University and is now a freelance researcher and writer.

'In the transnational, globalized world of the twenty-first century international organizations play an increasingly important role in world politics. Clive Archer skilfully explores that role—its history, development, and future prospects—in a clear and accessible way, as only he can as an expert in international cooperation, the European Union, and the Nordic zone of peace.'

Harvey Starr, *Dag Hammarskjöld Professor in International Affairs, University of South Carolina, US*

'An established leading text for decades, regularly updated and steadily building on the core working definitions, classifications and functions of international organizations: concise and comprehensive.'

Bob Reinalda, *Senior Researcher in Political Science, Radboud University, Nijmegen, The Netherlands*

# International Organizations
## Fourth edition

**Clive Archer**

Routledge
Taylor & Francis Group

LONDON AND NEW YORK

First published 1983

Fourth edition published 2015
by Routledge
2 Park Square, Milton Park, Abingdon, Oxon OX14 4RN

and by Routledge
711 Third Avenue, New York, NY 10017

*Routledge is an imprint of the Taylor & Francis Group, an informa business*

*British Library Cataloguing in Publication Data*
A catalogue record for this book is available from the British Library

*Library of Congress Cataloging in Publication Data*
  Archer, Clive
  International Organizations / Clive Archer. – 3rd ed
  p.cm
  Rev. ed. of: International organizations / Clive Archer.
  2nd ed. London; New York: Routledge 1992.
  Includes bibliographical references and index
  1. International agencies. I. Archer, Clive. International
  Organizations. II. Title.
  JZ4850.A73  2001
  341.2 – dc21

ISBN: 978-0-415-61475-7 (hbk)
ISBN: 978-0-415-61476-4 (pbk)
ISBN: 978-1-315-75151-1 (ebk)

Typeset in Garamond Three
by Florence Production Ltd, Stoodleigh, Devon, UK

# Contents

# Illustrations

## Tables

## Figures

# Preface to fourth edition

Previous editions of this book after the first edition have reflected major changes internationally. The period since the third edition in 2001 has seen the war on terror, the invasions of Afghanistan and Iraq, great power incursions into Georgia, Libya, Mali and Ukraine and further turmoil in the Middle East. China and some Global South states have continued their economic growth, but others found it hard to weather the post–2007 recession. Meanwhile the electronic media have thrived. Environmental degradation and climate change still haunt the planet.

These events add to the history but do not affect the working definition of international organizations (Chapter 1); neither have they upset the classification of these institutions (Chapter 2). Chapter 3 on the writings about international organizations has adopted the division of works in the third edition. Chapter 4 on the roles and functions of international organizations also reflects some of the events since 2001 mentioned above. The list of abbreviations and the bibliography have also been updated.

As with previous editions, all views expressed in this book – except when otherwise indicated – are mine and I am responsible for any mistakes. I am still indebted to those who helped me with previous editions. I am grateful to the anonymous commentators who provided suggestions for this edition, to Mark Webber and Lee Miles, and to Craig Fowlie and Peter Harris of Taylor & Francis for their help and encouragement. I am particularly thankful to my wife, Elizabeth, for her help with the index and for all her support.

# Abbreviations

## (Including selective UN operations)

| | |
|---|---|
| ACP | African, Caribbean and Pacific states |
| ANC | African National Congress |
| ASEAN | Association of South–East Asian Nations |
| AU | African Union |
| BINGOs | business international non–governmental organizations |
| BIS | Bank for International Settlements |
| CMEA | Council for Mutual Economic Assistance |
| DPKO | Department of Peacekeeping Operations (of the UN) |
| EC | European Communities |
| ECE | Economic Commission for Europe (of the UN) |
| ECJ | Court of Justice of the European Union |
| ECLAC | Economic Commission for Latin America and the Caribbean (of the UN) |
| ECOSOC | Economic and Social Council (of the UN) |
| ECOWAS | Economic Community of West African States |
| ECSC | European Coal and Steel Community |
| EEA | European Economic Area |
| EFTA | European Free Trade Association |
| EMU | Economic and Monetary Union (of the EU) |
| EU | European Union |
| FAO | Food and Agriculture Organization |
| FRA | European Agency for Fundamental Rights |
| GATT | General Agreement on Tariffs and Trade |
| GCC | Gulf Cooperation Council (Cooperation Council for the Arab States of the Gulf) |
| IBRD | International Bank of Reconstruction and Development |
| ICES | International Council for the Exploration of the Seas |
| ICJ | International Court of Justice |
| IDA | International Development Association |
| IEA | International Energy Agency |
| IFC | International Finance Corporation |
| IFOR | Implementation Force |
| IGO | intergovernmental organization |
| ILO | International Labour Organization |
| IMF | International Monetary Fund |
| INGO | international non–governmental organization |
| INTELSTAT | International Telecommunications Satellite Organization |

| | |
|---|---|
| INTERPOL | International Criminal Police Organization |
| IPPF | International Planned Parenthood Federation |
| ITO | International Trade Organization |
| ITU | International Telecommunications Union (formerly International Telegraphic Union) |
| IUCN | International Union for Conservation of Nature and Natural Resources |
| IULA | International Union of Local Authorities |
| IWC | International Whaling Commission |
| MINURSO | United Nations Mission for the Referendum in Western Sahara |
| MINUSMA | United Nations Multidimensional Integrated Stabilization Mission in Mali |
| MINUSTAH | United Nations Stabilization Mission in Haiti |
| MNC | multinational corporation |
| MNE | multinational enterprise |
| MONUSCO | United Nations Organization Stabilization Mission in the Democratic Republic of the Congo |
| NATO | North Atlantic Treaty Organization |
| NEAFC | North East Atlantic Fisheries Commission |
| NIEO | New International Economic Order |
| OAS | Organization of American States |
| OAU | Organization of African Unity |
| OECD | Organization for Economic Cooperation and Development |
| ONUC | Operations des Nations Unies au Congo (United Nations Operation in the Congo) |
| ONUCA | United Nations Observer Group in Central America |
| ONUMOZ | United Nations Operation in Mozambique |
| ONUSAL | United Nations Observer Group in El Salvador |
| OPCW | Organization for the Prohibition of Chemical Weapons |
| OPEC | Organization of the Petroleum Exporting Countries |
| OSCE | Organization for Security and Co–operation in Europe |
| PCIJ | Permanent Court of International Justice |
| PLO | Palestine Liberation Organization |
| QMV | qualified majority voting |
| SEATO | Southeast Asia Treaty Organization |
| SFOR | Stabilization Force |
| TGO | transgovernmental organization |
| TNC | transnational corporation |
| TNO | transnational organization |
| UIA | Union of International Associations |
| UN | United Nations |
| UNAMA | United Nations Assistance Mission in Afghanistan |
| UNAMID | African Union/United Nations Hybrid Operation in Darfur |
| UNAVEM | United Nations Angola Verification Mission |
| UNCED | United Nations Conference on Environment and Development |
| UNCHE | United Nations Conference on the Human Environment |
| UNCI | United Nations Commission for Indonesia |
| UNCLOS | United Nations Conference on the Law of the Sea |

| | |
|---|---|
| UNCTAD | United Nations Conference on Trade and Development |
| UNDOF | United Nations Disengagement Observer Force |
| UNEF | United Nations Emergency Force |
| UNESCO | United Nations Educational, Scientific and Cultural Organization |
| UNFICYP | United Nations Force in Cyprus |
| UNICEF | United Nations Children's Fund |
| UNIDO | United Nations Industrial Development Organization |
| UNIFIL | United Nations Interim Force in Lebanon |
| UNIIMOG | United Nations Iran–Iraq Military Observer Group |
| UNIKOM | United Nations Iraqi–Kuwait Observation Mission |
| UNIPOM | United Nations India–Pakistan Observation Mission |
| UNISFA | United Nations Interim Security Force for Abyei (Sudan) |
| UNMIBH | United Nations Mission in Bosnia and Herzegovina |
| UNMIH | United Nations Mission in Haiti |
| UNMIL | United Nations Mission in Liberia |
| UNMOGIP | United Nations Military Observer Group in India and Pakistan |
| UNOCI | United Nations Operation in Côte d'Ivoire |
| UNOMIL | United Nations Observer Mission in Liberia |
| UNOMSIL | United Nations Mission in Sierra Leone |
| UNOSOM | United Nations Operation in Somalia |
| UNPREDEP | United Nations Preventive Deployment Force (in Macedonia) |
| UNPROFOR | United Nations Protection Force |
| UNSF | United Nations Security Force in West New Guinea |
| UNSMIH | United Nations Support Mission in Haiti |
| UNTAC | United Nations Transitional Authority in Cambodia |
| UNTAES | United Nations Transitional Administration for Eastern Slavonia, Baranja and Western Sirmium |
| UNTAET | United Nations Transitional Administration in East Timor |
| UNTAG | United Nations Transition Assistance Group (in Namibia) |
| UNTMIH | United Nations Transition Mission in Haiti |
| UNTSO | United Nations Truce Supervisory Organization |
| UPU | Universal Postal Union |
| USSR | Union of Soviet Socialist Republics |
| WEU | Western European Union |
| WHO | World Health Organization |
| WMO | World Meteorological Organization |
| WTO | Warsaw Treaty Organization ('Warsaw Pact') |
| WTO | World Trade Organization |
| WWF | World Wide Fund for Nature |

# 1 Definitions and history

## Definitions

Both words in the title of this book have been a source of puzzlement for the student of international relations. It is worth examining them more closely before turning to the realities they represent when joined together. The term 'international', thought to be the creation of Jeremy Bentham, is often seen as a misnomer. Instead, it is claimed, the term 'interstate' or 'intergovernmental' should be used when describing an activity – war, diplomacy, relations of any kind – conducted between two sovereign states and their governmental representatives. Thus talk of an 'international agreement' between state A and state B to limit arms production or to control the selling of computer technology refers not to an understanding between the armament manufacturers of A and B nor to a pact between their computer firms, but to an arrangement by state A's governmental representatives with those of state B.

This state- and government-oriented view of the word 'international' has been increasingly challenged over the past four decades, as will be seen in Chapter 3. It is no longer used synonymously with 'intergovernmental' to mean 'interstate' or relations between the official representatives of sovereign states. Instead the term has come to include activities between individuals and groups in one state and individuals and groups in another state, as well as intergovernmental relations. The first types of relationships – those not involving activities between governments only – are known as transnational relations (Keohane and Nye 1971). Connections between one branch of government in one state (say a defence ministry) and a branch of government in another country (its defence ministry or its secret service, for example), which do not go through the normal foreign policy-making channels, are called transgovernmental. All these relationships – intergovernmental, transnational and transgovernmental – are now usually included under the heading 'international'.

The dual meaning of its singular form, and its interchanging in many books with the word 'institutions', confuses the use of the term 'organizations'. International relations, whether between governments, groups or individuals, are not totally random and chaotic but are, for the main part, organized. One form of the organization of international relations can be seen in institutions – 'the collective forms or basic structures of social organization as established by law or by human tradition' (Duverger 1972: 68) – whether these be trade, commerce, diplomacy, conferences or international organizations. An international organization in this context represents a form of institution that refers to a formal system of rules and objectives, a rationalized administrative instrument (Selznick 1957: 8) and which has 'a formal technical and material organization: constitutions, local chapters, physical equipment, machines, emblems, letterhead stationery, a staff, an administrative hierarchy and so forth' (Duverger 1972: 68). Inis Claude (1964: 4) makes the following distinction: 'International *organization* is a process; international *organizations* are representative aspects of the phase of that process which has been reached at a given time.'

Some writers confusingly refer to such international organizations as international institutions; also reference is often made to 'the institutions' of an organization, such as its assembly, council and secretariat. This use of 'institutions' to refer to the detailed structure of an international organization or as a synonym for international organizations is more restricted than the sociological meaning of the word. As can be seen from Duverger's definition, it has a wider use that encompasses the notion of a system of relationships that may not manifest themselves in formal organizations of bricks and mortar, headed notepaper, a ready acronym such as NATO or WHO, and an international staff. An institutional framework adds 'stability, durability and cohesiveness' to individual relationships which otherwise might be 'sporadic, ephemeral, and unstable' (Duverger 1972: 68). In personal life these institutions that bind people together may be represented by an organization such as the Mothers' Union, the Roman Catholic Church, or a trade union organization, but may also take the form of the less formal structures of the family, of a religion or of work conditions. At an international level, relations may be given a 'stability, durability and cohesiveness', in other words they may be organized, by the practice of diplomatic method or adherence to the tenets of international law or by regular trading – all institution in the wider sense – as well as by the activities of such international organizations as the World Movement of Mothers, the World Council of Churches or the International Labour Organization (ILO).

Regimes in international relations are defined as 'sets of implicit or explicit principles, norms, rules, and decision making procedures around which actors' expectations converge in a given area of international relations' (Krasner 1983: 2). They thus fulfil Duverger's wider definition of institutions but they need not be formalized in international organizations. However, it is normally the case that regimes in the areas of trade, finance, arms control or the environment *do* include international organizations. Krasner himself gives the example of the General Agreement on Trade and Tariffs (GATT) that helped regulate international trade. It was an international agreement rather than an organization but it was later formalized into an international organization, the World Trade Organization, established in 1995 (www.wto.org/).

International regimes and international organizations, together with diplomacy, have helped to create aspects of global governance which has been increasingly discussed since the end of the twentieth century. Finkelstein (1995: 369) gives a simple definition: 'Global governance is governing, without sovereign authority, relationships that transcend national frontiers.' A more involved explanation by Thakur and Weiss (2006) points to the embedding of international organizations, both international organizations (IOs) and international non-governmental organizations (INGOs), within this notion:

> the complex of formal and informal institutions, mechanisms, relationships, and processes between and among states, markets, citizens and organizations, both inter- and non-governmental, through which collective interests on the global plane are articulated.

It is worth noting that the concept of global governance has been taken up by international organizations such as the UN (www.unhistory.org/briefing/15GlobalGov.pdf), OECD (www.oecd.org/governance/oecdglobalforumonpublicgovernance.htm) and the Food and Agriculture Organization (www.fao.org/news/story/en/item/154300/icode/).

This book is concerned not so much with the broader notions of international organization, international institutions and international regimes, but with the more concrete manifestation of regularized international relations as seen in international organizations with their formal and material existence separate from, though for the most part dependent on, states and groups within states.

## International organizations up to the First World War

Accounts of the rise of international organizations rarely begin historically in 1919 at the Versailles Peace Conference, but it is a good time and place to start. Gathered together after the First World War were the representatives of the victorious powers ready to write a peace treaty; many national interest groups; and INGOs wanting to advance public health, the lot of the workers, the cause of peace or the laws of war. The states' representatives were also concerned to create a new, permanent world organization that would deal with the problem of peace and security and with economic and social questions. They drew on almost a century of experience of peacetime co-operation between European states and some half-century of the work of the public international unions. Their activity was underpinned by the existence of private international associations, was foreshadowed in the Hague conferences of 1899 and 1907 and in plans advanced before and during the First World War, and was moulded by the wartime experience of co-operation. The organizations they established – the League of Nations and the ILO being the leading ones – had structures determined by this background. This brief history will examine the lead-up to the creation of the League of Nations: the rise of INGOs, the parallel growth of public international unions with their major interest in economic and social questions, and the role of IGOs in dealing with peace and security up to 1919. The historical development of international organizations since that date will then be examined to demonstrate the growth of INGOs, economic and social IGOs, and IGOs involved with peace and security.

The gathering at Versailles in 1919 was primarily an intergovernmental meeting of heads of state and government, foreign ministers and their advisers. It was mostly concerned with the question of international peace and security, while economic and social questions were given only perfunctory consideration. The conference was faced with the task of writing a peace treaty and organizing relations between states after the most momentous breakdown in interstate relationships in history: the First World War. This war had arrived after a century of comparative peace since the defeat of Napoleon in 1815, during which time a number of forms of international organization had burgeoned. The rise of the phenomenon of intergovernmental organizations concerned with international peace and security and with economic and social issues needs some explanation.

An understanding of the reasons why these organizations started to grow in the nineteenth century can be reached by asking the question: why were there no interstate organizations prior to that time? The most obvious reason is that these organizations had to await the creation of a relatively stable system of sovereign states in Europe. The crucial turning point was the Peace of Westphalia, 1648, ending the Thirty Years'

War, which had torn apart late medieval Europe. Prior to 1648, the concept of a unified Christian Europe dominated the thinking, if not the practice, of political life in Europe (Bozeman 1960: 514; Davies 1997: 7–10 and chs 6 and 7; Hinsley 1967, chs 1 and 8). The waning temporal power of the Catholic Church headed by the papacy and of the Holy Roman Empire demonstrated the difficulties of unifying such a diverse geographical area as the continent of Europe, even when its peoples were threatened by the march of the Muslim Ottoman Empire. Despite this, a form of unity was offered by the doctrine of a God-given natural law above mankind, adherence to which provided an opportunity for Christian rulers and their subjects to belong to a greater commonwealth.

With the questioning and later rejection of natural law tenets by certain philosophers, and with the 'civil war' between Christian princes from 1618 to 1648, the prospect of a politically united Europe faded into the past. The Peace of Westphalia and the Treaty of Utrecht in 1713 laid the basis for the sovereign state system in Europe, a system later extended to the rest of the world. This system recognized the right of states with defined geographical boundaries, including more or less settled populations (territoriality), to have their own forms of government (non-intervention) and to conduct relations with one another on an equal legal basis (sovereign equality). Most rulers no longer utilized the natural law to guide relations between states but instead the concept emerged of an international law founded on the practice of states voluntarily making mutual agreements based either on treaty or on custom. 'The Westphalia conception includes the idea that national governments are the basic source of order in international society.' For international relations it means 'decentralised control by sovereign states' (Falk 1969: 68–9).

Given the existence of the sovereign state system, why did governments not create a network of international organizations throughout the eighteenth century? Claude (1964: 17) sets four preconditions before such action could be taken: the existence of a number of states functioning as independent political units; a substantial measure of contact between these subdivisions; an awareness of problems that arise from states' co-existence; and their recognition of 'the need for creation of institutional devices and systematic methods for regulating their relations with each other'. Only the first of these prerequisites manifestly existed before the nineteenth century. A form of diplomacy existed between the courts of the European powers, and trade and travel grew throughout Europe during the eighteenth century (Berridge 2002). The measure of contact built up between states in the 150 years following Westphalia could scarcely be described as substantial, and an all-too-common form of contact was warfare. It has been calculated that there were sixty-seven significant wars in the period from 1650 to 1800, a time particularly noticeable for the large number of major wars in which great powers participated on each side (Wright 1965: 636–51).

The international system that existed outside Europe before the area was integrated into the European system in the nineteenth century also showed little propensity for creating international organizations. The various arrangements of the Chinese Empire ranging from the feudal system of the Western Chou period (starting some 1,100 years BCE) to the imperial rule of the Manchus (from the latter half of the seventeenth century until the revolution of 1912); the divided warring India of the statesman Kautilya (about 300 BCE) to that of the decaying Mogul Empire of the seventeenth century; and the Muslim Ottoman Empire, were all familiar with war, trade, alliances, federations and even forms of diplomacy, but none produced the permanent institutions of international organizations. One possible exception is the Amphictyonic Councils of ancient Greece

> which were something between a Church Congress, an Eisteddfod and a meeting of the League of Nations Assembly ... Although the main purpose of these conferences, as of the permanent secretariat which they maintained, was the safeguarding of shrines and treasures and the regulation of the pilgrim traffic, they also dealt with political matters of common Hellenic interest and, as such, had an important diplomatic function.
>
> (Nicolson 1969: 18–19)

A forerunner of humanitarian international organizations can possibly be seen in the Knights of St John of Jerusalem (also known as the Order of Malta) who administered hospitals in the Holy Land during the Crusades from the twelfth century to the thirteenth century. They later had their headquarters in the Mediterranean islands of Rhodes, Cyprus and Malta before being based in Rome. However, it seems that this international order (drawn from citizens of many European states) exercised elements of sovereignty over areas in which it operated, and indeed claims a sovereign existence even today (Beigbeder 1992: 61–3).

Apart from these examples, the various polities in the systems mentioned, as in those of pre-nineteenth-century Europe, found that contact with other political units was either in a belligerent form or, if peaceful, could be satisfied by the skills of the merchants and the occasional envoy. In 1786 Thomas Jefferson, later to become US president, proposed an international naval fleet under the control of a council of ministers and an ambassadorial committee in order to control the pirates of the Barbery states in North Africa. However, the idea demanded co-operation between hostile European states and the establishment of a fleet funded by quotas at a time when national navies were often short of money (Szasz 1981).

The reasons why the nineteenth century provided such fertile ground in Europe for international organizations can be found in Claude's final two points: an awareness of the problems of states' co-existence and the recognition of the need for means different from those already used to regulate relationships. Governments' growing acceptance of new devices with which to conduct their relations arose partly out of the changed political situation post-1815 and partly from economic and social developments.

### Peace and security

First, the Vienna Congress of 1814–15 codified the rules of diplomacy, thereby establishing an accepted mode of regular peaceful relationships among most European states. This was an important development in one of the key institutions governing interstate relations, turning diplomacy from a rather discredited activity to one that served the international system as well as the individual state (Nicolson 1969, ch. 1).

The American Revolution, which led to the independence of the United States of America in 1776, and to the French Revolution of 1789, brought into play novel political factors on the international scene. Previously the important European states had been monarchies of one form or another; the interests of the state and those of the ruler were held to be convergent. Cromwell's Commonwealth in England deviated from this pattern and in 1689, when certain British political leaders considered King

James II unsatisfactory, a new dynasty was installed. Still it was the King's parliament, the King's army and the King's peace that existed in England. The two revolutions in America and France made a change by popularizing the state. The state no longer, even in legal theory, had to be the property or the trust of a monarch. It could be the instrument of popular will: 'Governments are instituted among Men, deriving their just Powers from the Consent of the Governed, that whenever any form of Government becomes destructive of these ends, it is the Right of the People to alter or to abolish it' (The American Declaration of Independence).

There were immediate and noticeable effects on international relations by these two revolutions: the victory of the American settlers weakened Britain; the new revolutionary France was soon at war with the rest of Europe, and Napoleon (the son of the Revolution and Madame Guillotine) had marched his armies across Europe from Iberia to Russia, from the Mediterranean to the Baltic. It took the combined might of Austria, Britain, Prussia and Russia to defeat Napoleon and to restore the pre-revolutionary monarchy to France.

The representatives of the victorious powers, meeting at Vienna in 1814–15, had the details of a peace treaty to prepare, but they also had wider problems for consideration. They had had to combine in order to defeat Napoleon and to prevent him from turning Europe into a French empire. Their temporary unity had overcome their foe and given them a chance to return to a system of sovereign states based on the Westphalian concept. The states represented at the Congress of Vienna took the opportunity of standardizing and codifying the rules of diplomatic practice and pronouncing on other problems in the international system, such as slavery. Their major contribution, however, was their mutual promise to 'concert together' against any future threat to the system. By Article VI of the Treaty of Chaumont (1814), Austria, Britain, Prussia and Russia

> agreed to renew at fixed intervals, either under the immediate auspices of the Sovereigns themselves or by their respective Ministers, meetings for the examination of the measures which at each of these epochs shall be considered most salutary for the repose and propriety of the Nations and for the maintenance of the peace of Europe.
>
> (Hinsley 1967: 195)

Previously, states' representatives had met to sign peace treaties at the end of a war, but the agreement that emerged after the Congress of Vienna was to meet in times of peace to prevent war. After 1815 the Great Powers met together to discuss questions such as Greek independence and revolution in the Italian peninsula. Furthermore, the gatherings were regular – 'at fixed intervals' – another novel concept for governments.

These congress meetings, as they were termed, saw a diplomatic struggle between Britain, represented by Foreign Minister Castlereagh, and the Holy Alliance of the reactionary rulers of Austria, Prussia and Russia over the aims and methods of common action. The Russian Czar's idea of the Great Powers intervening in Europe to uphold the status quo was opposed relentlessly by Castlereagh, who was more appreciative of the forces of change in Europe (Davies 1997: 762–3). Eventually what emerged from the congress system was the looser format of the Concert of Europe, with the Great Powers consulting together on problems as they arose rather than trying to pre-empt them at regular meetings. The concept remained of a group of powerful countries discussing questions of mutual interest at a gathering of ambassadors or members of government: this was an innovative improvement on traditional bilateral diplomacy. Despite this innovation, many of the decisions concerning war and peace during the nineteenth century were made in the chanceries of Europe with little prior discussion with other governments, except to arrange alliances.

During the third quarter of the nineteenth century there was a reversion to holding international meetings after conflict rather than using them to prevent a war. The Paris Peace Conference ended the Crimean War in 1856, Vienna in 1864 ended the Schleswig-Holstein War, Prague the Seven Weeks' War in 1866, and Frankfurt brought to a close the Franco-Prussian War in 1871. However, the thirty-five years before the start of the First World War saw the Great Powers of Europe again trying to avoid conflict by mutual agreement: the Berlin Congress of 1878, after the Russo-Turkish War, attempted a more long-term settlement of the Balkan question; the Berlin Congress of 1884–85 agreed on the division of Africa; and the Algeciras Conference in 1906 temporarily relieved pressure over rival claims in North Africa. But these gatherings did little to ease the basic tensions between the Great Powers: their growing empires and wish for expansion, their alliances and their increased military might.

The period from the end of the congress system in 1822 to the First World War was, however, not one of a straightforward descent into Armageddon. Apart from powers continuing the practice established by the Concert of Europe of meeting together to decide matters of general European concern, there were other landmarks which demonstrated the efforts of governments to take a more organized approach to the problems of peace and security. A factor pressing states in this direction was the internationalization of the European system. Northedge (1976: 73–5) has discerned seven major stages in this process of expansion, starting with the Treaty of Paris in 1783 by which the United States received international recognition. Of these seven steps, five were taken before the start of the twentieth century: the inclusion of the United States; the recognition in 1823 of the new Latin American states by Canning, Britain's Foreign Secretary; the admission of the Ottoman Empire (and Romania) into the Concert of Europe system by the Treaty of Paris, 1856; Japan's joining the system after the opening-up of that country by Commodore Perry in 1853; and the imposition in the mid-nineteenth century of diplomatic relations and unequal treaties by Britain on China, thereby making it a rather unwilling member of the internationalized European system.

This extension of the system faced the leaders of the major European powers with a dilemma. In seeking to control events within Europe, they could continue holding conferences among themselves, admitting to the negotiating chamber any other power with an obvious interest. Such intimate arrangements were less likely to work if the number of powers in attendance doubled or tripled, and if these representatives came from lands outside the central stage of Europe. Yet if general rules for the maintenance of the state system were to be successful, either the non-European states had to be forced to follow the wishes of the Great Powers (as happened with China in the mid-nineteenth century) or they would have to be given the chance to subscribe voluntarily to the tenets. The latter option was taken up in the Declaration of Paris at the end of the Crimean War in 1856; this established the principle of free navigation for traders on all international rivers and also dealt with the question of naval warfare, the abolition of privateering, rules for neutral flags in times of war and blockades. As Hinsley (1967: 233) comments:

To be effective these rules required the accession of other states beyond the signatories of the Declaration (the Great Powers, including Turkey, and Sardinia); fourteen other states acceded to them in 1856, Japan in 1886, Spain in 1908, Mexico, in 1909.

Furthermore, Protocol 23 of the Treaty stated:

> the desire that States . . . should, before appealing to arms, have recourse, so far as circumstances allow, to the good offices of a friendly power. The Plenipotentiaries hope that governments not represented at the Congress will unite in the sentiment which has inspired the desire recorded in the Protocol.

How much easier to bring other governments into general agreements from the beginning; and how much more sensible to have meetings about these matters convened separately from a congress primarily aimed at ending a war. Such thoughts were scarcely the main motivating force behind Czar Nicholas of Russia's call in 1898 for an international conference to discuss disarmament – he was more concerned with the ability of his own country to stand the financial strain of the arms race. Twenty-seven states attended this conference and, while most of them were European countries, China, Japan, Mexico, Siam (now Thailand) and the United States also sent representatives. The Second Hague Conference of 1907 drew a response from forty-four states, including eighteen Latin American countries (Brown 1909: 528).

Although the Hague meetings did not prevent the catastrophe of August 1914, they did produce some modest achievements and also pointed the way for the institutional development of organized international relations (Best 1999: 619–34). A panel of arbitrators was established with the intention of making their services available on a regular basis and the First Conference adopted a Convention for the Pacific Settlement of International Disputes. Precedents for such moves can be found in the Alabama Case (1871), when Britain and the United States settled a dispute by arbitration rather than conflict; the Pan-American Conference of 1889, at which seventeen North American and Latin American states tried to establish an arbitration tribunal for disputes but ended up with an agreement on ad hoc tribunals; and the Anglo-American Arbitration Treaty negotiated in 1897. The latter two attempts were not very successful – the Pan-American agreement was signed by eleven states and only ratified by one; the Arbitration Treaty was subject to stringent British reservations and failed to obtain the approval of the US Senate (Hinsley 1967: 267–8).

Despite these meagre results, the Hague conferences and the corresponding American efforts still represented an advance in the method of arranging relations between states (Best 1999: 619–34). Hinsley (1967: 266) points out the increase in the number of arbitration treaties post-1870 and the need to regularize international contacts by states new to the 'comity of nations' as being the driving force behind the legalistic approaches of the Hague and inter-American conferences. Claude (1964: 26), describing the Hague conferences as meeting in an 'atmosphere heavy with unreality', underlines the diplomatic difficulties in the way of any state wishing to turn down the Czar's invitation. Whatever the motivation for the Hague meetings, once government representatives were there, they experienced the innovation of conference diplomacy even with recommendations ('*voeux*') being passed by a majority vote. The legalistic notions behind the Hague concept – that the creation of the correct institutions to make judgments on international disputes would contribute significantly to peace – were later to inspire the Permanent Court of International Justice (PCIJ) and the International Court of Justice (ICJ) and the wide membership of the two conferences was a precursor of the League of Nations' Assembly. The verdict of Claude is that

> the abortive system of the Hague called attention to the emerging reality of a global, rather than a merely European, state system, the demands of small states for participation in the management of that system and the need for institutionalized procedures as well as improvised settlements, in the conduct of international relations.

> (Claude 1964: 28)

This is a superficially attractive opinion but it is perhaps far-fetched in typifying Hague as anything resembling a global state system – even an emerging one. It was more a demonstration that the European state system, with European-based law, European diplomacy and other European institutions, had been extended to include outsiders. While the conferences certainly brought out the demands of smaller states and 'the need for institutionalized procedures' – presumably new procedures such as arbitration – the continuation of Great Power diplomacy in Europe, North Africa, the Middle East and China demonstrated that the time was not then ripe for the general adoption of such changes. The concert system of the early part of the century may have lasted to the end of the nineteenth century, but by then it only masked struggles and complex alliances. It was too much to expect the Hague meetings to reverse completely this downward spiral. While the methods used at the Hague and some of the recommendations were useful models for later consideration, the two conferences primarily indicated the limits reached in the institutionalization of international relations by the end of the nineteenth century. A system so imbued by the primacy of the needs of individual governments and which had passed over the idea of collective action implied in the Concert of Europe for the more straightforward and ruthless advancement of state interest was scarcely a good breeding ground for institutional innovation.

## Economic and social questions

In the area of economic and social matters, the nineteenth century was also a period of growth in international co-operation. Another consequence of the French revolution and the Napoleonic Empire lay in the popularization of the state as already mentioned. It seems far-fetched to claim that during the post-Napoleonic period, 'the advance of democratic ideas, the belief that all human beings were of equal value, fostered the notion of egalitarian participation by all states in international organizations responsible for ensuring peace and progress' (Gerbet 1977: 11). However, the French – and indeed the American – Revolution made the state more responsive to the needs of a wider section of the population. The demands of the new middle class, let alone the working class, were not just for a nightwatchman state. Political liberalism in the nineteenth century built on strands of Christian belief in advancing ideas of social justice (Beigbeder 1992: 11–12). By the end of the nineteenth century, a number of European governments were increasingly intervening in the economies of their countries and were becoming more involved with the welfare of their citizens, a fact that was to be reflected in their international relationships. J.M. Keynes (1919) wrote of the pre-1914 world economy: 'the internationalization of economic life was almost complete'.

During the nineteenth century, the states of Europe were, of necessity, fashioning new means for co-operation over the issues of peace and conflict and were being faced with a growing need to co-ordinate action in the socio-economic areas of life. A further consequence of industrial development was an improvement in communications. The steamship replaced sail, the railway overtook the stagecoach, the telegraph was introduced in 1837, and by 1850 a submarine telegraph cable joined England and France. By increasing common links, these changes underlined the need for co-ordination between states and also made communications between governments easier. Faster travel allowed government delegations to convene together more readily; the telegraph gave them the possibility of consulting with and receiving instructions from home.

Commerce was being increasingly internationalized and many nineteenth-century activities of the public international unions or international agencies reflected this (Murphy 1994: 2–7). The representatives of states were brought together to manage aspects of public life normally associated with travel, communications, commerce or welfare, the good governance of which would otherwise be affected by state boundaries. In 1804 the Convention of Octroi set up a centralized supranational administration to subject the navigation of the Rhine to international control, but this was done at a time when Europe was dominated by Napoleonic France. The first post-Napoleonic agencies followed the opening-up of the international waterways to all traders by the Congress of Vienna (Articles 108–16 of the Final Act of the Treaty of Vienna). An international commission for the Elbe was established in 1821, one for the Rhine in 1831, and Article 15 of the Treaty of Paris, 1856, established a European Danube Commission to supervise the free navigation of that river, independent of national control as the 'system of national administrations had utterly broken down, incompetent to deal with the modern world of shipping and international trade' (Woolf 1916: 373).

The idea of having a group of experts and administrators performing particular functions on behalf of states was taken further by the establishment in 1868 of the International Telegraphic Bureau (later named the International Telegraphic Union – ITU) and in 1874 of the General Postal Union (later Universal Postal Union, UPU). Both organizations were a response to technological advances and the patent need to co-ordinate national developments in these areas.

As government involvement in the social and economic sphere of its citizens' lives grew, so did the requirement to ensure that these activities were not unduly confused by the existence of national borders. The International Bureau of Weights and Measures (1875), the International Union for the Publication of Customs Tariffs (1890) and the Metric Union helped to ease international trade, while the international health offices established in Havana and Vienna in 1881 and Paris in 1901 demonstrated increased government concern in matters of public health and a recognition that disease knew no frontiers.

A major innovation of these agencies was their secretariats. At the end of the seventeenth century, William Penn had included international civil servants modelled on the clerks of the English House of Commons in his proposals for a general European parliament. However, it is more often the bureaux of the public international unions that are seen as the forerunners of the secretariats of later universal organizations such as the League of Nations. The international aspect of the bureaux should not be overestimated; for the most part they were based on the nationals of their host country, though they did provide continuity and a sense of purpose. In many of these unions, representatives of a few selected member states formed a governing body which directed policy between the regular policy-making conferences of all the member states. This structure pointed up the tension between the desire of states not to be bound by actions to which they had not agreed and the need for the unions to function efficiently. In the end most of the organizations struck a balance by allowing the governing body to deal with non-controversial technical questions, responsibility for which the national governments were happy to delegate, while the conferences agreed on the broad policy lines.

In the latter half of the nineteenth century, the rise of the private international associations mirrored that of the public international unions. National humanitarian, religious, economic, educational, scientific and political organizations arranged international meetings. Probably the first such gathering was the World Anti-Slavery Convention of 1840 (see www.antislavery.org/english/what_we_do/our_history.aspx): it was this sort of association that spawned permanent organizations with the machinery of secretariats, boards and assemblies (Woolf 1916: 165). The interest of governments in their citizens' activities, outside those that might endanger the security of the state, was fairly minimal. There were few official restrictions on those who wished to travel and indulge in meetings of the International Institute of Agriculture, the International Law Association or the Universal Peace Congress, although the representatives of anarchist, socialist and working men's associations normally received police attention when they crossed frontiers. According to the Union of International Associations, while the number of intergovernmental organizations rose from seven in the 1870–74 period to thirty-seven in 1909, the number of international non-governmental organizations had already reached 176 by the latter date (Union of International Associations, 1974, vol. 15, tables 1 and 2).

The relationship between the international public and private associations has usually been symbiotic. While many of the private associations clearly rejected individual interests of little concern to the state, some of them demonstrated the necessity for governmental activity and co-operation across frontiers. The International Committee of the Red Cross, a private international union, promoted the intergovernmental Geneva Conventions of 1864, 1906, 1929, 1949 and 1977. In some cases a private union was a forerunner of a public international union; for example, the International Association of the Legal Protection of Labour led to the establishment of the International Labour Organization (ILO) in 1919. The Union of International Associations, established in 1910 because of the growth of private unions, laid down as conditions of membership that the association should possess a permanent organ; that its object should be of interest to all or some nations and not be one of profit; and that membership should be open to individuals and groups from different countries. Despite this distinction between private and public associations, a number of the organizations had mixed memberships with representatives of government bodies sitting together with individual members. Examples are the International Council of Scientific Unions and the International Organization for Standardization (International Council of Scientific Unions 2014; International Organization for Standardization 2014).

This rise of international public and private associations during the nineteenth century was a response to scientific and technological changes. An American writer observed that:

> Events in the international society have been following those in the national societies of which it is composed. The same new inventions, the same intensification and complication of social life have led to a great increase in international regulations which have to do with the relations of states in the economic and social fields and which affect the daily lives of individuals.
>
> (Chamberlain 1955: 87)

Another American academic has suggested that the link between particular international organizations and industrial change is more direct. Murphy considered that

> the greatest impact of the world organizations themselves has been on industrial change. They have helped create international markets in industrial goods by linking *communication and transportation infrastructure*, protecting *intellectual property*, and reducing legal and economic barriers to *trade*.
>
> (Murphy 1994: 2, original emphasis)

In particular, Murphy stressed the role of international organizations 'in the growth and development of industrial society for over a century' and the way they have contributed to 'the rise of the new leading industries of the next era of political order and economic growth' (Murphy 1994: 9). He outlined four stages in the building of a Public International Union as being:

1   The proposition of a design: someone has to suggest a new institution to solve a perceived international problem.
2   Sponsoring a conference: key governments or monarchs were needed to do this.
3   Support of an experimental Union by a powerful individual or government often resulted from the conference.
4   By developing a constituency of supporters benefiting from its activities, the Union could then become more permanent.

(Murphy 1994: 71)

The functional approach taken by both the private and the public associations – that it made sense to co-operate across frontiers on specific matters of a technical or administrative nature – was strongly affected during the First World War. On the negative side, the prosecution of the war throughout much of Europe put paid to a number of nineteenth-century public international unions such as the International Association of Public Baths and Cleanliness. Others became private unions, such as the International Geodetic Union (Murphy 1994: 82–3). However, conflict also brought more positive change. The pressures of the war economy forced the Allies to consider afresh the organization of important areas of economic life. On the political side it was found necessary in 1916 to co-ordinate the war effort through the Inter-Allied Committee, consisting of prime ministers, relevant ministers and the necessary experts, and which was advisory in character with its proposals subject to the approval of the governments involved. As the war continued, the Allies established a Supreme War Council, served by a permanent secretariat, which had authority over the range of inter-Allied councils covering the economic, military and political aspects of the war. On the economic side, the aim was to make the maximum use of limited resources by pooling them and distributing them where most needed. The executive committees of these councils consisted of government officials, such as Britain's Arthur Salter and France's Jean Monnet, who had a wide remit to organize provision of food and transport in a way that functioned best rather than to suit national sensitivities.

## The foundations of the League of Nations

The participants at the Versailles Peace Conference of 1919 had the dual task of making a settlement of victor over vanquished and of establishing a functioning international system after the disturbances created by a world war.

During the course of the war, various individuals, groups and governments had started work on plans for organizing post-war international relations so that 'the Great War' would be 'the war to end all wars'. President Wilson of the United States was committed to 'a general association of nations' and his adviser, Colonel House, drew up plans to this end (Armstrong *et al.* 2004: 16–18). An official British commission under Lord Phillimore had examined a number of schemes, including those of the sixteenth- and seventeenth-century philosophers, and had decided that while international relations could not be radically changed, a more organized form of interstate diplomacy was desirable, with states submitting disputes to a Conference of the Allied States. The French proposal, advanced by Leon Bourgeois, was more robust. It imagined an international tribunal that could pronounce on issues open to legal decisions, an international body of delegates of the League member states which would take decisions on disputes, and an international force with a permanent staff which would ensure the execution of the tribunal's decisions and overcome any armed opposition to the League. In his scheme, the South African statesman, Jan Smuts, stressed the need for a small council of League members to discuss international affairs and he placed store on deliberation and delay during disputes so that public opinion could be organized to cool down war passions.

At the Versailles Peace Conference, President Wilson himself chaired a special Commission on the League of Nations, at which the British–American–South African ideas, as expressed in the Hurst-Miller draft, were dominant. The statesmen moulding the new League found that the plans before them relied heavily on the experience of the previous hundred years – the congress and concert systems; the public international unions and their private counterparts, and the Hague meetings. They also had something else on their minds: the wartime experience. One side of the coin was the determination to prevent the collapse of international relations into general war; the other side was the experience of Allied co-operation during the war which helped the leaders to decide at Versailles on particular schemes for their post-war relationships.

The Covenant of the League of Nations reflected the somewhat jumbled hopes and fears of the leadership of the Allied and Associate powers that had won the war (see Armstrong *et al.* 2004: ch. 2 for an account of the negotiations leading to the League's establishment). The new organization had as its aim the promotion of international co-operation, peace and security. To achieve this, it required the form of relations between states to be open, lawful, just and peaceable.

In line with what had been sought at the Hague meetings of 1899 and 1907, the Covenant stressed the need to control the sinews of war. Whereas agreements of the nineteenth century had dealt with the laws of war and the Hague conferences had not produced any radical suggestions on the topic, the arms race preceding the war and the carnage of 1914–18 led to the inclusion of Article 8 in the Covenant. This recommended the reduction of armaments and the limitation of the private manufacture of armaments.

Article 10, by which the members of the League undertook 'to respect and preserve as against external aggression the territorial integrity and existing political independence of all Members of the League', was the work of President Wilson, who based this idea on the experience of the Pan-American Union formed some twenty years previously. The British watered this down by a more concert-like addition that, when the need arose, the members of the League Council would 'advise upon the means by which this obligation shall be fulfilled'. However, the British delegation was willing to see a 'musketeers' oath' placed in Article 11 by which 'Any threat of war . . . is hereby declared a matter of concern to the whole League and the League shall take any action that may be deemed wise and effectual to safeguard the peace of nations.' The British were also enthusiastic about the inclusion of Article 19, which allowed another element of the old European concert into the League system: the prevention of conflict by the prior consideration of situations that might threaten peace.

The core of the League system was Articles 12–16, which outlined how states in dispute should conduct their relations. The promise of the Hague conferences was to be fulfilled in the establishment of a Permanent Court of International Justice (Article 14) and a stress on arbitration, conciliation and mediation (Articles 12, 13 and 15). Articles 12–15 took up Smuts's idea of a breathing space, during which war would be precluded while countries attempted to settle their disputes peacefully, and public opinion would thereby be allowed to restrain any rush to war. States resorting to war in disregard of the processes established under Articles 12, 13 or 15 were deemed 'to have committed an act of war against all other Members of the League, which hereby undertake immediately to subject it to severance of all trade or financial relations'. This section reflects closely the wording of Jan Smuts in his 'The League of Nations: a practical suggestion' (Henig 1973: 34). There was a notion expressed by Lord Cecil, the British minister, that the war had shown such action, including blockades, to be a potentially powerful instrument for peace.

President Wilson's wish for 'open covenants, openly arrived at', as opposed to the secret agreements which he felt had contributed to the outbreak of the First World War, ended up in Article 18, whereby new treaties were to be registered with and published by the League's Secretariat.

To be truly global, the League system would have had to cover the colonized world as well as just the sovereign states. There was pressure from the Americans for an extension of the international system, yet in the end the colonial powers' refusal to consider such a trespass on their territory blocked these plans. All that remained was the compromise over the treatment of the ex-colonies of the defeated powers – the mandates system of Article 22 and a paragraph in Article 23 whereby League members would: 'undertake to secure just treatment of the native inhabitants of territories under their control'.

Article 22 also contained other clauses concerning economic and social questions, which reflected the growth in their international aspect as seen in the public and private international unions of the previous fifty years and in the effects of the war. An organization to secure fair and humane conditions of labour was to be established; traffic in women, children and drugs was to be controlled; the trade in arms to be supervised; freedom of commerce and communications to be ensured, particularly in the war-ravished areas; and steps taken internationally to control disease.

Such aims presumed a reshaping of international politics with new institutions to serve the purpose of peace. While schemes abounded for such innovations, the statesmen present at the Versailles Conference drew heavily on their own experience of co-operation during the war and of previous institutional developments. The Inter-Allied Supreme Council established during the war formed the basis of the Council of Ten, the inner negotiating group of the Versailles Peace Conference: its continuation can be seen in the Council of the League of Nations, which was created as a forum for the Great Powers (Hankey 1946: 26). While nostalgia for the Concert of Europe may have affected the thinking of those who advanced plans for a post-war organization, it seems more likely that the Great Powers determining the actual settlement just decided to carry on as they had done, relatively successfully, for the previous four years. The same can be said about the social and economic institutions associated with the League. While the ILO had the work of the International Labour Office at Basle (established in 1901) to build on, and the Red Cross organizations mentioned in Article 25 of the League Covenant had been functioning for some fifty years, the real stimulus to the inclusion of social and economic co-operation in the League's work was the wartime effort mentioned above. Indeed, people such as Salter and Monnet remained prominent in League efforts in this area.

The Hague conferences are often seen as the model for the Assembly of the League, with each state (regardless of size) having one vote and being able to make its contribution to the debates on the great questions of war and peace. This does not answer the question of how the smaller states (or, in truth, non-Great Powers) were willing and able to press their demand for such an Assembly and why the Great Powers agreed to this request. Again the answer can be found in the wartime experience. Apart from the fact that two small states – Serbia and Belgium – had figured in the immediate causation of war, by the time the war had ended, British Empire and Dominion states had made a noticeable contribution to the war effort, and a number of other smaller states had come in on the Allied side. Furthermore the entry of the United States into the war, the dominance of President Wilson at the Versailles Conference, and the insistence of American politicians on his writing into the Covenant a reference to 'regional understandings like the Monroe Doctrine' (Article 21) meant that there would most likely also be a strong Latin American presence in any post-war peace organization. The First World War started in Europe but ended as a global war: it was fought over four continents by troops from all continents. This made it impossible for any post-war institution such as the League Assembly not to be open to universal membership, albeit determined by the restrictions of Article 1 of the Covenant. However, the Assembly was by no means seen as the central institution of the League by framers of the Covenant: the powers given to the Council compared favourably with those of the Assembly, and the intention of a number of the Versailles peacemakers that the Assembly should meet only every four years whereas the Council would meet more frequently, demonstrated the original favour shown to the Council.

The Secretariat of the League is often seen as being based on the model of the bureaux of the public international unions of the nineteenth century. While these may have provided examples of how an international secretariat can work, this by no means explains why the model was adopted rather than the idea of a secretariat with a political role or the stronger executive allowed for by the ILO. Once more the answer lies in the wartime experience, specifically that of the international Secretariat of the Supreme War Council headed by Sir Maurice Hankey. The genesis of the Supreme War Council can be found in the British Empire-based Committee of Imperial Defence, established in 1902, which had Hankey as its Secretary and which also had a number of deputy secretaries with specialized knowledge. Its task was to make war plans and to co-ordinate with the Dominion governments (such as those of Canada and Australia) and its lineal successor was the wartime Imperial War Cabinet of which Hankey was again Secretary. It is perhaps not surprising that Hankey was the choice for the job of Secretary of the Supreme War Council, which by the end of the war brought together the representatives of the British Empire, France, Italy and the United States. The next step seemed logical:

> The machinery that had stood the terrible test of war inevitably became the nucleus of the Peace Conference . . . The International Secretariat of the Supreme War Council was brought up from Versailles and attached to the Secretariat-General of the Peace Conference.
>
> (Hankey 1946: 26–7)

When consideration was given to a secretariat for a newly emerging League of Nations, there was some support for 'a permanent organization presided over by a man of the greatest ability', as Lord Cecil wrote in his memorandum to the Imperial War Cabinet on 24 December 1918. He suggested a 'Chancellor' who, as well as heading the League Secretariat, would be the 'international representative of the League . . . the suggester, if not the director, of its policy'. He was in fact proposing a Secretariat with a political role and it was fitting that he chose a politician for the job – the Greek premier, Venizelos. However, Venizelos thought his own country needed him more than the League, as did Masaryk of Czechoslovakia and President Wilson, both of whom were apparently considered. This inability to persuade any active politician to take on such a thankless task, and French opposition to the plan, meant a return to the established model: the word 'Chancellor' was replaced by that of 'Secretary-General' in the draft Covenant and the faithful Hankey was offered the job. As Colonel House, President Wilson's adviser, explained: 'Hankey had during the war done the type of work contemplated for the Secretary-General.' When Hankey declined the position, another British civil servant, Sir Eric Drummond, was appointed in his stead (Barros 1979: 1–9). It seems that the drafters of the Covenant intended that the new Secretariat of the League, while remaining administrative rather than political, would also carry on the co-ordination role of Hankey's wartime office:

> There shall be placed under the direction of the League all international bureaux already established by general treaties if the parties of such treaties consent. All such international bureaux and all commissions for the regulation of matters of international interest hereafter constituted shall be placed under the direction of the League.
>
> (Article 24)

This somewhat underestimated the bureaucratic urge for self-protection of the existing agencies once the immediate pressures of war had ceased. These plans were finally undermined when the United States did not join the League. Existing international organizations of which the United States was a member were unwilling to risk its membership by too close a connection with the League.

## The League's activities

If the institutions of the League were fashioned by the immediate experience of wartime co-operation rather than by the ideas of seventeenth-century writers, the activities pressed by the members through these institutions were also more determined by memories of 1914–18 than by abstract concepts.

During the 1920s, the League provided a useful but modest addition to international diplomacy. Regular annual meetings between states' representatives allowed the discussion of threats to peace and security and a more long-term consideration of questions of disarmament, guarantees of frontiers and the evolution of the League system (Armstrong *et al.* 2004: 21–31). The Council – voicing the concern of the French and British governments – was able to dampen conflict between Greece and Bulgaria in 1925, was active in solving the Aaland Islands dispute between Finland and Sweden in 1921 and solved the Turkish-Iraqi dispute over Mosul. The League was by no means the only method used by states to place their relations with each other on a more peaceful and organized basis: the Locarno Treaty of 1925 guaranteed French–Belgium–German frontiers, thus allowing Germany to become a League member in 1926; the Kellogg–Briand Pact of 1928 allowed both League and non-League members to renounce war as an instrument of national policy; and by the end of the decade the Preparatory Commission for Disarmament, which included US and Soviet delegates, had started work.

On the economic and social side, the League provided valuable co-ordination for efforts that had previously been disparate and also provided machinery through which problems could be studied and eventually tackled on a cross-national basis (Armstrong *et al.* 2004: 30–1). Refugees from Russia and Turkey were aided; protection of minorities was placed on a regular international footing. The importance of co-operation on economic questions had become accepted after the experience of the Depression and by 1939 the Bruce Report recommended that the League Assembly strengthen its economic programme and establish a Central Committee for Economic and Social Questions to this end.

However, in the end the system created in 1919 could not prevent the Second World War in 1939. Rather than an organization helping to achieve collective security, disarmament, the peaceful settlement of dispute and respect for international law, the League eventually became an empty shell abandoned by countries unwilling to involve themselves outside their domain or give teeth to the League's Covenant. The failure of the United States to join the League undermined the League's claim to universality and its hopes of taking effective action in areas outside Europe, in Manchuria, Ethiopia and Latin America. French policy was aimed at securing their country against future German attack, by a system of alliances if need be, and France attempted to make the League more of a collective security organization which would serve its own interests in Europe. British leaders in the interwar period showed themselves unwilling either within the League or outside it to commit themselves to the automatic defence of other countries: the logic of the alliance and of collective security.

A more serious threat came from those governments who were unsatisfied with the Versailles settlement: originally the Soviet Union, then Mussolini's Italy and finally Nazi Germany and imperial Japan in the 1930s. These revisionist powers all had a deep-seated dislike of the post-1919 status quo which, in the cases of Germany, Italy and Japan, led them to reject the institutions of the existing international system: treaties, diplomacy, international law, the international economic order, and international organizations such as the League. In the case of the Soviet Union, the distaste for the European bourgeois democracies and their associated forms of international relations became attenuated over time by the need to secure the Soviet motherland from outside attack, even if this meant membership of the League or alliances with non-socialist states.

Of the major Allies and associated states that had fought the First World War, Russia had undergone a revolution and had retracted into a protective shell, both the United States and the United Kingdom had withdrawn their troops from the European continent after the immediate post-war hiatus, and the French Third Republic became crippled by internal political divisions. During the 1930s, the European political system which had helped to create the League of Nations came under attack from the revisionist states. Japanese attacks on China and its occupation of Manchuria from 1931 onwards underlined the unwillingness of League members to act in the Asian and Pacific areas without US support. Full-scale military aggression by Italy against Ethiopia (Abyssinia) in 1935 brought only desultory League economic sanctions which were undermined by British and French concern not to push Italy into the arms of Germany. Hitler's withdrawal of Germany from both the League and the Disarmament Conference in 1933 presaged a whole series of aggressive measures which went unchecked by the League's remaining members. Brierly (1946: 84–92) has argued that it was not the League system that failed. Indeed, it can be seen as having achieved a good deal of success, especially given the unfavourable conditions: it is scarcely surprising in this period of uncertainty, isolationism and economic protectionism that international institutions created to further international co-operation were so severely tested.

As Mazower (2012: 136) comments, 'from any perspective, the League was an extraordinary diplomatic innovation, a realization of the dreams of many nineteenth century internationalists and a moment of truth for others'. The whole League system can be seen as a crucial link which brought together the strand of pre-1914 international organizations and wartime co-operation into a more centralized and systematic form on a global scale, thus providing a stepping stone towards the more enduring United Nations. The economic and political crises of the late 1920s and 1930s also changed attitudes among politicians and business leaders – at least in Europe and North America – and made them more open to an active liberal internationalism that underpinned many of the institutions emerging from the Second World War.

## Organizations from 1945 to 1989

The Second World War is often seen in negative terms as far as international organizations are concerned: the League of Nations and the ILO had just a residual presence in Geneva; a few other technical or humanitarian agencies (in particular the International

Committee of the Red Cross) were kept going by the hard work of the neutral states and their citizens. Yet the war years provided the furnace within which some of the most important post-war organizations were fashioned. The experience of wartime co-operation was crucial in determining the institutions and aims of the United Nations (UN) and the various economic organizations that resulted from the Bretton Woods negotiations of 1944–46. The wartime summit conferences and the intense diplomatic activity between Britain, the United States and the Soviet Union culminated in these three states, together with China, deciding on the basic structure of the UN at the Dumbarton Oaks meeting of 1944 and the Yalta Summit of February 1945.

### The formation of the United Nations

While the institutions of the UN superficially resemble those of the League – Council, Assembly, Court, Secretariat – there are important differences, not just ones of detail. The UN was negotiated while the war was still being fought, with the failures of the 1930s and the burdensome task of defeating the Axis Powers on the minds of Allied politicians. Emphasis was placed on carrying over wartime Great Power co-operation into peacetime, with a council that would be dominated by the Big Three (the United States, the USSR and the United Kingdom) plus France and China, and which would have prime responsibility for the maintenance of peace and security. This political solution contrasted to the legalism of the League Covenant but was also a reflection of reality: it had been the joint Anglo-American–Soviet forces that had saved the world from the German–Japanese–Italian Axis domination. The role of the other states was not forgotten; after all, many small states and Commonwealth countries had again played an honourable and important role in the war effort and a number of the European governments-in-exile in London had contributed to the debate about post-war institutions.

There was no going back from the League Assembly in making plans for the UN but at least it could be made clear that the Council body was to bear the prime responsibility for peace and security matters. It was recognized that the new organization would need a secretariat, if only to carry out the administrative duties. However, the introduction of an executive and political role (Articles 98 and 99) needs some explaining. The forerunner of the executive role can be seen in the Secretariat of the ILO, especially when Albert Thomas was Secretary-General (Phelan 1949), while Cecil's idea of a Chancellor and President Roosevelt's notion of a world moderator may have been a model for the political role of the UN's Secretary-General. Furthermore the powers meeting at Dumbarton Oaks had the practical example of the United Nations Relief and Rehabilitation Agency's Director-General available – in this case the Director-General had a non-voting seat on the Central Committee of the United States, USSR, United Kingdom and China, and he had wide executive powers (Royal Institute of International Affairs 1946: 18–21).

Preparation for the formulation of the United Nations was extensive, particularly in the United States where numerous private organizations produced proposals which were fed into the official planning process (Russell and Muther 1958: 215–24). All the major powers at Dumbarton Oaks and at the later San Francisco Conference which drafted the UN Charter were aware of the need to avoid the 'mistakes' of the League of Nations – the confusion of responsibility for peace and security between Council and Assembly; a legalistic approach to international peace and security; the restrictions of all members having a veto. However, the reality of wartime co-operation determined the nature of what was decided: the UN was to be primarily a peace and security organization based on the concept of the Four Policemen – that is, the United States, USSR, the United Kingdom and China as protectors of the world against a recurrence of Axis aggression. The San Francisco Conference of all the founding members added important elements to this core: the economic and social aspects of the organization were filled out (the League's Bruce Report providing the groundwork), and trusteeship was added to the Charter, as was the Declaration Regarding Non-Self-Governing Territories (Chapter XI).

The creation of the UN contrasts to that of the League of Nations. The League's creators – Clemenceau, Lloyd George, Wilson and their advisers – had a number of draft proposals before them, based on work during the war. However, the political decisions were made after the end of hostilities and were tied to the peace settlement. As suggested above, the League established by the leaders of the major victor powers scarcely looked brand new, more the practice of nineteenth-century wartime and peace conferences continued, institutionalized, and given some purpose. By comparison, the birth of the United Nations seemed the result of the more deliberative consideration of future needs. It was based less on existing practice than had been the case with the League. After all, the experience of the major powers with the League had not been happy: the United States had not joined; the USSR had been expelled in 1939 for invading Finland; China had seen the League powerless to act against Japanese invasion of its territory; and Britain had chosen appeasement and then rearmament rather than action through the League to combat the advance of Hitler in the late 1930s. Despite this, these four countries recognized at the Moscow Conference of October 1943

> the necessity of establishing at the earliest practicable date a general international organization, based on the principle of the sovereign equality of all peace-loving States and open to membership by all such States, large or small, for the maintenance of international peace and security.
>
> (Royal Institute of International Affairs 1946: 13)

There was even a lively debate between the British and American governments as to the basis of such an organization – whether it should have a strong regional element, as advocated by Churchill, or whether the emphasis should be universalist, as Roosevelt came to believe. Unlike the case of the League, there was not the range of inter-Allied institutions on which to base the organization of the UN. The major exception was that of the Security Council, which grew naturally from four-power wartime co-operation, though even here it was recognized that non-permanent members chosen from the lesser powers should be included. In contrast to the League, the work of the drafting of the United Nations Charter was undertaken while the war was being fought and the document was signed at San Francisco on 26 June 1945, some six weeks before the end of the war in the Far East. The proposals germinated in Allied chancelleries, particularly in the various US government departments. The blueprint worked out by the Big Four at the tough negotiations at Dumbarton Oaks and the confrontation of this draft with the demands of the other allied countries meeting at San Francisco was bound to produce a hybrid. The US Senate Committee of Foreign Relations provided an appropriate epitaph for these efforts when referring to the Charter:

While it may be that this is not a perfect instrument, the important thing is that agreement has been reached on this particular Charter, after months and even years of careful study and negotiation, between the representatives of 50 nations.

(cited in Russell and Muther 1958: 939)

Like the League Covenant, the UN Charter reflected the circumstances of the time in its vision of how to obtain peace and security – by the mechanisms of peaceful change and settlement and by Great Power enforcement of the peace. With the experience of the League behind them, the Allies knew not to provide for just a particular peace (as seemed to be the case in 1919) but to fashion instruments able to deal with the unforeseeable future. The Charter was far more successful in doing this than the League Covenant. Of course, the Charter was blessed with the signatures and ratification of the major victorious powers, something the Covenant never achieved, but there were more basic differences. The Covenant contained a particular formula for maintaining peace – a rather legalistic machinery which became dated even before the end of the 1920s. The Charter also established machinery that soon became outmoded – the Military Staff Committee of Articles 46 and 47 being the prime example – but on the whole it left the task of obtaining and maintaining peace and security to the political decisions of the UN membership made at the appropriate time. Rather than re-establish the tripwires of Articles 11–16 of the Covenant, which were avoided by some states and trampled on by others, the Charter provided a set of tools (Chapter VI – Pacific Settlements of Disputes; Chapter VII – Action with Respect to Threats to the Peace, Breaches of the Peace and Acts of Aggression; Chapter VIII – Regional Arrangements) which members could take up in order to help fashion a settlement of their problems.

### Post-war developments to 1989

The way that the UN had worked in the post-war world and the mode of development of other international organizations has been affected by the international environment since 1945. Michalek (1971: 387) has written that 'the successes or failures of international organizations stem not so much from their formal-legal covenants as from changing configurations and distributions of power, systemic issues and forces, and the attitudes and resources of member states'. A brief examination of these developments from 1945 to 1989 – the end of the Second World War to the end of the Cold War – will help to set the historical context for the behaviour of international organizations during that period.

The international system that emerged in 1945 was still one based on the sovereignty of states and it seemed that the European system had emerged victorious despite being challenged by the Axis Powers. The work of the San Francisco Conference and the statements of the Great Powers at conferences from Moscow, November 1943, to Potsdam, August 1945, pointed to a belief in the tried and tested system of diplomacy, international law and international institutions. Developments in the international system since 1945 have severely tested the efficacy of the old European mode of adjusting relations between states and have, to a certain extent, amended it to suit new demands.

A former British diplomat who had much to do with the organization wrote: 'The United Nations is a mirror of the world around it, if the reflection is ugly, the organization should not be blamed' (Gladwyn 1953: 390), while a Romanian ex-ambassador made the point more generally: 'international organizations have always mirrored the world power structure of the given period' (Brucan 1977: 95). What sort of post-war world to 1989 has the UN – and other international organizations – reflected?

First, it was a world which saw a substantial increase in the number of states and in the range of state types, measured by a variety of indicators. During the life of the League, sixty-three states had been members and in 1945 fifty-one governments signed the UN Charter. Another twenty-five states joined during the following ten years and by the end of 1960 there were 100 members. In 1982 membership reached 157, covered all the inhabited continents, and included mini-states such as the Seychelles and Grenada as well as giants such as China and the Soviet Union. By 1991 the membership figure for the UN totalled 169. The political spectrum ranged from right-wing military dictatorships, through the parliamentary democracies to states with Marxist governments. The economic development of the membership was as varied as the consumerist United States and poverty-stricken Bangladesh, welfare-state Sweden and broken-backed Somalia. Powers such as USSR, United States, France and the United Kingdom had worldwide connections; some members, South Africa for example, could be regarded as regional powers, while most countries had significant relationships only with their immediate neighbours, their former colonial power and the United States. A growing number of states should have provided the possibility of a large number of international organizations, and a wide variety in the nature of states suggests that this would be mirrored in those organizations. However, the poverty of many states and the increased unwillingness of the richer states to finance the IGOs in fact led to a decline in their number during the late 1980s. The total number of IGOs in 1985 was 378 but this had declined to 300 by 1989 (Union of International Associations 1999).

This growth in the number of states in the system has resulted in the universalist institutions of the UN and its associated agencies being underpinned by a variety of international organizations with more limited membership. Some of these were confined to particular geographic areas – the Organization of American States, the League of Arab States, the Organization of African Unity (OAU, later African Union) – while others were geographically and ideologically defined: NATO, the OECD, the Association of South East Asian Nations (ASEAN). The functional areas covered were varied, ranging from the economic interests of Mercosur (the economic association of the 'southern cone' states of Latin America) to the cultural, social and juridical remit of the Nordic Council and the obvious concern of the International Whaling Commission and the South East Atlantic Fisheries Organization. The universalist UN dealt with issues that motivated the League – international peace and security – and developed a prominence in areas that the League at first neglected: economic and social issues, the position of colonial peoples. The wide range of other IGOs reflected these concerns. The Bretton Woods institutions – the IMF, IBRD, GATT, IDA, IFC – provided the organized basis of the post-war, non-communist economic system. The OAU, OAS and the League of Arab States helped in peacefully settling disputes and provided much of the inspiration for the UN's work on decolonization. However, some organizations demonstrated the different interests of the growing number of sovereign states that cannot be satisfactorily accommodated at the UN, whether they be the security concerns of NATO and the then-existing Warsaw Treaty Organization; the desire for a better price for their oil exports expressed in OPEC; or the wish to develop a regional identity as demonstrated in the Nordic Council, the Caribbean Community and the European Communities (later European Union).

Scientific progress allowed greater ease in communications in the decades following 1945. Also there was more to communicate among countries: there were more people, more industrial and agricultural production, more money, more writings and so on. Governments continued to intervene in economic and social affairs and also in educational, scientific and cultural matters. Faster travel and transport and the advent of telecommunications and information technology (IT) meant that contacts between peoples, groups and governments were more numerous, regular and widespread. Keohane and Nye (1971: xii) identify four major types of global interaction:

1   communication, the movement of information, including the transmission of beliefs;
2   transportation, the movement of physical objects, including war material and personal property as well as merchandise;
3   finance, the movement of money and instruments of credit;
4   travel, the movement of persons.

These interactions resulted in a growth in the number of intergovernmental technical, economic and social organizations and the spread of organizations between individuals and non-governmental groups.

The rise of INGOs allowed for by the increase in global interactions has been one of the noticeable developments in international relations in this period. Article 71 of the UN Charter authorized the Economic and Social Council to 'make suitable arrangements for consultation with non-governmental organizations which are concerned with matters within its competence' and by 1990 there were some 640 INGOs that had consultative status with ECOSOC. As well as these INGOs, which by nature concern themselves with economic, social, educational, cultural and scientific questions, a whole range grew up in other spheres, and developed similar symbiotic relations with the UN specialized agencies. The trade union and employee organizations have an established relationship with the ILO and scientific and specialist associations were drawn into a consultative status with the Food and Agriculture Organization (FAO) and UNESCO. The 1972 Stockholm UN Conference on the Human Environment was a gathering place for many non-governmental ecology groups, and such organizations as Friends of the Earth, the International Union for Conservation of Nature, and the WWF continued to act as shadows to UNESCO and the United Nations Environment Programme (Boardman 1981: 118–23; Willets 1982, *passim*, www.un.org/en/civil society/index.shtml). On a more regional scale, the European Communities' structure encouraged INGO activity both through its Economic and Social Committee and by its general decision-making procedure. This led to Communities-wide interest groups being formed to represent producer, consumer and worker interests at a European level (Archer 2008: 43–4).

Even excluding the INGOs associated with the European Union and EFTA, the total number of these organizations mushroomed from 176 in 1909 to 1,470 in 1969, to 4,676 in 1985 and 5,825 in 1999 (Union of International Associations 1999: table 2; see also Boli 2006: 334). Many of them had little direct influence on IGOs, let alone on governments. They were either weak in membership and organization or were concerned with activities of seemingly little interest to the authorities; for example, chess, stamp collecting, esperanto, nudism. Yet their very number can be seen as presenting a potential power in the mobilization of social forces separate from the agents of government. They represented the glue for civil society working across frontiers. Because of this, the spread of INGOs has been an important political as well as social factor in international life.

The creation of a near-global economy in this period went hand-in-hand with the extension of another form of non-governmental activity across frontiers – the multinational or transnational corporation. Such firms were partly responsible for scientific and technical achievements and the internationalization of economic factors, but they were also encouraged by the more general trend in this direction.

One of the major post-war developments in the political world that the United Nations very quickly mirrored was the division between the Soviet-led bloc and the US-led bloc: the East–West Cold War. Such a divide between the major powers restricted the functioning of the UN and some of its agencies, in the type of peace and security questions that they handled in the Cold War period (basically from 1948 to 1989), and in the creation of bloc-oriented organizations such as the North Atlantic Treaty Organization (NATO) in 1949 and the Warsaw Treaty Organization in 1955.

With the increase in the number of states (brought about mainly by the process of decolonization), international organizations started to reflect another factor – the growing importance of the Afro-Asian-Latin American states, often then called the Third World (the First being the West and the Second the then Soviet bloc). The creation of a group of states standing outside both the East–West military and political divisions is often dated from the Bandung Conference of non-aligned states held in April 1955. In 1960 sixteen African states became independent and joined the United Nations. This helped establish the Third World in international forums, not just as a non-aligned grouping but also as an economic force with its own demands concerning the ending of the Western-oriented, market-based global economy and the adoption of a New International Economic Order (NIEO). In this context the Third World often appeared under the nomenclature of the Group of Seventy-Seven (or G77), originally adopted by the Third World state attending the first United Nations Conference on Trade and Development (UNCTAD). The demands of these states were felt both within previously existing organizations and by the creation of new organizations that supported the needs of G77 states, such as ASEAN or the OAU.

The North–South divide that emerged during the 1960s was by no means a story of two contending monolithic blocs. Both sides had serious internal divisions: the 'North', until the 1990s, included the then Soviet-group countries which claimed a special position in relation to the Third World by virtue of their non-colonialist past. Even the European Communities contained former colonialist states with strong connections with the South, such as France, and also critics of neo-colonialism such as Ireland. The OPEC oil states espoused the cause of the G77 during the 1970s while many had considerable wealth, some of which was obtained at the expense of the world's poorest states which had to import oil. Some Third World states' economies were integrated into the semi-global economy led by the West while others, such as North Korea and Cuba, stayed outside the system. Contacts across the North–South divide were often expressed in institutional form – the Lomé Conventions between the European Communities and a number of African, Caribbean and Pacific (ACP) states; and the Commonwealth of Nations.

So while the East–West and North–South divisions can be seen as major developments in the Cold War world until 1989, interstate relations cannot be reduced to such slogans. The history of relationships between the Western countries and the Soviet bloc from 1945 to 1989 contained an important strand of co-operation which waxed and waned over this period. In the immediate months following the end of the Second World War, both the Soviet and the US governments were anxious not to be the first to break up the wartime alliance, but the period from 1947 to 1954 was one of the deepest confrontation between the two sides. While the demise of Stalin, the USSR's leader, saw a lifting of Cold War feeling in the mid-1950s, crises in the Middle East, Berlin and (in 1962) Cuba stressed the adversarial side of East–West relations. The conscious attempt to decrease tension between the two sides made in the late 1960s and the 1970s – *détente* – demonstrated that even when the systems were in competition and were rivals, agreement could be reached over important areas of international relations. When the Cold War looked frozen solid – at the time of the Korean War (1950–54) – the major powers kept contact with each other both bilaterally and through international organizations such as the UN.

The onset of renewed adversarial East–West relations at the end of the 1970s and start of the 1980s was reflected in a freezing of activities in the main international organizations such as the UN. The end of the Cold War can be traced to an acceptance in the mid-1980s by the new Soviet leadership of Mr Gorbachev that an 'arms race' with the West could not be won and could only be sustained at great expense to the Soviet economy. The subsequent change in relations between the East – the Soviet bloc – and the West – mainly the United States and Western Europe – meant an increase in co-operation and a revival of international organizations. The melt-down of the Soviet bloc from 1989 to 1991 changed the power calculation in these institutions so that there was more of an American hegemony.

## Post-Cold War organizations

Since the end of the Cold War, international organizations have had to adapt to a continuation of some factors seen during the Cold War, plus new elements. The end of the Cold War with the collapse of the Warsaw Treaty Organization in 1990 and of the Soviet Union in 1991 meant that security was seen in new terms and that new methods were needed to maintain it. Security was no longer considered as coming from the balance of power of two blocs – one led by the United States and the other by the Soviet Union – but as a more malleable concept that could refer to anything from the security of individuals, groups, or states to the global environment. Old institutions were adapted to maintain new forms of security. The UN was freed from the stalemate that the Security Council suffered during the Cold War and, for example, agreed to back US-led collective action in the Gulf War of 1990–91 to counter the occupation of Kuwait by Saddam Hussein's Iraq. The UN then went on to use a number of operations in areas as far apart as the Balkans, West Africa, East Asia and Central America that used the tools of peacekeeping, peacemaking (to help resolve conflicts peacefully) and peacebuilding to heal areas after conflict (United Nations 2011). In the forty years from the first operation in 1948 to 1989, there were fifteen UN peacekeeping operations, of which five were still active at the start of 2012. In the twenty-four years from the start of 1989 to the end of 2013, there were fifty-eight operations with fifteen still current at that date (United Nations 2013a; see also Table

4.2). Furthermore, the nature of UN operations diversified especially since the early 1990s with the more active use of peacemaking – bringing together hostile parties using diplomatic means (United Nations 2011) – and peacebuilding which involved supporting peace efforts in states emerging from conflict (United Nations Peacebuilding Commission 2012; Berdal 2009: 135–69). The reason for UN involvement within states was enhanced by the UN General Assembly's acceptance in 2005 that a state had the responsibility to protect ('R2P') 'its populations from genocide, war crimes, ethnic cleansing and crimes against humanity' and the UN also had the right to take action in pursuit of such ends (United Nations Office of the Special Advisor on the Prevention of Genocide 2012). This led to UN-backed operations such as that against the Al-Ghaddaffi regime in Libya in 2011, but also criticisms of the newly found UN activism by states such as China, Russia and Malaysia that wanted to protect their sovereign rights from what they regarded as Western influence (Berdal 2009: 167–9). Indeed, attempts to use the R2P concept in the case of chemical weapons used in the Syrian civil war in 2013 led Russia and China to oppose UN-backed military intervention in this case though they did accept oversight of Syria's dismantling of those weapons by an Organization for the Prohibition of Chemical Weapons (OPCW)-UN joint mission (United Nations 2013b; United Nations 2014).

The above statistics reflected a complex change in the nature of world conflict. During the Cold War period, conflict grew up to the 1970s mainly as a result of the decolonization process. In the 1970s and 1980s conflict increased partly as groups vied over who should control various post-colonial states and partly as the Superpowers sustained armed conflicts in the Third World. The UN's role in these disputes was limited as many of the former were internal to states – and therefore not seen as the business of the Security Council – and the action in the latter was restricted by the very existence of the superpower veto in the Security Council. The end of the Cold War and of superpower division ended wars by proxy in places such as Angola and Eritrea and several wars, both between and within states, simply finished (Human Security Report Project 2010: 2). However, a number of conflicts also started during the 1990s, though overall there was a net decline in the total of conflicts and a considerable fall in the number of deaths per conflict (Human Security Report Project 2010: 2–3). Indeed a detailed Canadian report points to increased international activism, especially by the UN and other international organizations such as the OSCE, as one of the major contributors to the fall in these figures (Human Security Report Project 2010: 13). However, there has been a resurgence in both state-based and non-state armed conflict since 2003, much of which has been associated with conflicts in Iraq, Afghanistan, Pakistan and Somalia (Human Security Report Project 2010: 18–19). This seems to suggest that the '9/11' attack on the United States and its response in the 'War on Terror' has opened a new bout of conflict that affects a larger number of states than before and which can be seen in increased civil unrest and community tensions, factors that have been aggravated by the world economic depression that started in 2008 and by a longer term heightened competition for economic resources. Another round of conflict finds its source in the uncertain frontiers of the Russian Federation. The government of President Putin has expressed a wish, when talking about Russians in Ukraine, to 'always defend their interests using political, diplomatic and legal means' (Putin 2014). This consideration for Russian-speakers has led Russia to engage militarily in both Georgia and Ukraine, thereby increasing tension with Western powers. As Russia has seen these events as being ones either of a bilateral nature or internal to the Russian Federation, the role of international organizations has been limited, despite efforts by the UN and OSCE to get involved.

Economic and social development since the end of the Cold War has also seen an increased demand for the institutions of management of these factors across frontiers and, indeed, globally. World population has grown from 5.3 billion in 1990 to over 7 billion by March 2014. In 2009 world economic output declined for the first time since 1945 and world trade dropped by a massive 25 per cent over the 2008 figure (OECD 2011), after a long period of global economic expansion and growth in world trade. Furthermore, economic power seemed to shift from the previous power-houses of North America, Europe and Japan to countries that had both access to raw materials and a growing industrial base – the BRICs (Brazil, Russia, India, and China). This was recognized in the management of international affairs as the old Bretton Woods system, assisted by the occasional meeting of the G7 (Canada, France, Germany, Italy, Japan, the United States and the United Kingdom), later the G8 (the G7 plus Russia), was supplemented by the G-20. This group consists of the finance ministers of the G7, the four BRICs, Argentina, Australia, Indonesia, Mexico, Saudi Arabia, South Africa, Republic of Korea and Turkey, as well as the European Union (G-20 2010). The groups have secretariats, regular meetings and often a managing threesome ("troika") of the chairing country plus its predecessor and successor, and are thus well on the way to becoming international organizations. However, after the Cannes meeting of the G-20 only offered kind words to tackle the consequences of the Eurozone economic crisis in November 2011, the usefulness of these meetings is in doubt (G-20 2011). This was perhaps a factor in the 2012 G20 pushing a 'growth and employment' action plan and branching out into environmental issues (G-20 2012).

Indeed the world economic crisis from 2008 tested international organizations to their limits. In particular, the European Union found its institutions buffeted by the spreading financial problems, often made worse by the inability of member states to agree on harsh measures. The EU's recipe was that of proposing deeper integration as a long-term solution while in the short run managing crises by a series of meetings of the Eurozone states and their main political leaders. The International Monetary Fund (IMF) also increased its activity, suggesting that the eventual way out of crisis was more co-operation (International Monetary Fund 2012) and more active involvement in domestic affairs by organizations such as the EU and IMF. Unrest in a number of states suggests that people of the worst affected states are reluctant to tolerate harsh economic medicine seemingly doled out at the behest of international bodies and the longer the recession lasts, the greater will be the tension between international economic organizations and their members' citizens.

International organizations have also been involved in social developments on a regular basis. The UN specialized agencies have continued their work and have been supplemented by a greater emphasis on relations with and use of civil society, as often manifested in INGOs. The report of the Panel of Eminent Persons in 2004 to Kofi Annan, then secretary-general of the UN, described constructively engaging with civil society as 'a necessity for the United Nations, not an option' (United Nations General Assembly 2004: 3). This is a response to what Clarke (1998) calls the 'associational revolution' triggered by the growth in the numbers and importance of INGOs and their contribution to political life and change in countries. However, as Davies (2008) points out, the move to transnational civil society is by no means a smooth one and the world since 1989 has seen moves towards nationalism and regional fragmentation in world society with INGOs being involved in poor policy-making and raising unattainable expectations. Nevertheless, INGOs have entrenched themselves in a range of human activity and are particularly active in the field of modern technology and global policy-making (Willetts 2010). The revolution in information and communication technology (ICT, or IT (Information Technology)) has produced IT divisions in the world, often mirroring existing economic ones, which some international organizations, such as the World Bank and the International Telecommunications Union, have attempted to address (World Bank 2012). IT has also offered opportunities to civil society and INGOs both to inform and to mobilize themselves, quite often in a way that sidesteps both government and IGOs (Moore and Selchow 2012).

## In summary

International organizations do not exist in a political vacuum. They are part of the modern state system and their institutional forms and activities reflect the hopes and fears of the governments of states within that system. This brief history of the rise of international organizations demonstrates how closely they have been tied to the life of modern industrial society and the expansion of the European international system to the rest of the world. With the growth in the number of states, the activities of government and groups within the state, and the number of potential areas of conflict – and prospects for co-operation – the climate for international organizations has been generally favourable in the post-Second World War period. After the end of the Cold War, the picture has been more varied but it is clear that IGOs and INGOs have entrenched themselves as part of global and regional governance and that states expect to work through international organizations on a range of subjects from the economy and the environment to security and IT.

This is not to say that with a future different configuration of states, the role of these organizations might not decline. A world empire would have little use for them, preferring the use of force or bilateral diplomacy – it was noticeable that Nazi Germany had no time for international organizations. A world in which war becomes more endemic than at present may have need for international organizations but may find that they are physically unable to function. A world of continental federations may have use for organizations to ease relations between the continents, but within each federation 'international' organizations may have turned into new political federal institutions. A world in which humankind decides to confront universal problems – such as overpopulation, starvation, pollution and destruction of the environment – by the use of effective international organizations will see a shift in the balance of political activity from the sovereign state to a number of strengthened globally functional (but also highly political) institutions.

## A working definition

This chapter started with an examination of the words 'international' and 'organization' and continued with an account of the historical rise of those institutions known as 'international organizations'. It is now possible to define 'international organizations' within the context of that account. This can be done by examining the essential characteristics of international organizations and adding some of the more noticeable elements which, while not necessary preconditions in the identification of international organizations, are often important contributory factors that distinguish them. After undertaking this all-embracing definition, the next chapter will disaggregate international organizations, looking at the ways various *kinds* of organization may be typified.

*The Yearbook of International Organizations* (www.uia.org/yearbook) defines intergovernmental organizations as 'an organization composed primarily of sovereign states, or of other intergovernmental organizations. IGOs are established by treaty or other agreement that acts as a charter creating the group.' This definition has the advantage of being widely encompassing yet at the same time excluding certain groups of organizations that might otherwise be seen as IGOs.

Wallace and Singer (1970: 245–7) distinguished intergovernmental organizations by three criteria:

1    The organization 'must consist of at least two qualified members of the international system' and should have been 'created by a formal instrument of agreement between the governments of national states'. Bilateral international organizations are included on the grounds that they are still international organizations and because otherwise certain multilateral organizations (e.g. the Rhine River Commission) would have to be excluded for the periods when their membership was reduced to two.
2    'The organization must hold more or less regular plenary sessions at intervals not greater than once a decade.'
3    The organization should have a permanent secretariat with a permanent headquarters arrangement and which performs ongoing tasks.

Plano and Riggs (1967: 12–13) gave eleven essential features of nineteenth-century intergovernmental institutions. These are the 'basic characteristics and the procedures' of early international organizations which 'have become commonplace features of modern international institutions'. Volgy et al. (2008: 839) see formal IOs as 'entities created with sufficient organizational structure and autonomy to provide formal, ongoing, multilateral processes of decisionmaking between states, along with the capacity to execute the collective will of their members (states)'. However, this requires a good deal of research into the workings of an entity before deciding on its status. Other writers have produced less exhaustive though more precise criteria for international organizations. Bennett (1977: 3) listed their common characteristics as being

1    a permanent organisation to carry on a continuing set of functions;
2    voluntary membership of eligible parties;
3    a basic instrument stating goals, structure and methods of operation;
4    a broadly representative consultative organ;
5    a permanent secretariat to carry on continuous administration, research and information functions.

The Russian international lawyer, G.I. Tunkin, referred to international organizations as 'permanent bodies' that states create 'to handle matters entrusted to them' and which result from international agreements and possess 'a certain degree of international legal personality' (Osakwe 1972: 24–30).

Another author of the Soviet period, Grigorii Morozov, defined an international organization 'in the light of the basic tenets of the socialist conception':

In its most general form as a stable, clearly structured instrument of international co-operation, freely established by its members for the joint solution of common problems and the pooling of efforts within the limits laid down by its statutes. . . . The aims and activity of an international organization . . . must not have a commercial character or pursue profit-making aims.

(Morozov 1977: 30)

Paul Reuter (1958: 214) considered an international organization as a group normally, but not exclusively, of states 'which can permanently express a juristic will distinct from that of its individual members'. Charles Pentland (1976: 626) described international organizations as institutions with 'formalized sets of relationships expected to persist for a considerable time' whose institutional quality 'is found in their legal, institutional fabric, their political organs and bureaucratic structures, and their physical and symbolic presence'. Pierre Gerbet's definition is succinct:

The idea of an international organization is the outcome of an attempt to bring order into international relations by establishing lasting bonds across frontiers between governments or social groups wishing to defend their common interests, within the context of permanent bodies, distinct from national institutions, having their own individual characteristics, capable of expressing their own will and whose role it is to perform certain functions of international importance.

(Gerbet 1977: 7)

Virally, the French writer on public international law, after examining other definitions, issued his own to the effect that international organizations 'can be defined as an association of States, established by agreement among its members and possessing a permanent system or set of organs, whose task it is to pursue objectives of common interest by means of co-operation among its members' (Virally 1977: 59).

What then are the irreducible essential characteristics of international organization and what are the other elements which often typify such organizations? The outstanding features have three headings:

1  *Membership.* An international organization should draw its membership from two or more sovereign states, though membership need not be limited to states or official state representatives such as government ministers. (Further distinctions between interstate, intergovernmental and international non-governmental organizations will be made in Chapter 2.) Wallace and Singer's case for choosing two as the minimum membership is accepted here in preference to the *Yearbook of International Organizations* and Morozov's choice of three.
2  *Aim.* The organization is established with the aim of pursuing the common interests of the members. It may end up not undertaking this task or favouring the interest of one member over that of another, but it should not have the express aim of the pursuit of the interests of only one member, regardless of the desires of others.
3  *Structure.* The organization should have its own formal structure of a continuous nature established by an agreement such as a treaty or constituent document. The nature of the formal structure may vary from organization to organization but it should be separate from the continued control of one member. It is this autonomous structure that differentiates a number of international organizations from a series of conferences or congresses.

So an international organization can be defined as

> a formal, continuous structure established by agreement between members (governmental and/or non-governmental) from two or more sovereign states with the aim of pursuing the common interest of the membership.

Other factors are often associated with most international organizations: their institutions usually consist of a plenary gathering of all the membership (often called an assembly or conference), a more regular meeting of a limited number of members, quite often with executive powers, and a permanent secretariat of an international nature. 'International' in this context can mean being drawn from several countries, or being chosen to serve the organization regardless of nationality, or being financed by the organization's other institutions. Some organizations also have institutions with judicial or quasi-judicial powers. This book will adopt the *Yearbook of International Organizations* and the Morozov proviso that the international organizations dealt with are to exclude those established with the purpose of making a profit for the members. This rules out international business corporations, cartels and transnational or multinational enterprises. However, these will make an appearance in the next chapter before being removed from the remit of the book. The following chapter will consider the various types of international organizations as determined by aims, activities and functions, membership and structure.

# 2 Classification of international organizations

The definition of an international organization as a formal, continuous structure established by agreement between members, whether governmental representatives or not, from at least two sovereign states with the aim of pursuing the common interest of the membership, covers a wide range of institutions even if profit-making associations are excluded. Although useful observations can be made even about the total spectrum of international organizations, a more helpful and informative study is possible if various types of international organizations, with common features separating them from other international organizations, can be identified.

In this chapter, international organizations will be examined from three perspectives which tend to break down the totality into subgroups. The three headings provide a description of types defined by membership, by aims and activities, and by structure.

## Membership: what are the building blocks?

From the discussion in Chapter 1 about membership and the description of the history of international organizations, it should be clear that their existence is closely associated with that of the sovereign state but that membership of some international organizations is not necessarily drawn from sovereign states or their governmental representatives. The first distinction between the kinds of international organizations is those which are interstate or intergovernmental and those whose membership is non-governmental. A further category could be made of international organizations with mixed membership.

### Intergovernmental organizations (IGOs)

According to the UN Economic and Social Council, 'Every international organization which is not created by means of inter-governmental agreements shall be considered as a non-governmental international organization' (Economic and Social Council, Resolution 288(x) of 27 February 1950). This suggests a distinction between inter-governmental organizations (IGOs) and international non-governmental organizations (INGOs, sometimes shortened to NGOs). There is still some discussion as to whether intergovernmental organizations are the same as interstate organizations. Three points can be made about this latter distinction:

- Some organizations allow membership by countries which are not sovereign states but which have governments and which are usually non-self-governing territories. Examples of international organizations that have accepted such members are the

International Telecommunications Union (ITU), the Universal Postal Union (UPU) and the World Meteorological Organization (WMO) (Klepacki 1973: 5). These are still regarded as being 'interstate'.

- Klepacki also divides international organizations into those having interstate organs, made up exclusively of heads of state, and those having intergovernmental organs with governmental representatives. This seems a little elitist and will not be followed here.

- The international lawyer Jenks (1945a: 18–20) claims a fundamental distinction between organizations based on a treaty between states and one between governments. An interstate treaty includes all the institutions of the state – administrative, executive, legislative and judicial – whereas an intergovernmental organization is established purely by the administrative branch of government.

Bowett (1970: 11) comments on Jenks's distinction that 'in practice [it] is not regarded as having this significant difference in effect', and the political scientist should perhaps extend Bowett's words to refer to all the distinctions between interstate and inter-governmental. Any interstate agreement has to be made by an agent for those states, and it matters little whether his or her nomenclature is that of head of state or head of government. Indeed in many countries, including the United States and Russia, this distinction is no longer made, whereas in some states where it is made, the head of state no longer has treaty-making powers; for example, in Sweden. It will be the practice of this book, unless otherwise stated, to use the terms 'intergovernmental organization' and 'interstate organizations' interchangeably.

## Beyond intergovernmental organizations

The traditional notion of international organizations being established between governments is based on the sovereign state view of international relations, which contains three important elements: that, with few exceptions, only sovereign states are the subjects of international law; that sovereign states are equal in their standing in international law; that sovereign states are institutionally self-contained and international law cannot interfere with the domestic jurisdiction of their governments. This doctrine has important consequences for international organizations.

In theory, such organizations, if they were to be recognized as having any standing in international law, should only consist of sovereign states in their membership. However, as has been seen, the UPU, ITU and WMO all allow non-self-governing territories to become members; even the League of Nations opened its membership to 'Any fully self-governing State, Dominion or Colony' (Article 1.2), a position that fell short of admitting only sovereign states.

Second, the notion of the sovereign equality of states would allow states to have equal voting power in any international institution such as an assembly or a council of an organization. The creation of executive councils in the early public international unions placed some states in a constitutionally favourable position in those organizations and that situation was entrenched in the League Covenant, with the Council having permanent members.

Finally, the inviolability of sovereignty can be protected within international organizations by the doctrine that states cannot be bound by agreements to which they are not party. This would effectively rule out decisions by anything short of unanimity (with abstaining states not being bound) and by executive secretariats or councils which could act without the express consent of all the membership. Certainly any interference with questions of domestic jurisdiction by international organizations would not be allowed. Even Articles 15 and 16 in the League Covenant produced a fear among some sections in the United States that member countries might be obliged to carry out actions against their will but in support of the League. Clearly the UN Charter, allowing majority decisions, breaks with the unanimity principle. Furthermore, although Article 2.7 of the Charter states that 'Nothing contained in the present Charter shall authorize the United Nations to intervene in matters which are essentially within the domestic jurisdiction of any state or shall require the Members to submit such matters to settlement under the present Charter', it continues with the important exception that 'this principle shall not prejudice the application of enforcement measures under Chapter VII'.

Against these seeming shortfalls from the 'sovereign state' model of international relations, it could be argued that states were exercising their sovereign rights in allowing non-sovereign states to become members of international organizations; in agreeing to restricted membership institutions or executive secretariats; and in allowing majority voting or exceptions to the domestic jurisdiction clause. The state-centric model of international relations would allow interactions between the government of one state and the domestic society of another state, but would insist that international politics is about relations between the governments of two or more states and not between the members of those states' societies (Figure 2.1). Thus international organizations are interstate, intergovernmental organizations by this reckoning.

This is clearly not the case. What are commonly and reasonably called 'international organizations' often contain members that are not states or governmental representatives but are drawn from groups, associations, organizations or individuals from within the state. These are *non-governmental* actors on the international stage and their activities give rise to *transnational interaction*. Figure 2.2 typifies international relations seen from a viewpoint that admits the importance of transnational relations.

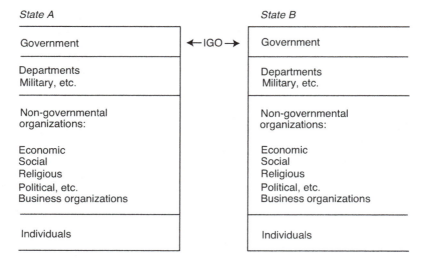

*Figure 2.1* Intergovernmental relations and organizations

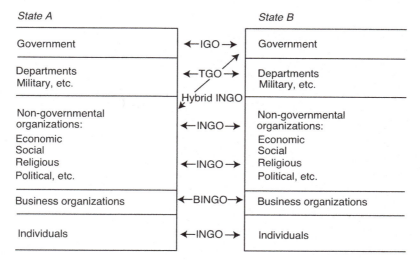

*Figure 2.2* Transnational relations and organization

Keohane and Nye (1971: xii) have defined transnational interactions as covering 'the movement of tangible or intangible items across state boundaries when at least one actor is not an agent of a government or an international organization'. They list four major types of global interaction – communications, transport, finance and travel – and note that many activities contain several of the types simultaneously.

When such relationships between more than two participants become institutionalized by agreement into a formal, continuous structure in order to pursue the common interests of the participants, one of which is not an agent of government or an international organization, then a *transnational organization* (TNO) has been established. In contrast to an intergovernmental organization, a TNO must have a non-state actor for at least one of its members.

Three sorts of TNOs are commonly identified in the literature:

1   *The genuine INGO* which is an organization with only non-governmental members. Such organizations bring together the representatives of like-minded groups from more than two countries and examples are the International Olympic Committee, the World Council of Churches, the Soroptimist International, the Salvation Army International and the Universal Esperanto Association.

2   *The hybrid INGO* which has some governmental and some non-governmental representation. If such a hybrid organization has been established by a treaty or convention between governments, it should be counted as an IGO, an example being the ILO which has trade union and management (i.e. non-governmental) membership as well as governmental representatives. However, some INGOs have a mixed membership and are not the result of a purely intergovernmental agreement. An example is the International Council of Scientific Unions, which draws its membership from international scientific unions, scientific academies, national research councils, associations of institutions and governments (Judge 1978: 57). Increasingly IGOs are involving elements of 'civil society' represented by citizens' groups, consumers and users or pressure groups. These are often organized by

INGOs and may have a formal or semi-formal presence at meetings of the IGOs as do environmental groups at various UN conferences on the environment. However, there are sometimes parallel activities orchestrated by INGOs and less formally organized groupings that are less sympathetic to the work of the activity. This was the case with the Seattle meeting of the World Trade Organization in December 1999, which was disrupted by demonstrations, and that of the IMF and World Bank in Prague in September 2000 that saw a series of protests in which some INGOs, such as Greenpeace International, participated.

3   *The transgovernmental organization* (TGO) which results from 'relations between governmental actors that are not controlled by the central foreign policy organs of their governments' (Keohane and Nye 1971: xv). Such relationships are fairly common if the term 'governmental actors' is widely defined to include anyone engaged in the governmental process of a country – in the legislature, judiciary or executive, at local government level or as part of a regional government. Much of these contacts tends to be informal or non-institutionalized but organizations do exist such as the International Union of Local Authorities (IULA) which brings together the local government authorities of the European Union; the International Council for the Exploration of the Sea (ICES), which has established a network of co-operation between government marine research laboratories; Interpol (the International Criminal Police Organization); and the Inter-Parliamentary Union.

A fourth category of TNOs is sometimes made: that of the business international non-governmental organizations (BINGOs), alternatively called multinational enterprises or corporations: MNEs, MNCs.

Before deciding whether to include this group, the nomenclature should be sorted out. All the descriptions used above have their critics. The use of 'BINGO', though no doubt having its attractions, would exclude those international business organizations that are definitely governmental (such as the former-Soviet airline Aeroflot) or which have a strong governmental stake (such as the Norwegian petroleum company Statoil). The use of the word 'multinational' (or 'international') to describe large corporations functioning in several countries (such as Shell, Unilever and Microsoft) has been challenged on the grounds that it makes them sound as if their management is recruited internationally and their decision-making is not centred in any one country. This does not seem to be true of the leading US companies with overseas interests: a survey of these in 1970 revealed that only 1.6 per cent of their top-level executives were non-Americans (Barnet and Muller 1975: 17). Even with the rise of Indian and Chinese MNCs, this sector is still dominated by the United States; a later study of the control network of transnational corporations showed thirteen of the top twenty 'control-holders' to be based in the United States (Vitali *et al.* 2011: 33). The United Nations Group of Eminent Persons reported the 'strong feeling that [the word] transnational would better convey the notion that these firms operate from their home bases across national borders' without any form of state control. Another UN discussion produced the distinction between

> 'transnational corporations' for enterprises operating from their home bases across national borders . . . [and] the term 'multinational corporations' for those established by agreement between a number of countries and operating in accordance with prescribed agreements.
>
> (Judge 1978: 354)

Multi- or transnational business enterprises have been excluded from the rest of this study on the following grounds:

- Both the ECOSOC Resolution 288(x) of 27 February 1950 and the definition used by the *Yearbook of International Organizations* exclude them from the term 'international organization'.
- Using the definition of an international organization established at the end of Chapter 1, multinational corporations (MNCs) cannot really be described as 'formal, continuous structures established by agreement between members (governmental and/or non-governmental) from two or more sovereign states'. In reality the transnational corporation (TNC), as defined by the UN document quoted above, is an extension across frontiers of a business domiciled in one country.
- If an MNC is tightly defined as a corporation 'established between a number of countries and operating in accordance with prescribed agreements', then it would certainly come much closer to being defined as an international organization. An example is the Scandinavian Airline System. However, it has been decided to keep in line with the *Yearbook of International Organizations* and exclude profit-making organizations from the description.

The exclusion of MNCs is not to deny that they have much in common with international organizations, especially organizationally (Wells 1971: 113; Rittberger and Zangl 2006: 9). Also, a number of MNCs may join together to form an international non-governmental organization; for example, a users' group designed with a representational, promotional or educational purpose (e.g. International Chamber of Shipping, Oil Companies International Marine Forum). A more borderline case is that of international cartels and the various freight and shipping conferences which do not themselves make a profit but whose clear aim is to advance the profit-making capacities of their members. Shipping conferences, for example, are varied in their structure and permanence but their general aim is to include a number of shipping lines plying a defined ocean route and to come to an agreement about the conditions used for that route: uniform charges, freight tariffs, working conditions and so forth.

In summary, it should be remembered that MNCs, while not defined here as international organizations, are nevertheless 'clearly important international actors' (Wells 1971: 113) as will be seen in the later review of the literature on international organizations (Chapter 3).

Meanwhile two different sorts of 'building blocks' making up international organizations have been identified – the governmental members and the non-governmental members. The mix of these produces different types of international organizations.

### *The European Union: IGO, sui generis or complex?*

The European Union (EU) encompasses within its institutions, governmental, non-governmental and sub-national actors, but is the European Union an international organization? Or is it something that has to be classified by itself – *sui generis* – or perhaps a complex of IGOs and INGOs?

The EU can been seen as 'a formal and continuous structure' which has been set up by the member states 'with the aim of pursuing the common interest of the membership'. If that is the case, then it fulfils the criteria set out at the end of Chapter 1 of being an international organization.

There are three reasons why the EU might *not* be seen as an international organization. The first is that it has gone beyond being an international organization and is a confederation or even a federation (Burgess 2000). The second is that it no longer pursues just – or even primarily – the common interest of the membership but more the common interest of the Union. Finally, a case could be made that it is not *a* structure but a matrix of structures that provide a new form of governance for the area it covers. These cases will now be briefly examined.

The notion that the EU has been transformed into a sort of super-state or federation seems particularly weak. It is a view that has sometimes been advanced in an attenuated form by some federalists, though more in hope than as a reflection of reality (Pinder 1991; Burgess 2000). More often the warnings about the state-like institutions and activities of the EU have come from those opposing the building of a European federation and who saw in the institutions of the EU at least the genesis of such a behemoth. The British Conservative prime minister from 1979 to 1990, Margaret Thatcher, was suspicious of the federalist motivations behind the European Commission of Jacques Delors (Thatcher 1993: 551–90). But does this mean that the EU became a federation?

The case against the EU even nearing a federal status can be made on several grounds. First, it has no federal constitution. The various treaties establishing the EU and its predecessors – the Treaties of Paris, Rome, Maastricht, Amsterdam, Nice and Lisbon – were all international treaties made between sovereign governments and they lacked any federal vocation. Although the Treaty of Lisbon set out what were Union competences and those where the EU shared responsibilities for policies with member states, there is still no clear division of powers within the EU (Sieberson 2008) and no hierarchy of legislation whereby constitutional matters may be given a higher standing than other issues, for example. The European Court of Justice can only rule on matters covered by the 'Community' aspects of the treaties, being excluded from most of the intergovernmental elements of the treaties. Second, the institutions of the EU are not federal. There is no federal government in Brussels, equivalent to that in Washington DC for the United States or Ottawa for Canada. The main decision-making institution is still the Council of the European Union (previously the Council of Ministers) consisting of the representatives of the member states, though the European Parliament has gradually gained a joint decision-making power with the Council for certain EU legislation. Finally, it is not treated by other states as a federation. However much they may recognize the role of the EU in trade and other negotiations, they still have diplomatic representation to the member states of the Union. Each member state has a seat in the UN General Assembly with two – the United Kingdom and France – having permanent seats in the Security Council.

However, there may be a case for the EU being regarded as a confederation whereby each of the composite states is still sovereign though there is also a central government with some powers. Writers such as Saeter (1991) and Warleigh (1998) regard the EU as becoming more confederal with a greater sharing of power between those institutions that are concerned with the Union as a whole (the European Commission, the European Parliament and the European Court of Justice) and those that represent the interests of the member states, primarily the Council of the European Union. Chryssochoou (1994: 530) has typified the EU political system as 'inverse federalism' whereby 'political authority tends to be diffused as much as possible to the executive branches of the constituent units, rather than to the common central institutions', which suggests a variation on confederalism. One problem associated with typifying the EU as a confederation of one form or another is that there have been precious few examples of confederations. Most have not lasted long before becoming federations (as in the case of the Swiss Confederation, which nevertheless kept that name) or falling apart (in the case of the confederacy in the southern states of the United States). At best the EU can be regarded as a 'confederacy in the making'. Indeed, one US commentator saw the new treaty proposed by France's President Sarkozy and the German Chancellor, Angela Merkel, in December 2011 as Europe's 'Articles of Confederation moment', the comparison being with the Articles agreed by the north American states in the late 1770s before opting for a federation (Horn 2011).

Might it not be the case that the EU pursues the common interest of the Union rather than, primarily, that of its members? The distinction between the two – common and individual interests – is a moot point in any organization and is particularly hard to distinguish within the EU. However, the EU does have prominent institutions whose task is to address and uphold the Union interest. The European Commission was given powers under Article 211 of the European Community Treaty 'to ensure the proper functioning and development of the common market' and, according to Article 213, it is to consist of members whose 'independence shall be beyond doubt' and who should be 'completely independent in the performance of their duties'. Furthermore, in performing their duties, they shall not 'seek nor take instructions from any government or any other body', neither shall governments try to influence them 'in the performance of their tasks'. Likewise the judges of the Court of Justice of the European Union are appointed from persons 'whose independence is beyond doubt' (Article 223). Unlike other international organizations, the regulations and decisions of the European Union are directly applicable in the member states without any need for national legislation (Article 249). This contrasts with the judgments of the European Court of Human Rights of the Council of Europe (a body separate from the European Union), which have to be accepted and implemented by the member governments.

Against this, it can be argued that the EU is still basically pursuing its members' interests. As mentioned above, the Council of the European Union – in which the states are represented – is at the heart of the EU decision-making process, with the Commission having the right of proposition and only very limited powers to make decisions. Although Qualified Majority Voting (QMV) within the Council can oblige a state to accept decisions to which it is opposed, the extension of this process – for example, at the Lisbon Inter-Governmental Council of 2007 – has to be supported by all member states. In December 2011, the United Kingdom was able to prevent the other then twenty-six member states from pursuing a closer fiscal union by changing the treaties of the European Union, obliging them to achieve their aim by a separate agreement. Also the rule of unanimity has been maintained in areas such as accepting new members, constitutional changes and legislation in areas seen by members as affecting their vital national interest. Furthermore, though both the Commission and the Court are supposed to be independent of government influence, their members are nominated by the member states (in effect the governments) and some Commissioners have not been re-nominated for a second term because their 'home' government considered that they had 'gone native', meaning that they took too much of a Community or Union view of matters.

In short, the European Union has two faces. The one looks inward and is a reflection of the wishes of the member states with all the limitations that implies. Its façade is the Council of the European Union, the European Council of the Heads of State or Government (admittedly with Commission representatives participating) and the meetings of the national civil servant representatives in the Committee of Permanent Representatives (Archer 2008: 34–40). It frowns upon activities that upset the vital national interests of any member state and in extreme cases still wields the national veto to prevent such action being taken. More positively it ensures that the activities of the EU achieve for the member states what they could not garner by their own separate efforts. The other face looks outwards and is more the feature of the Union collectively. It is the common policies, the EU as an actor in international negotiations and on the world stage, and is represented by the European Commission. It attempts to build policies that represent more than just the lowest common denominator of the interests of the member states. It aims to create 'an ever closer union among the peoples of Europe' (Common Provisions, Treaty of Maastricht). There is a continual tension between these two faces and sometimes one is more dominant than the other.

Wessels (2005) and Miles (2011) have dealt with the EU's duality through their advancement of fusion approaches in which they argue that political and economic elites within states have recognized that the nation state 'is alive but not well', and is in a process of transformation whereby international interdependence makes it difficult to achieve welfare solutions for citizens. On this basis, these elites are willing to see the participation of their respective states in the construction of new forms of international (mainly supranational) governance. This is because they accept the need to develop policy instruments and deliver solutions through international organizations that cannot be achieved by national means and instruments alone. According to Wessels (2001: 199), fusion explains the process 'by which national and community actors increasingly merge resources in joint institutions and complex procedures', with competencies being blurred across the international, national and subnational levels of governance and making accountability is increasingly hard to trace. Thus fusion explains why the competencies of international organizations can often be blurred with those of participating states and hard to trace across the gradually merging levels of international governance. The outcome is a fusing EU without a clearly defined political aim, which goes beyond the limitations of intergovernmental co-operation, yet falls short of establishing a fully fledged constitutional settlement akin to a Federal Europe (Miles 2011: 193).

Reflecting this dual nature of the European Union and also the various layers at which it carries out its government-like activities, the EU can be seen more as a matrix of organizations – some of them international, some transnational – rather than just one international organization. Within the complex covered by the term 'European Union', there are:

- sovereign member states (http://ec.europa.eu/enlargement/policy/from-6-to-28-members/index_en.htm);
- intergovernmental conferences such as the one held in Lisbon in July to October 2007 (www.consilium.europa.eu/treaty-of-lisbon/igc-2007?lang=en);
- a European Parliament that is directly elected by the citizens of the member states and whose members sit by political party (www.europarl.europa.eu/portal/en);

- a Court whose decisions can be directly applicable to citizens of the member states (http://europa.eu/about-eu/institutions-bodies/court-justice/index_en.htm);
- institutions that resemble those of an IGO (the Council and the Commission) (http://europa.eu/about-eu/institutions-bodies/council-eu/index_en.htm; http://europa.eu/about-eu/institutions-bodies/european-commission/index_en.htm);
- a network of international organizations that have been created by the EU or which are dependent on it, such as the European Environment Agency based in Copenhagen and the European Union Agency for Fundamental Rights (FRA) (http://europa.eu/about-eu/agencies/regulatory_agencies_bodies/index_en.htm);
- and a system that links the EU to the regions of the member states, mainly through the Committee of the Regions (http://europa.eu/about-eu/institutions-bodies/cor/index_en.htm).

It is thus more complicated than any international organization, including the UN system which – though more extensive – is clearly a system of interrelated international organizations. In its actions, the EU has been described as a system of multilevel governance, in which the state – though important – 'no longer monopolizes European level policy-making or the aggregation of domestic interests' (Marks *et al.* 1996: 346–7). The EU can best be regarded as a complex that has a number of institutional forms and undertakes a variety of tasks, some familiar to many IGOs, some state-like. Furthermore, it has a wide range of relations with non-member states and uses and interacts with a gamut of international organizations (Jorgensen 2009). In this book, reference will be made to the institutions and activities of the EU precisely because some of them resemble those of an IGO but also because of the unique nature of the EU. It therefore offers a contrast as well as a comparison with many 'straightforward' IGOs.

## Membership: regionalism versus universalism

Another important aspect of the membership of international organizations is the catchment area from which it is drawn. The two extremes of spread of membership are, first, those of the most limited kind with two members drawn from a geographically contiguous area which has many other factors – economic, social and political – in common. The Benelux Customs Union with its associated institutions is perhaps the best example of this limited end of the membership spectrum: the three members of Belgium, the Netherlands and Luxembourg fulfil the criteria of having relatively similar socio-political and economic backgrounds and are certainly geographically contiguous. At the other extreme are the universal organizations which have membership drawn from practically all the sovereign states in the world: the United Nations and many of its specialized agencies fall into this category.

The distinction made in types of international organizations based on membership is often that between regional organizations and global or universal organizations (see, for example, Schiavone 2008: 401–3). This is a distinction that informs us not just about the extent of membership but also about the aspirations of the organization. Most academic writings on this question have discerned a tension between the trend towards regional organizations and that towards universal aspirations.

In discussing this subject, attention will be predominantly given to IGOs, as their membership is more easily defined. However, the general points made can be mirrored in the INGOs.

The major problems arising here are the definition of a region (and thus of a regional organization) and the delineation of one region from another. Matters would be simplified if the world resembled a peeled orange which divided neatly into segments. This would at least make a geographical typology of international organizations easier: those covering a particular segment would be defined as regionalist and those covering the whole, universalist.

However, there seems to be no one satisfactory definition of a region. Bruce Russett (1967: 2) cites two American social scientists: Rupert Vance, who called a region 'any portion of the earth's surface whose physical characteristics are similar', and Howard Odum, whose 1938 study claimed that a region should have 'a relatively large degree of homogeneity measured by a relatively large number of purposes or classifications'. In the social sciences, regions have not been defined just by geographical characteristics but have also been tested on economic, social, cultural and political grounds. Cantori and Spiegel consider regions

> to be areas of the world which contain geographically proximate states forming, in foreign affairs, mutually interrelated units. For each participant, the activities of other members of the region (be they antagonistic or co-operative) are significant determinants of its foreign policy.
>
> (Cantori and Spiegel 1970: 1)

Karl Kaiser (1968: 86) defines a subsystem as 'a pattern of relations among basic units in world politics which exhibits a particular degree of regularity and intensity of relations as well as awareness of inter-dependence among the participating units', and thus a regional subsystem is a partial international system 'whose members exist in geographical propinquity'. Norman Padelford (1955: 25) also allows for the intermix of geographic and political elements in his definition of regions as 'spatial areas which come to be spoken of as "regions" as a result of usage stemming from the practices of groups of states, utterances of statesmen, or the terms of treaties or agreements between groups of states'. In this description, the stress is placed on the *behaviour* of state representatives; whether an area becomes defined as a region is a result of states' activities. Such activities may give rise to an international organization which institutionalizes the relations of the member states in a regional context.

Another view of regions places less emphasis on 'objective' factors but stresses more the intentions of those that use these geographical terms. One view sees geography as an instrument in the domination by the centralized nation states of the 'marginalized peoples and nations'. In this view, '(g)eography is about power' (Ó Tuathail 1996: 1–2). A particular region can be an area contested in discourses. This allows regions to be built by politico-cultural debate that can create the notion of a particular region. Neumann compares the creation of regions to that described by Andersen (1983) for nations – being 'imagined communities' – whose existence is preceded by region-builders, 'political actors who . . . imagine a certain spatial and chronological identity for a region, and disseminate this imagined identity to others' (Neumann 1994: 58). Saarikoski (1995: 228) makes the distinction between the more objective process of regionalization and region-building. The former is 'a "natural" and passive process without a conscious or programmed human activity' whereby a subjective identity emerges over a period of time, during which the political and cultural frontier areas create an objective essence (Saarikoski 1995: 228–9). Region-building is 'an active process with a conscious human subject', often based on regionalization (Saarikoski 1995: 229) and can either be made from above (by the political powers) or below (by the citizens and subjects) (Saarikoski 1995: 230).

Another problem in dealing with international regions is that of delineation: where does one region end and another begin? If the world divided easily into segments, then the answer would be self-evident, but not even the continents provide such neat packages in international relations. The AU and the OAS both cover their continents in membership terms and are exclusive to their continents. However, Morocco withdrew from the AU in 1985 when the Sahrawi Arab Democratic Republic was admitted, and Cuban membership of the OAS has been suspended since 1962. It seems difficult to decide what *size* a region should be – or, indeed, who should define that size. This can often lead to the term being used very loosely with boundaries 'zones rather than lines', ending in 'transition seldom in definite boundaries' (Russett 1967: 5). Otherwise non-geographic factors (political, cultural) can be used to delineate members of a region. An example of the latter case is the Nordic region, where membership is not only drawn from the Scandinavian peninsula but includes Denmark (though not Germany to which Denmark is physically joined) and Iceland, far out in the North Atlantic, because of their cultural and historic links with the peoples of the Scandinavian peninsula.

Quite often the problem of delineation is sidestepped by identifying a region's 'core area' and its 'periphery' with sometimes 'intrusive' outsiders (Cantori and Spiegel 1970: ch. 1). Even here the definition is by no means clear. To take the Nordic case again, a geographical core area would include Norway, Sweden and Finland while the cultural-political core area is readily recognized as being made up by Denmark, Norway and Sweden.

Bruce Russett (1967: 11) has tackled the problem of regionalism in a comprehensive fashion, focusing on five aspects: regions of social and cultural homogeneity; regions sharing similar attitudes or external behaviour; regions of political interdependence; regions of economic interdependence; regions of geographic proximity. If these five factors are utilized for regional international organizations, it can be said that some organizations are 'more regional' than others. An organization of which the members have strong similarities in each of the five categories could be classified as strongly regional, while an organization 'scoring' in only one category would be one with a weak regional profile (see Table 2.1 for examples). This helps to move away from the sterile argument in the classification of international organizations: 'Are they regional or universal?'

The entrenchment of this regional/universal dichotomy in writings on international relations seems to be a result of the values attached to the ideal organization of each type: the perfect regional organization brings together states of similar backgrounds to solve problems they could not otherwise deal with at a national level and which would be ineffectively tackled by a wider institution; it can produce a security community between members who will no longer expect to resort to force in their mutual relations and can provide a form of selective security against outside threats (Deutsch 1957); it can perhaps produce political entities which will act as components for a future world government (Carr 1945: 45; Etzioni 1964; Gladwyn 1966: 694–703). The perfect universal organization would, in contrast, stress the indivisibility of world peace and prosperity; it would help link the rich and the poor areas of the world; it would be the basis of a collective security system whereby all countries would unite

*Table 2.1* Degrees of homogeneity among five IGOs

| Organization | Russett's factors | | | | | |
|---|---|---|---|---|---|---|
| | A | B | C | D | E | Total |
| Benelux | 3 | 3 | 3 | 3 | 3 | 15 |
| European Union | 2 | 2 | 3 | 3 | 2 | 12 |
| Arab League | 2 | 1 | 1 | 1 | 2 | 7 |
| Commonwealth of Nations | 1 | 0 | 1 | 1 | 0 | 3 |
| UN | 0 | 0 | 0 | 1 | 0 | 1 |

| Key | | Scores | |
|---|---|---|---|
| *Russett's Factors* | | 0 | No or negligible homogeneity |
| A | Social–cultural homogeneity | 1 | Weak homogeneity |
| B | Attitudes and behaviour | 2 | Medium homogeneity |
| C | Political interdependence | 3 | Strong homogeneity |
| D | Economic interdependence | *Totals* | |
| E | Geographic proximity | 15 | Strongest 'regional' identity |
| | | 0 | Weakest 'regional' identity |

to protect any one that was threatened (the Independent Commission on International Development Issues 1980: introduction; Yalem 1965: ch. 1). Depending on the stance taken, regional organizations are seen as better or worse in attaining desired ends such as international peace and security, economic growth and prosperity.

Inis Claude (1964: ch. 6) remarks that 'the constitutional problem of achieving a balance between regional and universal approaches to international organization is far from solved' but points to the complementary elements of the two. Indeed, the UN Charter has a good number of references to the regional element in articles 23(1), 33(1), 47(4), 52, 101(3), with Article 52(1) being the most specific:

> Nothing in the present Charter precludes the existence of regional arrangements or agencies for dealing with such matters relating to the maintenance of international peace and security as are appropriate for regional action, provided that such arrangements and agencies and their activities are consistent with the Purposes and Principles of the United Nations.

Clearly the superiority of the UN in matters of peace and security is maintained, especially as Articles 52(3) and 53(1) underline that regional arrangements should not impair the peaceful settlement of disputes and peace enforcement activities of the Security Council. This dominance and the subordination of regional agencies has been challenged as '"regions" are becoming the most relevant actors in the global security architecture' (Hettne and Söderbaum 2006: 229). After all, regional organizations, being close to any conflict, 'are able to more efficiently assess potential conflicts and direct their limited organizational resources to more effectively prevent and mediate conflict' (Hansen *et al.* 2008: 298). Pevehouse and Russett (2006: 994) have narrowed down the most effective of such organizations in reducing 'the risks of militarized inter-state conflict' to those 'comprised mostly of democratic states'.

More generally, it may be useful, as Russett suggested in his 1967 study, to refer to organizations with a limited membership, with one of the limitations being geography rather than the present classification of 'regional', which can cover anything from a three-member, tightly knit group to a fifty-member multicontinent organization. It should also help in drawing some of the normative sting associated with the term 'regionalism', whether positive or negative.

## Aims and activities

Perhaps the most common way of classifying international organizations is to look at what they are supposed to do and what they actually do. These two interrelated aspects of the behaviour of the organizations get to the heart of their existence and it is by these that they are best classified.

Most international organizations, be they IGOs or INGOs, usually have their aims stated in the basic document by which they have been established. This is not to say that an organization has no other aim except the stated ones. Neither does it hide the fact that each member of the organization may harbour slightly different aims in creating the organization or in joining it. The proclaimed aim is the most apparent statement of the intentions behind the existence of an organization.

The activities that an organization is intended to undertake are also often laid down in its basic documents and they are normally seen to be the fulfilment of the stated aims. This is an area that can be judged by the record of the organization, enumerating the sort of activities it has undertaken. These may vary from the study of 'the scientific, technical, social and economic aspects of poplar and willow cultivation' of the International Poplar Commission of the FAO (www.fao.org/forestry/ipc/en/); the aim 'to promote, coordinate and harmonize all activities of the coconut industry' of the Asian and Pacific Coconut Community (www.apccsec.org/); to 'the development and consolidation of the regional integration process' of the Latin American Integration Association (www.aladi.org/nsfweb/sitioIng/).

The preamble of the Charter of the United Nations, in a lyrical passage that caused much heart-searching and dictionary-thumbing at the San Francisco Conference, declares:

> We the people of the United Nations determined
> to save succeeding generations from the scourge of war, which twice in our lifetime has brought untold sorrow to mankind, and
> to reaffirm faith in fundamental human rights, in the dignity and worth of the human person, in the equal rights of men and women and of nations large and small and
> to establish conditions under which justice and respect for the obligations arising from treaties and other sources of international law can be maintained, and
> to promote social progress and better standards of life in larger freedom, and for those ends
> to practice tolerance and live together in peace with one another as good neighbours, and
> to unite our strength to maintain international peace and security and to ensure by the acceptance of principles and the institution of methods, that armed force shall not be used, save in the common interest, and
> to employ international machinery for the promotion of the economic and social advancement of all peoples
> have resolved to combine our efforts to accomplish these aims.

While this passage may not prepare the reader for the present operations of the UN, it does give an insight into the breadth and depth of activity intended for the organization by its founders. In contrast, some statements of aims are succinct and limited; for example, Article 1(i) of the agreement establishing the International Institute of Refrigeration states:

> The Contracting Parties resolve to collaborate closely in the study of scientific and technical problems relating to refrigeration and in the development of the uses of refrigeration which improve the living conditions of mankind.
>
> (Peaslee 1975: 278)

As can be seen from the two examples of the UN and the International Institute of Refrigeration, the aims of international organizations range from the general and extensive to the specific and particular. The same can be said about an organization's activities, which may range from the establishment of a free trade area down to the study of poplars and willows.

Organizations have been readily defined by their activities. Virally (1977: 65) notes the distinction both between general and specialized organizations and between political and technical ones. Nye (1972: 430) uses a threefold division: military security; political organizations; economic organizations. Padelford (1954: 205) again has three types: '1. economic and technical arrangements; 2. arrangements for defence purposes; and 3. arrangements providing an organization framework for the consideration of broad political issues'. Haas and Rowe (1973: 15) divided 'regional organizations' by their substantive mandate, distinguishing between those devoted to economic objectives, those with military and diplomatic activities, and 'multipurpose organizations covering all or some of these aims in addition to mandates concerning cultural co-operation, human rights, and social or technological questions'. Rittberger and Zangl (2006) provide a variation in their division of activities: security, welfare and economic relations, the environment, and human rights. However, Schiavone (2008: 3) warns that 'any clear-cut classification of organizations according to main objects of activity . . . would prove to be less than accurate and lead to glaring inconsistencies in a number of cases, because of the overlap of functions and responsibilities'. Likewise, Pentland (1976: 628–9) cautions against relying too much on formally stated objectives when classifying international organizations according to their activities. He notes that many organizations are 'flexible and multifunctional and that it is best to group them according to the issues in which they are most actively and consistently involved'. He goes on to use the distinction between 'high' and 'low' politics. High politics concerns 'diplomatic and military problems relating directly to the security and sovereignty of states and to the fundamental order of the international system'. Low politics refers to 'the great volume of daily business conducted between states within that political order – concerning economics, social, cultural and technical issues'. Pentland then distinguishes between 'high political organizations . . . most directly concerned with the sovereignty and security of their members' and low political organizations, subdivided into those dealing with economic management or development, those within the narrow technical or functional sectors of international relations, and those concerned with social and cultural questions.

This distinction between high and low political issues, although a traditional one, is far less useful now in the twenty-first century. In the post-Cold War world and in times of perceived limitations on the availability of resources – even in the richer parts of the world – the security of a country may depend more on economic factors than on the immediate diplomatic and military ones. It is interesting to note that Western summits of heads of state and government drawn from the most powerful European and North American states plus Japan (the Group of Seven or G7) and Russia (Group of Eight, G8) were traditionally concerned with economic management issues, but now have chosen to deal directly with the emerging economies in the wider G20 (including countries such as Brazil, China and India), which they regard as 'the premier forum for international economic cooperation' (www.g20-g8.com/g8-g20/g8/english/home.18.html). This left the G8 to deal with some of the 'higher' issues including security and international terrorism, though in 2014 this became entangled in the cooling relations between the G7 and Russia over Ukraine. The Organization of the Petroleum Exporting Countries (OPEC), the International Energy Agency (IEA) and the International Monetary Fund (IMF) can be seen to be involved in 'problems relating directly to the security and sovereignty of states and to the fundamental order of the international system'. Likewise the institutions of the EU, and the EC before it, have traditionally dealt with just the 'low political' issues mentioned by Pentland but have also been 'directly concerned with the sovereignty and security' of its members. The blurring of the distinction has been confirmed since the start of the 2008 financial crisis when a range of institutions and organizations, such as those connected with the EU, the IMF, the G8 and the G20 have all attempted to address these economic problems. The resulting economic crises in a number of states has led to security problems in those countries – riots in Spain and Greece, among others – and revolutions in others such as Egypt and Tunisia in 2012.

There are certainly two ways in which international organizations may usefully be classified by aims and activities. The first is to take the discrete areas of activity within which the organization acts and to evaluate it on a 'general–specific' scale. The results of such a classification can be seen in Tables 2.2 and 2.3, in which a number of headings are drawn from those used by writers already mentioned. The aims and activities of five selected IGOs and five INGOs are listed under these heads, giving a clear idea of the range of the organizations. A study in the late 1950s examined the field of activities covered by both IGOs and INGOs founded between 1693 and 1954. Perhaps the most noticeable trends were those of the steady growth of the percentage of economic, food, agricultural, trade, commodities, industrial and education organizations, and the decline in new legal, juridical, administrative, cultural, religious, philosophical, ethical, peace and, more surprising, scientific and technological organizations (Speeckaert 1957: xiii).

Tables 2.2 and 2.3 disguise the gap between the aspirations and the achievements of each organization: OPEC seems to have helped achieve 'a steady income to the [petroleum] producing countries' and 'a fair return on their capital to those investing in the petroleum industry' (Article 2c), though it is more arguable whether it has succeeded in bringing about 'the co-ordination and unification of the petroleum policies of Member Countries' (Article 2a); 'the stabilization of prices in international oil markets' (2b); or 'an efficient, economic and regular supply of petroleum to consuming nations'. However great the shortfall between the aims and activities of an organization, both can help in the classification of international organizations by the extent of their intended and actual activity.

Their aims and activities may also typify international organizations in another way: by consideration of the orientation of activities involved. Cantori and Spiegel (1970: 362),

*Table 2.2* Aims and activities of five IGOs by functional area

|  | UN | NATO | IMF | OPEC | Nordic Council |
|---|---|---|---|---|---|
| Political | x | x |  |  | x |
| Economic | x | x | x |  | x |
| Social | x | x |  |  | x |
| Labour | x |  |  |  | x |
| Legal | x |  |  |  | x |
| Military | x | x |  |  | x |
| Food & Agriculture | x |  |  |  |  |
| Trade & Commodities |  |  | x | x | x |
| Education | x |  |  |  | x |
| Culture | x |  |  |  | x |
| Human rights | x |  |  |  | x |
| Science & Technology |  | x |  |  | x |
| Health | x | x |  |  | x |
| Transport |  | x |  |  | x |
| Other |  |  |  |  |  |
| Communications |  | x |  |  | x |

*Table 2.3* Aims and activities of five INGOs by functional area

|  | IOC | WFUNA | ITUC | LI | ICS |
|---|---|---|---|---|---|
| Political |  | x | x | x |  |
| Economic |  | x | x |  | x |
| Social |  | x | x |  |  |
| Labour |  |  | x |  |  |
| Legal |  |  |  |  | x |
| Military |  |  |  |  |  |
| Food & Agriculture |  |  |  |  |  |
| Trade & Commodities |  |  |  |  | x |
| Education | x | x | x | x | x |
| Culture | x | x |  |  |  |
| Human rights |  | x | x | x |  |
| Science & Technology |  |  |  |  | x |
| Health | x |  |  |  | x |
| Transport |  |  |  |  | x |
| Other |  |  |  |  |  |
| Communications |  |  |  |  | x |

*Key:*
IOC       International Olympic Committee
WFUNA   World Federation of United Nations Associations
ITUC     International Trade Union Confederation
LI          Liberal International
ICS        International Chamber of Shipping

when dealing with 'regional' organizations, identify three kinds of orientation: organizations aimed at settling disputes between members 'either through the diplomatic process or through more elaborate peacekeeping machinery'; organizations designed 'to present a common military and, perhaps, diplomatic front against an outside actor or actors'; and those intended to deal with economic relations and other technical problems.

This division can be adapted and broadened to cover international organizations generally. When examining the aims and activities of organizations, the sort of relationships they are intended to create among their members should be considered. Three major divisions are identifiable:

1   Organizations that aim at encouraging *co-operative* relations between members which are not in a state of conflict. The organizations would be intended to increase already existing co-operation or to turn a relationship of indifference into one of co-operation.
2   Organizations intending to decrease the level of *conflict* between members by means of conflict management or conflict prevention. Such an organization would help to move an existing relationship from that of conflict (or potential conflict) to that of less conflict, indifference, or even co-operation.
3   Organizations with the aim of producing a *confrontation* between members of differing opinions or between members of the organization and specific non-members. This can either harden already existing attitudes or can move them from the co-operative or indifferent points on the scale to that of conflict.

Many organizations incorporate an element of divisions 1 and 2 in their aims and activities; others include 3 with some elements either of 1 or 2, or of 1 and 2. This admixture is shown for five IGOs in Table 2.4. By far the greatest orientation in the stated aims and activities of these five organizations as portrayed in their basic documents is that of co-operation, which is an understandable finding. It should, however, be noted that the stated aims and activities of organizations are not always reflected in their actual behaviour. The good intentions of co-operation are sometimes laid aside and the instruments of conflict management do not work every time. The actual behaviour of organizations is considered in Chapter 4.

*Table 2.4* Aims and activities of international organizations

|  | *Co-operation* | *Conflict management* | *Confrontation* |
|---|---|---|---|
| UN | Arts 1.2–1.4, 10, Ch. IX | 1.1, 2.3, 2.4, Ch. VI, 52 | Ch. VII, 53 |
| NATO | Arts 2–5 | 1,2 | |
| IMF | Arts 1–VI, VIII 4–6, XXI–XXXII | Art VIII, 2–3 | |
| OPEC | Arts 2, 4, 7d | | |
| Nordic Council | All provisions | | |

## Structure

One of the easiest ways used to classify international organizations is by the structure of their institutions and the comparative power of these institutions. Since the rise of international organizations in the mid-nineteenth century, their institutions have become increasingly complex. Originally organizations such as the UPU and ITU had a permanent administrative bureau with a policy-making meeting of member countries' representatives every few years and this seemed to be the most common pattern for the international service unions, although the International Union for the Publication of Customs Tariffs, established in 1890, has only a bureau supervised by the Belgian Ministry of Foreign Affairs, there being no provision for the meeting of member governments' representatives. Another pattern, clearly established with the creation of the League of Nations, was to have a secretariat, a plenary gathering of members' representatives and a body – the council – which was drawn from a selected number of states. The International Labour Organization (ILO), set up in 1919, had two innovations in its structure: it included representatives drawn from non-governmental groups, in this case employers and employees, who sat together with governmental representatives at the General Conference and the meetings of the governing body. Separate organs representing economic and social groupings have become more common in organizations established post-1945, as in the European Economic and Social Committee of the European Union (www.eesc.europa.eu/). The ILO also established an administrative tribunal in 1927, an example followed by post-war institutions such as the UN, NATO, OECD and the WEU.

Juridical institutions dealing not so much with administrative disagreements within the organization but more with disagreements between members date back to the dispute-settling powers of the top bodies of the International Commission for the Navigation of the Rhine and the Moselle Commission, to the peaceful settlement of disputes undertaken by the Permanent Court of Arbitration and the work of the Permanent Court of International Justice. There now exists a range of legal institutions attached to international organizations for the purpose of settling disputes or controversies: the UN's International Court of Justice, the European Court of Justice (of the European Union), the European Court of Human Rights and European Commission of Human Rights (of the Council of Europe) are perhaps the best-known examples. A further institutional innovation has been that of parliamentary organs consisting of either a number of elected representatives from member states' parliaments – as in the case of the Parliamentary Assembly of the Council of Europe, the Nordic Council, the NATO Parliamentary Assembly or the Parliament of the European Communities previous to 1979 – or of directly elected members, the post-1979 European Parliament providing the one example.

As the number of international organizations has grown, so have the possibilities of institutional innovation. Some organizations have gone through their own process of institutional development during the past twenty years: the Nordic Council has obtained a secretariat and added a council of ministers to its original parliamentary base; the Commonwealth of Nations now has a permanent secretariat. Others have been attracted by simplicity: the South African–Botswana–Lesotho–Swaziland Customs Union had, under its 1969 Agreement, a Customs Union Commission composed of representatives of all the contracting parties meeting annually, though since 2000 the revitalized Southern African Customs Union now has a council of ministers, commission, tribunal as well as a secretariat and various committees (www.sacu.int/about.php?id=396). At the other extreme, the United Nations is now a network consisting of the Security Council, General Assembly, Economic and Social Council, Secretariat, International Court of Justice and the various commissions, committees, conferences, boards and specialized agencies attached to these principal organs.

On what basis can institutional structure provide a typology of international organizations? Three basic questions about the institutions, suggested by Reuter (1958: 248), help in providing an answer:

1   What provision is made in the organs to balance the interests of one member against those of another or one group of members against another group? How, then, is institutional power distributed?
2   How is the balance between the power and influence of the member states and that of the organization's institutions reflected in its structure?
3   What is the balance between governmental and non-governmental representation?

Examining each of these questions separately, it can be seen how the answers may help to provide a classification of organizations by their structure.

### Institutional power of members

In looking at both the legal status of international organizations' members and functioning of organs, the interstate organs are of crucial interest. How is power divided between deliberative, plenary organs on which all members are represented and executive-governing organs which do not always have representatives of all members on them? Klepacki (1973: 31) points out that both the constitution and the practice of leading IGOs provide 'permanent representation in the executive-governing organs of states playing a leading role in the realm which constitutes the main sphere of action of a particular organization'. Examples are the permanent seats given to the Great Powers in the Council of the League of Nations and the UN's Security Council (though it is arguable whether these can be called 'executive-governing' organs without qualification); those given to the large capital subscribers of the IMF, the IBRD, the International Development Association (IDA), the International Finance Corporation (IFC) and the Bank for International Settlements (BIS); and the distribution of ten of the twenty-eight governmental seats on the Governing Body of the ILO to the major industrial states. However, an organization may have an executive-governing organ on which all members are represented equally or may only have plenary deliberative organs in the interstate section. The AU has an executive council, which is responsible to the supreme organ of the Assembly of the Union which consists of heads of state and government, but all members are equally represented on the Executive Council (www.au.int/en/).

Another structural way of affecting the distribution of power and influence between the members within an organization is by means of the voting mechanisms. One possibility is to allow parts of a state separate representation – this was the course adopted in 1944 by the UN and its specialized agencies to allow the then Soviet Union extra votes in the form of representation by two of its constituent republics – Byelorussia and the Ukraine. A more usual method is to weight the votes, something done within

IMF, IBRD, IDA and IFC in accordance with the economic strengths of the members as reflected in their subscriptions to the capital of the organization. The representation of national delegations to the parliamentary and economic and social organs of certain organizations is frequently moderated by population size; in the European Union, Cyprus, Estonia, Luxembourg and Malta each has six representatives in the 2014 European Parliament while the Federal Republic of Germany has ninety-six; France, seventy-four; and Italy and the United Kingdom have seventy-three each; the Danish, Finnish, Norwegian and Swedish delegations to the Nordic Council each have twenty members although their populations are, respectively, about five and a half, over five, five and almost nine and a half millions, but Iceland, with 300,000 plus people, has seven seats.

Sometimes the majority needed for decisions within institutions can be varied. Before the First World War, the UPU and other public international unions accepted two-thirds majorities. Although the League of Nations worked on the unanimity principle, a motion passed by a two-thirds majority, while not a decision, was respected as an indication of the members' wishes (*voeux*). The UN and many of its associated agencies have accepted majority voting – the General Assembly takes most of its decisions by a simple majority of members present and voting, while 'important questions' are decided by a two-thirds majority (Article 18). Given that the United States and Russia have only one vote each, they could find themselves being dictated to by a majority of much smaller states. To alleviate this position in the Security Council, while decisions are taken by the affirmative vote of nine of the fifteen members, the permanent members are given the right of veto, that of blocking any decision with which they disagree.

It is difficult to reflect accurately the political reality of relationships in voting formulas. An elaborate system of weighted voting was devised for the Council of Ministers of the European Communities (later European Union) to allow it to take majority decisions, but this system was originally rarely used because of the members' wish to protect their essential national interests by the use of the veto, if necessary, and the general acceptance that Union decisions are best taken with the support of all member states. Sometimes arrangements become outdated: the veto rights which the United Kingdom and France were allowed in the UN Security Council seem superfluous now they are no longer major colonial powers. In many cases, institutional arrangements show little propensity to reflect power relationships: those of NATO have not indicated the dominance in the organization of the United States.

To sum up: international organizations may be classified by whether their institutions differentiate between one member and another; whether some institutions have only limited membership; whether they have weighted voting, majority or unanimity decisions; and whether certain members have veto rights. It can then be estimated whether the institutions of a particular organization are more or less egalitarian.

### Member states/institutions

The bureaux of the early public international unions were often allowed a good deal of independence in the limited functional area of their competence. While the periodic meetings of interstate organs could exercise sovereign control over general policy, the implementation of this policy and the day-to-day running of affairs had to be left to the bureaux – the secretariat. There was little or no tension between the organ representing the individual sovereign states and that embodying the collective needs. Once organizations started to deal with more than technical questions and once they obtained permanent bodies, meeting frequently, that represented the member governments, there was a greater possibility of a conflict between the demands of the individual members and those of the organization's institutions.

An important element in this equation is the extent to which the international functionaries or officials are controlled by the member states. In the early public international unions, the bureaux were quite often run by one member state: Switzerland in the case of the UPU and ITU, Belgium for the International Union for the Publication of Customs Tariffs. The former two offices acted within the general policy limits set by the member states, meeting at regular intervals, while the latter was not inhibited in such a way; its task was so specific and obvious from the 1890 Brussels Convention (amended in 1949) that it needed no further control. The advent of the League of Nations brought the notion of an international secretariat to the fore; that is, civil servants with a loyalty to the organization rather than to their original home country. The UN took over this concept in Article 100:

1   In the performance of their duties the Secretary-General and the staff shall not seek or receive instructions from any government or from any other authority external to the Organization. They shall refrain from any action which might reflect on their position as international officials responsible only to the Organization.
2   Each Member of the United Nations undertakes to respect the exclusively international character of the responsibilities of the Secretary-General and the staff and not to seek to influence them in the discharge of their responsibilities.

The UN Charter also gave, as well as executive and administrative responsibility, political powers to the Secretary-General in Article 99:

The Secretary-General may bring to the attention of the Security Council any matter which in his opinion may threaten the maintenance of international peace and security.

In practice, the secretaries-general have exercised a political role even without reference to Article 99. Both the first and second holders of the office – Lie and Hammarskjold – accumulated a great amount of responsibility using their own interpretation of their duties, sometimes in opposition to members of the Security Council.

However, there have been serious constraints on the independence of action of the UN Secretariat. Members of the permanent staff have not always come up to the standard of Article 100 – former Soviet and some Third World members kept obvious connections with their home governments. Also short-term secondment of national civil servants has been used so that 'the UN Secretariat has gradually and painfully evolved a series of compromises with the original concept of a largely international civil service' (James 1971: 70). A damning report by the retiring Under Secretary-General for Oversight Services in 2010 stated that the Secretariat of the UN was 'in a process of decay' and 'drifting into irrelevance' (Ahlenius 2010: 2).The earlier independent role of the Secretary-General seems to have been moderated after the problems experienced by

Dag Hammarskjold in the Congo from 1960 to his death in 1961. For example, the role of the Secretary-General in the operations in former-Yugoslavia during the 1990s was severely curtailed by the Security Council and its members.

The European Union has, in the European Commission, a body made up of international functionaries which has important executive-governing powers. Members of the European Commission are obliged to act in the interests of the Union rather than in the interests of any one country and they have at their service an international staff. Whereas the High Authority of the European Coal and Steel Community and the Commission of the EEC under its first president, Walter Hallstein, tended to consider the needs of the whole of the Community area – that is, to take a supranational view of their task – the French government's stand against this independent attitude in 1965–66 brought a greater stress on satisfying national needs. Indeed the Commission of Romano Prodi complained that at the Nice Intergovernmental Conference of December 2000, at which a number of reforms of EU institutions were decided, it was side-lined by the French government that hosted the conference. The Treaty of Lisbon has tended to limit the impact of the European Commission in favour of institutions representing the member states, such as the Council of the European Union.

Both the Secretary-General of the UN and Commissioners of the EU have been open to another form of control by the interstate organs; their tenure is renewable and they are chosen by the member states. The opposition of the Soviet Union to both Lie and Hammarskjold limited the diplomatic and mediating role that they could perform between East and West, and in the end Lie was forced to resign and Hammarskjold almost certainly would not have had his term of office renewed had he lived. Similarly, members of the High Authority of the ECSC in the past and of the Commission of the Economic and Atomic Energy Communities and the European Union were and are chosen by member states. It is accepted that every four years the government of each member state names one, though under the Lisbon Treaty this will be one for two-thirds of member states from 2014. A past president of the Euratom Commission, Etienne Hirsch, did not have his term of office renewed in 1962 because he had incurred the displeasure of his home government – the French government of President de Gaulle. A similar fate befell Lord Cockfield, the British-nominated commissioner in the mid-1980s, because the British prime minister, Margaret Thatcher, thought that he had 'gone native' and taken on an EC agenda rather than one in tune with British needs (Thatcher 1993: 547).

While there have been important developments in the creation of institutions that can take independent decisions in vital political areas in some international organizations – notably the UN and the EU – this process has met resistance among key member states. Likewise, the 'international' nature of the functionaries of these and other organizations has been held in check. Dag Hammarskjold described 'two of the essential principles of an international civil service: 1 its international composition, and 2 its international responsibilities', and it is the achievement of these that has been an uphill task in the face of criticism and opposition from members wishing to maintain the dominance of interstate organs. Even the international secretariats of the specialized agencies have been feeling the strain of having to ensure 'equitable geographical distribution' in their recruitment to satisfy new members even though this may mean a decline in the standards of appointment (Symonds 1971: 113).

### Governmental/non-governmental

The major indicator here is the extent to which organs of an international organization contain non-governmental representation as opposed to governmental. At one end of the scale are those INGOs that have no governmental representatives on any of their institutions, while at the other end of the scale are the IGOs without any non-governmental representation. In the middle but to the INGO side are those organizations such as the Inter-Parliamentary Union (which have special links to governments) and the Consultative Group on International Agricultural Research (with governmental, foundation, bank and EU membership). To the IGO side are those intergovernmental organizations which have non-governmental representation in the institutions, such as the European Union and the ILO.

A classification of international organizations by an examination of their structures would demonstrate whether the institutions are more or less egalitarian, what degree of independence the institutions have from their membership, and the balance between governmental and non-governmental participation. A division using these elements produces examples as in Table 2.5.

*Table 2.5* A division of international organizations based on structural characteristics

| | | Governmental | | Mixed | | Non-governmental | |
|---|---|---|---|---|---|---|---|
| | | *Organ's dependence on members* | | | | | |
| | | *More* | *Less* | *More* | *Less* | *More* | *Less* |
| | *More* | NATO | Arab League | ILO | EFTA | Rotary | Nordic Association |
| Egalitarian nature of institutions | *Less* | IMF | UN | EU | International Council of Scientific Unions | WWF | |

## Summary

This chapter has examined three of the most common classifications of international organizations: by membership; by aims and activities; and by structure.

When considering *type of membership,* a distinction was made between organizations made up of governmental representatives (IGOs) and those with non-governmental members (INGOs), though there are a number of international organizations with mixed membership (e.g. ILO). Also identified are international organizations between governmental actors that are not controlled by the central foreign policy organs – transgovernmental organizations (TGOs). Excluded by the definition of international organizations are the business international non-governmental organizations (BINGOs) and other multinational enterprises (MNEs), partly on the grounds of their being based in one country but mainly because their aim is the making of profit. However, they are important transnational actors. The peculiar nature of the European Union was examined and it seemed to be a complex governed by states, regional governments, IGOs and INGOs.

The *extent of membership* introduces the question of regionalism versus universalism. The definition of a region in itself presents problems, though it is generally agreed that the concept denotes more than geographical closeness – it normally indicates economic, social, cultural and political ties as well. There is also an increasing belief that regions are based on perceptions by elites as well as by peoples. This does not help in the task of defining any one region: certainly international organizations are best typified as being more or less regional rather than regional or universal. It is most helpful to refer to organizations with limited membership as opposed to those, such as the UN, that have extensive membership. This also helps avoid some of the normative elements attached to the word 'regional'.

The *aims and activities* of international organizations show what they are meant to do and what they actually do, thus providing the fairest way to classify them. Both aims and activities may be ranged along a 'general-specific' scale and can also be divided according to whether they are oriented towards co-operative relations between members, lowering their level of conflict, or producing confrontation between members (and, in some cases, specific non-members). International organizations may have elements of all three in their basic documents, though the co-operative aspect seems to be the strongest.

An examination of the *structure* of international organizations is the easiest method of classification. The historical growth of the numbers and complexity of international organizations have provided a wide range of structures. A study of these structures can examine how institutions differentiate between one member and another; whether they are more or less egalitarian in their treatment of members; the degree of independence the institutions have from the member governments; and the balance between the governmental and non-governmental elements in the institutions.

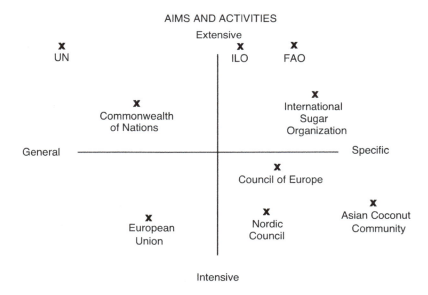

*Figure 2.3* A cross-classification of IGOs

A combination of the above elements can be used to classify international organizations. For example, the extent of membership factor can be placed together with the general/specific range of aims and activities, producing the sort of outcome seen in Figure 2.3. Whichever way types of international organizations are identified, the question to be asked is whether the classification helps in understanding the nature of international organizations. To do this, membership characteristics, behaviour or form should be disentangled in such a way that the factors that make for different international organizations are understood as well as those elements that unify institutions under the one heading of 'international organizations'.

# 3 Writings on international organizations

The student of international organizations is not short of written material on the subject – most textbooks on international relations contain a chapter or section on them and, as shown in Chapter 1, there are a number of books and articles devoted exclusively to the phenomenon. There are also some bibliographies dealing with international organizations – Yalem (1966), M. Haas (1971), Atherton (1976), Church and McCaffrey (2013: 27–40) and the Union of International Associations (2014). Table 3.1 lists the websites that provide either bibliographies of international organizations or links to international organizations. There are at least four periodicals (*The Review of International Organizations*; *Global Governance: A Review of Multilateralism and International Organizations*; *International Organization*; and *Yearbook of International Organizations* – see Table 3.1 for websites) which provide a rich source of material and observation. Reinalda's history of international organizations (2009) is both exhaustive and extensive; MacKenzie (2010) is particularly good on the early period and Herren (2009) gives a historical overview for German readers. Schiavone's dictionary and directory (2008) provides information on a wide range of organizations and Alvarez's article (2006) covers historical and legal developments. The major problems are those of access (how to reach the necessary book, article or website) and of choice (which publications to leave out, which to read and note).

Kratochwil and Mansfield (1994) have provided a survey of the history of the literature on international organizations, suggesting that it reflected the world it studied in the period between the two world wars (1919–39), but that this linkage of theory and practice did not continue after the end of the Second World War in 1945. They had identified four foci in the literature since that time:

> work on formal institutions;
>
> work on institutional processes such as decision-making within international organizations;
>
> a concentration on the organizational role of international organizations;
>
> a pre-occupation with international regimes.
>
> (Kratochwil and Mansfield 1994: 4–8)

They thus divide writings on the subject more by the aspect of international organizations emphasized. This chapter will aim at categorizing the approaches more by their intellectual background. The divisions will therefore reflect those made more

*Table 3.1* Websites for publications on international organizations

---

*General*

— Elizabethtown College PA, *The WWW Virtual library: International Affairs Resources*: a thorough gateway to online resources in the subject, including international organizations.
www2.etown.edu/vl/

— Global Policy Forum: New York-based not-for-profit group that monitors UN and has consultative status with the UN; has good section on NGOs (see section below).
www.globalpolicy.org/

— International Organization section of International Studies Association: brings together academic members of this mainly US-based association who are interested in the study of IOs and provides news of section's activities.
www.isanet.org/ISA/Sections/IO.aspx

— Union of International Associations: Geneva-based organization that has done the most over the years to research into and support international organizations. Publishes the *Yearbook of International Organizations*, reference to which can now be found on the UIA's website.
www.uia.org

— UN's home page: access to the UN's institutions and the range of issues with which it deals.
www.un.org/

— Yahoo's Government, International Organizations site provides an alphabetical list of IO sites with some odd ones there and other more obvious candidates absent.
dir.yahoo.com/Government/international_organizations/

*Non-governmental organizations*

— Global Policy Forum's section on NGOs is thorough and provides useful links.
www.globalpolicy.org/ngos.html

*Journal publications*

— *Global Governance A Review of Multilateralism and International Organizations*: a relative newcomer that tackles the issues of global governance.
journals.rienner.com/loi/ggov

— *International Organization*: the well-established journal on the subject that now has greater emphasis on the politics of international economic relations.
journals.cambridge.org/action/displayJournal?jid=INO

— *The Review of International Organizations*: it analyses the policies of international agencies.
springer.com/social+sciences/journal/11558

— *Yearbook of International Organizations*: the journal of the Brussels-based UIA that, for more than sixty years, has counted, classified and written about international organizations.
www.uia.org/yearbook

---

Note: All sites were accessed on 25 March 2014.

generally in the study of international relations under the headings of realist, reformist and radical. These are very much catchwords and often hide more than they describe.

The three major sections need a little more explanation. This division of writers on the subject into three groups to some extent reflects Martin Wight's headings of realist, reformer and revolutionary (1968, 1991). That representing the more traditional 'realist' view of international organizations is based primarily on the state-centric model of international affairs. The international system is seen as a state of nature in which each state has to be self-reliant to survive. Realism reflects a general conservative outlook that is suspicious of progress. It looks to national interest, rather than moral imperatives, to drive international relations and calculates in terms of comparative power, often defined in military terms. Reformist views of international relations typify them as international society, however imperfect. Humankind is seen as basically co-operative and progress is detected in its activities. Co-operation involves trade, institutions and laws; the role of the state is not as central as in the realist world, neither is it seen as a unitary actor but as representing a number of groupings. It accepts the role and importance of international institutions and non-state actors. It also tends to reflect a liberal outlook that places emphasis on human rights rather than state power. The third set of writings is perhaps the most disparate and is called radical as it challenges the very roots of the realist and liberal approaches, seeing them both as being tied to a state-centred system. It is revolutionary as it is often critical of the existing world order to the extent of wanting it replaced by something better. The state system is seen as outmoded and a form of control and the international system is interpreted as reflecting an unjust distribution of power and wealth. This group includes those with a Marxist approach, and also encompasses other critical approaches to both the practice and the study of international relations. Furthermore, it covers those that see the world from a global perspective, wishing to ignore the divisions that states produce. These divisions should not be regarded as watertight – there is clearly some overlap between the first and second approaches. Within each section, disagreement over the role and importance of international organizations may be found, but the three sections represent particular ideas as to the nature of international organizations. They are seen, respectively, as institutions between states and governments; institutions between societies as well as states; and institutions that form part of a system that itself is under challenge. An attempt has been made to choose the major writers typifying these main lines of thought about international organizations and to include those authors who offer interesting points of dissent.

This chapter is by no means a comprehensive survey of the literature: it is bound to be selective, not just because a full account would be indigestible for the reader but also because of the limitations on the author. This means that material is drawn from that originally written in the major European languages, with English and American literature dominant. It does not mean that material written in other languages is of little value – clearly this is not the case. Because of the international nature of the political science community, important contributions originally written in, say, Romanian or Chinese will normally filter through with translation into English or one of the other European languages. Despite this probability, the reader should note that linguistic constraints, the nature of publishing and what might be called the 'cultural imperialism' of the European and North American area all mean that ideas from the Global South (African, Asian and South American regions) fight an uphill battle to be widely disseminated in print. So this chapter is bound to have a built-in cultural bias however careful the author may have been.

## Realists

Realist views of international organizations consider them to be part of the institutionalized relationship between states and governments. They have a state-centric view of the political world and have little interest in INGOs. Their main concern is how international relations can best be managed rather than how the system may be reformed or improved. A good summary of realist writers is that they have in common 'shared assumptions about the primacy of states as international actors, the separation of domestic and international politics, and who describe the latter in terms of anarchy and a concomitant ubiquitous struggle for power and security' (Griffiths 1992: 217). Textbooks tend to refer back to the writings of Thucydides in Ancient Greece, Machiavelli in medieval Italy and Thomas Hobbes living through the seventeenth-century English civil war – all three writing in times of turmoil and strife – as expressing the basic wisdom of realist thought (Jackson and Sørensen 1999: 70–6; Wohlforth 2008: 131–49). In the modern era, the traditional realist writers have also reflected troubled times.

### *The traditional realists*

These writers had their intellectual roots in the 1930s, the Second World War and the Cold War and are sometimes known as the power politics school. They are represented here by E.H. Carr and Georg Schwarzenberger in Britain and by Reinhold Niebuhr and Hans Morgenthau in the United States. Their starting point was the existence of the contemporary state system, in which there is no common authority over and above the sovereign state, and where there is international anarchy in the sense of a lack of government at the international level. As stated, this viewpoint has consequences for their appreciation of the role of international organizations in interstate relations.

E.H. Carr's writings reflect the disillusionment with the League of Nations in the 1930s over its – or rather its members' – failure to prevent the invasions of Abyssinia (Ethiopia) and Manchuria, and with the conquests by the Nazi and fascist states in Europe. He considered that it was misguided to suppose that a more rational, and more moral, mode of conducting interstate relations, such as by use of the League and the PCIJ, would necessarily have led to a more satisfactory world order, especially if it were not based on the realities of existing power relationships. The League, and the structure it purported to uphold, was only as strong as those countries willing to support it. As the most powerful League supporters (France and the United Kingdom) found an increasing number of states (Germany, Japan, Italy) ranged against the League system and as the United States and the USSR were either unwilling or unavailable to help, Britain and France compromised their support of the League to keep the wolves from their own doors. Indeed, Carr was prepared to support such policies as the Munich Agreement of September 1938 (at which Britain and France effectively handed over Czechoslovakia to Hitler's Germany) as 'the nearest approach in recent years to the settlement of a major international issue by a procedure of peaceful change' and as a recognition of the preponderance of German power in central Europe (Carr 1939: 282).

Furthermore he concluded that there were two major shortcomings in international morality, a morality on which the League of Nations was supposedly based. First, there was discrimination in the international community between the way in which the cases of certain countries were treated. There was, for example, a different attitude by the British and French governments to Poland or Abyssinia being attacked: the former was unacceptable, the latter case only regrettable. Second, there was 'the failure to secure general acceptance of the postulate that the good of the whole takes precedence over the good of the part' (Carr 1946: 166). Without such acceptances it was hard to imagine an organization such as the League working, unless it were based on the overwhelming predominance of power of its supporters. Carr's emphasis on power does not mean that he jettisoned the role of morality in international affairs. He recommended a judicious blend of morality and power, though compared with the national order, 'in the international order, the role of power is greater and that of morality less' (Carr 1946: 168). Indeed Knutsen (1992: 268) considers, with much justification, that Carr was not a 'realist' but 'draws upon the Rousseauean tradition of social thought and gives a dialectical account of the evolution of International Relations'. Though this may be so, his writings reflect much realist thought of the interwar period.

The major work of Georg Schwarzenberger, *Power Politics* (1941), also took the failure of the League and the interwar system as a point of departure. On the question of collective security, the rock on which the League of Nations was built, Schwarzenberger remarked, referring to bilateral pacts of mutual assistance:

> The very need for treaties of this sort proved that League members either assumed that the system of the Covenant would be inadequate, inoperative or too slow to be of use, or that the other members of the League would not honour their obligations under the Covenant. Thus they offer the most open refutation that can be imagined of the solution envisaged by the drafters of the Covenant in a world imbued with century-old traditions of power politics.
>
> (Schwarzenberger 1941: 252)

During the latter part of the 1930s, supporters of the League had turned their interest from the central question of peace and security to the more peripheral areas of the economic and social activities of the League and of agencies such as the ILO. Such an interest is shown by Lord Cecil in the conclusion to his autobiography published in the same year as Schwarzenberger's book. Schwarzenberger was not convinced by the faith placed in such functional links:

> Organizations of a technical, commercial and professional kind, such as the International Postal Union, the Bank for International Settlements, white slave control or the Interparliamentary Union are, within a system of power politics, limited to that sphere of international relations which is irrelevant from the standpoint of 'high' politics.
>
> (Schwarzenberger 1941: 388)

Writing during uncertain times, Schwarzenberger was not aiming to adopt a merely negative stance. Indeed, he desired international relations to be based on a community spirit and founded on the rule of law, but he thought that nothing was more dangerous to this objective than the belief that 'half-way houses like the League of Nations or limited plans for economic co-operation are adequate to bring about this vital transformation' (Schwarzenberger 1941: 11). International order and the rule of law in interstate relations presupposed national communities based on 'justice, freedom, truth and love', Christian virtues to which he recommended Western states return (Schwarzenberger 1941: 434).

A strong Christian element is also to be found in the works of the American writer Reinhold Niebuhr who, nevertheless, is to be counted among the realist school. Niebuhr contrasted growth in man's technical achievement with the lack of advance in political areas:

> Our problem is that technics have established a rudimentary world community but have not integrated it organically, morally or politically. They have created a community of mutual dependence, but not one of mutual trust and respect.
>
> (Niebuhr 1948: 379)

Niebuhr examined the case for world government, noting that almost all the arguments for it rested on the 'presupposition that the desirability of world order proves the attainability of world government' (Niebuhr 1948: 380). He identified two faults which undermined arguments for world government: governments are not created by fiat but need a community for their base; governments 'have only limited efficacy in integrating a community' (Niebuhr 1948: 380). Given the absence of such a community of interest in the world, Niebuhr preferred the imperfections of the Charter of the United Nations to an international organization that would attempt world federation but would accomplish something a lot less spectacular. However, he did note that 'the international community is not totally lacking in social tissue' (Niebuhr 1948: 386). He listed economic interdependence, fear of mutual annihilation and moral obligation as unifying factors in the modern world. Pitted against these were the economic disparities in the world, the negative effect of fear of destruction, and the lack of common convictions on particular issues: 'in short, the forces which are operating to integrate the world community are limited' (Niebuhr 1948: 388). Writing during the initial night-frost of the Cold War, he tempered his realistic view of the world with an appreciation that satisfaction with the status quo is in itself dangerous: 'we might also gradually establish a genuine sense of community with our foe, however small. No matter how stubbornly we resist Russian pressures, we should still have a marginal sense of community with the Soviet Union' (Niebuhr 1948: 388). For this reason, Niebuhr placed emphasis on international organizations such as the UN not as being nascent world government but, in the Security Council, as being 'a bridge of a sort between the segments of a divided world' (Niebuhr 1948: 382). The Christian Niebuhr recognized that while individuals may be moral, the morality of groups is much inferior: 'it may be possible, though it is never easy, to establish just relations between individuals within a group purely by moral and rational suasion and accommodation. In intergroup relations this is practically an impossibility' (Niebuhr 1936: xxii–xxiii). Mankind might dream of peace and brotherhood but has to content itself with a more modest goal: 'a society in which there will be enough justice, and in which coercion will be sufficiently non-violent to prevent his common enterprise from issuing into complete disaster' (Niebuhr 1936: 22).

Perhaps the most famous member of the power politics or realist school is Hans Morgenthau, author of the classic *Politics among Nations* (Morgenthau 1960), first published in 1948. Morgenthau was a German-born international lawyer who emigrated in 1937 to the United States where his post-war work had a deep influence on international relations thinking and practice. Although he did not specifically devote any book to the problems of international organizations, his works were so broad as to envelop the general problems of relations between states and the specific questions of interstate organizations. The three major elements that typify Morgenthau's writings (and the realist school generally) are

> the beliefs that nation states are the most important actors in international relations,
>
> that there is a clear distinction between domestic and international politics,
>
> and that international relations is predominantly about the struggle for power and peace.
>
> (Vasquez 1979: 211)

These basic tenets are reflected in Morgenthau's treatment of international organizations which are seen purely as interstate institutions, important in so far as they are used in the search for power or in solving the problem of peace.

A crucial sentence in *Politics among Nations* points to a central idea in Morgenthau's work: 'The main signpost that helps political realism to find its way through the landscape of international politics is the concept of interest defined in terms of power' (Morgenthau 1960: 5). Thus 'International politics, like all politics, is a struggle for power' (Morgenthau 1960: 27) and 'When we speak of power, we mean man's control over the minds and actions of other men' (Morgenthau 1960: 28). Furthermore, 'All politics, domestic and international, reveals three basic patterns; that is, all political phenomena can be reduced to one of three basic types. A political policy seeks either to keep power, to increase power, or to demonstrate power' (Morgenthau 1960: 39). These policies are seen in three forms: the politics of status quo, the politics of imperialism and the politics of prestige. Morgenthau then evaluated 'national power' and limitations on it in the form of balance of power, international morality and world public opinion, and international law. He considered world politics in the mid-twentieth century and the problem of peace. He examined attempts to obtain peace through limitation (disarmament, collective security, judicial settlement, peaceful change, international government), through transformation (into either a world state or a world community) and through accommodation by diplomacy. In his work, Morgenthau touched on the role of international organizations, especially in his sections on international law, on peace through limitation and on world community.

Morgenthau stressed that on the basis of international law there has been built 'an imposing edifice, consisting of thousands of treaties, hundreds of decisions of international tribunals, and innumerable decisions of domestic courts'. These regulated relations between states arose from:

> the multiplicity and variety of international contacts, which are the result of modern communications, international exchange of goods and services, and the great number of international organizations in which most nations have co-operated for the furtherance of their common interests.
>
> (Morgenthau 1960: 277)

While most international law has been respected, Morgenthau remarked that when rules are violated, they are not always enforced; and that even when enforcement is undertaken, it is not always effective. Mentioning the Briand-Kellogg Pact, the Covenant of the League of Nations and the UN Charter, he considered that:

> These instruments are indeed of doubtful efficacy (that is, they are frequently violated), and sometimes even of doubtful validity (that is, they are often not enforced in case of violation). They are, however, not typical of the traditional rules of international law.
>
> (Morgenthau 1960: 277)

In the section on international government, Morgenthau noted that since the start of the nineteenth century, each of the three world wars (the Napoleonic War, the First and Second World Wars) had been followed by an attempt to establish international government: the Holy Alliance, the League of Nations and the United Nations. The first two attempts foundered because of the varied interests of states involved, in particular because of disagreements about the status quo they were supposed to be supporting. According to Morgenthau:

> conflict between the British and French conceptions and policies did not, however, wreck the League of Nations, as the conflict between Great Britain and Russia had the Holy Alliance. It rather led to a creeping paralysis in the political activities of the League and to its inability to take determined action against threats to international order and peace.
>
> (Morgenthau 1960: 469)

The League could only be said to have exercised governmental functions in the area of the maintenance of international order and peace 'in the rare instances when either the interests of the great powers among its members were not affected or the common interests of the most influential among them seemed to require it' (Morgenthau 1960: 471).

The United Nations was also seen by Morgenthau as being based on unsure foundations, but for a different reason from that for the League: after the Second World War, the victorious powers 'first created an international government for the purpose of maintaining the status quo and after that proposed to agree upon the status quo'. However, 'Since such agreement has never existed during the life span of the United Nations, the international government of the United Nations, as envisaged by the Charter, has remained a dead letter' (Morgenthau 1960: 493–4). He referred to a 'paralysed' Security Council with the General Assembly and Secretary-General of the UN both displaying 'weakness' (Morgenthau 1960: 492–3) and with the whole organization achieving 'little enough' (Morgenthau 1960: 496). In his view:

> The contribution the United Nations can make to the preservation of peace, then, would lie in taking advantage of the opportunity that the coexistence of the two blocs in the same international organization provides for the unobtrusive resumption of the techniques of traditional diplomacy.
>
> (Morgenthau 1960: 497)

In examining the possibility of creating a world community based on a range of international organizations such as UNESCO and the other specialized agencies, Morgenthau made the point that the creation of such a community 'presupposes at least the mitigation and minimization of international conflicts so that the interests uniting members of different nations may outweigh the interests separating them' (Morgenthau 1960: 536). On the UN agencies, Morgenthau considered that:

> the contributions international functional agencies make to the well-being of members of all nations fade into the background. What stands before the eyes of all are the immense political conflicts that divide the great nations of the Earth and threaten the well-being of the loser, if not his very existence.
>
> (Morgenthau 1960: 528)

In summary, Hans Morgenthau accepted that international organizations have a place in international relations, though he was careful not to overstate their importance in the search for power and peace in the world. He saw their contribution as being modest and as part of the general intercourse between states and their governments, and he gave no real consideration to international non-governmental organizations. Furthermore, functional international organizations, while recognized as being useful, were not given any particular role in solving the problem of peace. Even the United Nations was only given credence in this context as 'the new setting for the old techniques of diplomacy' (Morgenthau 1960: 497).

The realist or power politics school's view of international organization is open to three major criticisms. First, it could be claimed that from a moral viewpoint, the power politics school is greatly lacking as it accepts too easily the status quo in international politics and does not allow international organizations a positive role in creating a better world. However, this is to forget that in the writings of a number of the realist school – Carr, Schwarzenberger and Niebuhr – there is a moral and often Christian aspect. Hans Morgenthau was just as concerned with the moral aspects of politics as were his contemporaries who rejected the power politics precepts. The depth of his concern can be seen in his book *Truth and Power: Essays of a Decade 1960–70* (Morgenthau 1970).

Second, the whole realist school, typified by the works of Morgenthau, can be challenged exactly on its major claim, namely its realism. To what extent does the school offer a useful description and explanation of international relations? Vasquez (1979) has outlined how international relations articles published prior to 1970 were dominated by the realist paradigm, yet their hypotheses proved to be inaccurate and even did less well than 'non-realist' hypotheses in their predictive power. Such findings tend to undermine the strength of what was, during the 1960s, the 'intellectually hegemonic' perspective in Western academia (Katzenstein *et al.* 1998: 658). This vulnerability of realism, 'because its empirical validation was never compelling' must then also raise doubts about its rather dismissive treatment of international organizations as being marginal in international relations.

The third major criticisms of the school's treatment of international organizations has been its emphasis on 'high politics', the question of peace and war, to the neglect of 'low politics' such as economic, technical and cultural relations. International organizations are seen just as instruments of policy for states; international non-governmental organizations are hardly considered. Nowadays a neglect of economic relations and INGOs seems an even greater omission.

In defence of this attitude, it should be remembered that most of the power politics writings occurred before the massive expansion of INGOs from the 1960s onwards. The school is rooted in the reaction to the infirmity of the Western democracies when faced by Hitler and Mussolini in the 1930s and it found its feet in the immediate post-Cold War period. It is therefore understandable that it stresses 'high politics' and is antipathetic to international organizations which were seen to be connected with the discredited League of Nations and its intellectual supporters, or with the original intentions of the United Nations before these were stalemated by Great Power dissension.

### Neo-realists

The output of the realists flagged in the 1970s, together with the global power of the United States and in the face of new approaches to the study of international relations. The neo-functionalist and interdependence branches of reformist approaches (see next section) seemed to have taken into account the rise in transnational, non-state elements in international relations and the importance of economic factors in relations across international frontiers (Katzenstein *et al*. 1998: 658–62).

By the 1980s another brand of realism – the neo-realists – had digested the new elements in international relations and reasserted some familiar aspects. Bolstered by the response to the reversion to traditional security thinking by the Reagan administration in the United States (1981–89), these authors tended to stress the conflictual nature of international affairs, that this conflict was primarily between nation states in the modern world, and that power and security was a prime consideration in human motivations (Gilpin 1984: 227). The 'new' element in their writing is a matter of some debate (Baldwin 1993; Kegley 1995; Keohane 1986a), but they had in common a desire for more intellectual rigour in their work than some of the 'old realists', a willingness to deal with relations in a world where US hegemony was in question, and a preparedness to include economic factors in their calculations.

How then did the neo-realists treat international organizations? On the whole they viewed them with the same jaundiced eye as did Morgenthau. International organizations were seen as instruments of state policy, at most common forums. Their role as independent actors in the international system was not something that most of the neo-realists readily accepted. Indeed, their doyen, Kenneth Waltz, forcefully reasserted the position of the sovereign state in international politics:

> for a theory that denies the central role of states will be needed only if non-state actors develop to the point of rivalling or surpassing the great powers, not just a few of the minor ones. They show no sign of doing that.
>
> (Waltz 1986: 89)

Waltz, like others such as Gilpin (1981), was concerned with international politics structured by the uneven distribution of power. International institutions therefore reflected the realities of this situation and the major international organizations, such as the United Nations or the Bretton Woods institutions, could be expected to bear the imprint of the main hegemonic power (in these cases, the United States). If they tried to break away from this straitjacket – as did the General Assembly of the UN in the 1970s – they would find themselves side-tracked by that power.

The neo-realists accepted that hegemonic power could and would decline, but were less able to deal with the consequences of this decline on the structures of international relations. How might they (including international organizations) change 'after hegemony'? It was to this question that Robert Keohane addressed himself. He first admitted that: 'Realism is particularly weak in accounting for change, especially where the sources of that change lie in the world political economy or in the domestic structures of states' (Keohane 1986b: 159). He then referred to his own earlier works on complex interdependence for inspiration (Keohane 1986b: 160). He saw the need to supplement, though not replace, realist writings with theories, and he stressed the importance of studying international institutions which, in particular, would deal with the question of how co-operation can take place in world politics without hegemony (Keohane 1984: 14). By the early 1990s Keohane found a synthesis in the 'institutionalist argument that borrows elements from both liberalism and realism' (Keohane 1993: 271). This assumed that states were the principal actors in world politics and acted in their own self-interests, both traditional realist tenets. Relative capabilities – how power, wealth and other resources were distributed between the various states – were important and states had to rely on their own actions to ensure relative gains from co-operation. From the liberal side, Keohane's institutionalism borrows a greater emphasis on the role of international institutions 'in changing conceptions of self-interest' (Keohane 1993: 271).

During the period from about 1945 to 1965, international institutions were shaped by the prevailing American hegemony. Keohane identified as a problem the decline in resources that the US government had been willing to devote to the maintenance of this system (especially its economic aspect) since the mid-1960s. As US hegemony declined, there would be an increased need for international regimes – sets of rules, norms and institutions – so that states could rub along together. Keohane saw the regimes left by American hegemony as a good starting point for future co-operation and thought that these should be adapted to meet the needs of the new situation (1984: 244–6). This would at least make co-operation possible, would provide information for all about policies, intentions and values, and would create dependability in international relations (Keohane 1984: 259).

Keohane's work has been criticized by the staunch neo-realists. Joseph Grieco (1993: 301–38) provided a comprehensive refutation of Keohane's leanings to a more liberal position and thereby advances a classic statement of neo-realist concerns. He admits that institutionalism has made important contributions: it has shown how the anarchical structure of international relations has created the problem of cheating for international co-operation. Second, it has focused on how international institutions help states manage that problem and its symptoms. Third, it has caused the neo-realists to look more carefully at the relative gains problem. This is the case where states are less concerned with the absolute gains than with their gains set beside those of other states which are seen as potential rivals. In other words, it is better to agree to an arms control treaty allowing your state to build three extra missiles and your opponent to build two extra missiles than to tolerate a situation where you can build five more missiles (a better absolute gain than the three) but your rival can build seven (they have a stronger relative gain compared with the arms control treaty outcome). Finally, neo-realists have had to re-assess their views of the significance of international institutions in the system.

This view of international institutions encompasses the neo-realist understanding of the role of international organizations in the international system. As mentioned, the realists view them as instruments of the sovereign states. Neo-realists have refined this understanding by portraying them as reflecting the hegemony of the most powerful members. They can also provide forums with the potential to be somewhat more efficient than traditional diplomacy or irregular conferences, though a danger comes when they try to be actors in their own right. The successors of the traditional realists, such as Waltz (1979: 70–1) and Mearsheimer (1990) saw the European Union's predecessor, the European Communities (EC), as flourishing because of the bipolar division of Europe by the United States and the Soviet Union during the Cold War. The expectation was that, with the end of the Cold War, the EC project would not advance but rather sink into disuse. Though the EC faced a number of crises in the early 1990s, it did transform itself into the European Union (EU) with an Economic and Monetary Union (EMU) and a Common Foreign and Security Policy. Grieco (1993: 331) explained this in terms of states constituting collaborative rules for a common interest, with the weaker states trying to construct rules that allow them 'effective voice opportunities' to 'ameliorate their domination by stronger partners'. The weaker states – such as Belgium, Portugal or even France in the EU – were trying to bind the stronger – Germany in this case – into a form of relationship that avoids domination. The neo-realists would no doubt point to the domination of Germany in deciding the outcome of the euro currency crisis of 2011 to 2014 as being a triumph of power over institutions within the EU. Nevertheless Grieco (1993: 335) admitted that realism 'has not offered an explanation for the tendency of states to undertake their co-operation through institutionalized institutions'.

This challenge has been taken by those who have increasingly sought to link a fairly realist understanding of world politics with domestic politics in the leading state actors. An example is John Richards's study of the regulation of the international aviation markets in which he claims to 'refine the realist understandings of power in international bargaining' (1999: 33). Basically national politicians create and sustain international institutions, including international organizations, 'to maximise domestic political advantage' (Richards 1999: 9). His contention is that 'international institutions will be created when they are politically efficient (that is, increase electoral support) for national politicians' (Richards 1999: 3). Richards rejects a collective goods approach to international institutions (such as that of Zacher with Sutton 1996) that sees such institutions as correcting the workings of the market internationally and therefore producing economic benefits all round. However, he also rejects the 'hard realist' approach that claims that institutions, including international organizations, merely reflect the power capabilities in the international system as in Krasner's statement that 'stronger states have simply done what they have pleased' (1991: 337). Richards still claims that international institutions are the instruments of states. Because such institutions as the international organizations that regulate international travel define property rights internationally, they alter the market place, leaving gains for some and losses for others. This being so, the building of such institutions internationally is bound to trigger a 'fierce domestic political battle' (Richards 1999: 9). Thus what happens to and in international organizations can be used by domestic politicians to maximize their own domestic advantage. This is a view that may attract support within the United States, though may be less resonant in some of the smaller and weaker states.

A similar view has been taken by the liberal intergovernmentalists who have examined the European Union (EU). Moravcsik (1993, 1998) has pointed out that governmental strategies within the EU have been dominated by preferences and power. Unlike many realists, Moravcsik attaches importance to national preferences as 'shaped through contention among domestic political groups', as well as to interstate bargaining and institutional choice (1998: 20–4). Co-operation and integration were thus seen as useful strategies if they furthered a government's control over its domestic affairs and agenda. Moravcsik thus sees the EU as 'a successful intergovernmental regime designed to manage economic interdependence through negotiated policy co-ordination' (1993: 474).

The neo-realists have been attacked on many grounds, not least for providing no advance on the works of the 'old realists' (see Ashley 1984). Like their realist predecessors, the predictive power of their work has been challenged, particularly their inability to foresee the end of the Cold War and of the Soviet Union (Scholte 1993: 8). Scholte also criticizes them for not addressing global issues, such as welfare questions and pollution, that dominate the world of the late twentieth and early twenty-first centuries. This questions the descriptive ability of the neo-realists: is what they describe any more 'realistic' than their realist predecessors? They have, on the whole, been as uninterested as their predecessors in the role of international organizations. The main exception until the 1990s was Robert Keohane whose earlier works on interdependence served him well on that score. Even here, the criticism can be made that his view is basically conservative and was concerned little with the interests of the Global South (African, Asian and South American regions). Some of the writers on economic co-operation and integration in the 1990s accepted many of the neo-realist assumptions about national interests in international organization. They have brought to the field a more refined view of the relationship between governments and international organizations, and have left behind the Cold War realist emphasis on the military aspects of power.

## Reformists

The realist writers, despite their differing valuations of the worth of certain international organizations, have in common a state-centric approach to international relations. Though some were concerned that governments should reflect more the (inevitably) good intentions of their citizens in international affairs, or that world organizations should have more power to deal with warlike or renegade states, their focus of attention is the international governmental organization (IGO). A noticeable development in international relations literature since the Second World War has been the movement away from this state-centred view towards one that admits the importance of international actors other than the sovereign state. These include IGOs in their own right (rather than as meeting places or instruments of their member states), INGOs, transnational organizations, political groups and individual citizens. Although many publications just describe these new phenomena which have become more active in the last forty years, there is also a prescriptive element to some of the writings. They tend to prescribe increased non-state activity in international relations as a way of underpinning closer relations between states and societies or undermining hostile attitudes by governments (Gordenker and Weiss 1998; Weiss and Gordenker 1996; Willetts 1996). While this general reformist viewpoint is similar to realist approaches in accepting the importance of the state relations in international politics, it does not accept either the monopoly of the state in the system or that states are unitary, rational actors. In summary the key aspects of a reformist approach to international relations includes a number of the following:

- The belief in reason in human nature and in progress: the frequency and level of war can be reduced, for example.
- International relations can be co-operative rather than conflictual.
- Though states are important in international relations, they are not the only actors.
- States are not unitary actors, with their decisions internationally reflecting internal divisions and interests. They do not therefore necessarily maximize the 'interests' of the state.
- The international system, especially parts of it, contains the elements of international society and relies on a variety of international institutions, including international organizations.

The reformist approach to the study of international relations has consequences for the consideration of international organizations and it has made a noticeable contribution to the literature on the subject, especially since the 1950s. However, there is a background to the above ideas that can be seen in the earlier writings of Grotius, Locke, Bentham and Kant (Jackson and Sørensen 1999: 108–11; Viotti and Kaupi 1999: 200–4; Lawson 2012: 39–41). An understanding of the current reformist approaches to international organizations can be helped by reference to some of the writers on international law, which will form one section below.

### International lawyers

Much of the literature about international organizations is descriptive, often dealing with several organizations and giving particular emphasis to the League of Nations and UN, sometimes dealing with one organization such as NATO, the AU or the EU. Leading works in this area are those of the international lawyers who give particular consideration to the constitutions of international organizations, their legal personalities and institutional problems. Indeed, it was probably the Professor of Public Law at Edinburgh University, James Lorimer, who first coined the expression 'international organization' in 1866 (Lorimer 1890: 31).

Contributions to the study of international organizations have been made by British legal experts and historians such as Zimmern in his study *The League of Nations and the Rule of Law* (Zimmern 1939) and J.L. Brierly's comparison of the newly emerged United Nations with the structure and aims of the then dying League. Brierly demonstrated a strong preference for the intrusion of international law into economic and social affairs so that the generic grievances of states may be removed (Brierly 1946: 93). Hersch Lauterpacht published *The Development of International Law by the Permanent Court of International Justice* in 1934, and this was later matched in the United States by Judge Manley O. Hudson's *International Tribunals, Past and Future* (1944). Wilfred Jenks, the Legal Adviser to the ILO, contributed not just on that organization (Jenks 1962a) but also more general works on international organizations (Jenks 1945a, 1945b, 1962b). He stressed the need to marry the craft of the international lawyer with the prudence of the politician to develop an effective system of international organization:

> Institutional development is primarily the responsibility of statesmanship; it must
> be guided and controlled by a true appreciation of political forces. . . . The greatest
> of legal traditions is still to be created; its texture will be largely determined by
> the quality of the craftsmanship which international lawyers place at the disposal
> of statesmen during the next generation.
>
> (Jenks 1945a: 71–2)

Later international institutions' textbooks were provided by two European international lawyers. Henry Schermers, Professor of Law at the University of Amsterdam,
in his two-volume work, restricted himself to 'international institutional law' which
'by concerning itself with the structure and functions of international organizations
. . . tries to explain the present development and to promote the harmonious growth
of international organization' (Schermers 1972: 2). He dealt with the participants in
international organizations, the general rules for their organs, and the activities of these
organs from primarily a legal viewpoint. A similar approach was adopted by the British
international legal expert D.W. Bowett, whose book *The Law of International Institutions* (1970) placed greater emphasis on particular institutions – the League, the UN
and its specialized agencies, the regional organizations, the juridical institutions – as
well as dealing with general questions such as the international personality of the
organizations and their impact on the doctrine of the sovereign equality of states. For
a blend of sociology, history and international law, the work of Paul Reuter, Professor
of International Law at Paris University, is unsurpassed. In *International Institutions*
(1958), he examined the phenomenon of international organization rather than just
the organizations and institutions, and therefore spent some time on the nature of
international society, the origins and foundations of international institutions as well
as the position of states in international society.

Some post-Cold War studies have moved away from what they regarded as 'esoteric
descriptions of the law' and have instead examined 'international law's influence on
political behavior' (Ku and Diehl 1998b: 3). One of the bases of such an approach is
that '(i)nternational organizations, non-governmental organizations, multinational corporations and even private individuals have come to play an increasing role in
international relations, and accordingly international legal rules have evolved to engage
these new actors' (Ku and Diehl 1998b: 3). International law is seen as both an
operating system and a normative system for international relations. As the former, it
'sets the general procedures and institutions for the conduct of international relations
. . . (i)t provides the framework for establishing rules and norms, outlines the parameters
of interaction, and provides the procedures and forums for resolving disputes among
those taking part in these interactions' (Ku and Diehl 1998b: 6–7). As a normative
system, international law 'gives form to the aspirations and values of the participants
of the system . . . [It] is a product of the structures and processes that make up the
operating system . . . [It] takes on a principally legislative character, by mandating
particular values and directing specific changes in state behavior' (Ku and Diehl 1998b:
7). More traditional approaches to international law tended to describe the role of
international organizations as part of the operating system. Legal texts published since
the end of the Cold War have looked increasingly at the position of international
organizations – not least those of the UN system – in a normative framework, especially
in functional areas such as human rights (Alston 1998), the environment (Kiss 1998),
the global commons (Joyner and Martell 1998) and women's issues (Berkovitch 1999;

Wright 1993: 75–88). There is also reference to the tension between law and politics, the member states' domestic factor and the role of process in decision-making in international organizations (Scharf 2007: xxii).

International lawyers have given extensive consideration to particular institutions. The League of Nations attracted special attention as lawyers played an important role in its drafting and as it had as its aims the promotion of international co-operation and the achievement of international peace and security:

> by the firm establishment of the understandings of international law as the actual rule of conduct among Governments, and by the maintenance of justice and a scrupulous respect for all treaty obligations in the dealings of organized peoples with one another.

> (Preamble to the Covenant)

Furthermore the central part of the Covenant dealing with the keeping of peace (Articles 12–16) adopted a legalistic approach in defining an act of war in disregard of Articles 12, 13 or 15 as being an act against all League members (Article 16 (1)). In other words, the cardinal sin was the breaking of the legal agreement made with other states. International lawyers in particular were concerned with how international law might be agreed, judged and enforced: in the interwar period they turned much of their attention to the activities of the Permanent Court of International Justice and the League of Nations. Judge Hersch Lauterpacht, for example, considered that all international disputes were justiciable and thus open to solution by the judicial process in international law. He considered the League to be a useful step in the development of international law and the sanctions allowed for in Article 16 of the Covenant as marking 'the first step' towards the collective enforcement of international law (Lauterpacht 1970: 19).

The League had its advocates among other legal writers. Alfred Zimmern, writing in 1938, set the League's activities and institutions against the backdrop of the gathering storm in Europe. He still found much to say for it: it had developed and expanded the old diplomatic system, had encouraged co-operation in many areas, and at least represented an attempt to eliminate war even during a period of what Zimmern called 'earthquakes' (1939: 491–509). Lord Robert Cecil, one of the founders of the League as well as a lawyer and Conservative politician, admitted when writing in 1941 the failure of the organization in preventing aggressive powers. Nevertheless, he hoped that it would be reformulated after hostilities with a core of confederation of European states, 'the central object of which should be the preservation of the European peace'. Peace in the rest of the world would depend pretty well on the then just-existing Covenant with some small changes. Cecil did admit that 'another piece of machinery' could do little unless the peoples and governments 'really put the enforcement of law and maintenance of peace as the first and greatest national interest (Cecil 1941: 349–51).

The hopes of those who yearned for legal solutions to international disputes clearly declined as the UN Charter, with its emphasis on political solutions to what were political disputes, replaced the optimistic legal formulas of the League Covenant. The UN Charter was not to be without its international legal commentators. Indeed, two early standard books on the UN are by distinguished lawyers, Kelsen (1950) and Goodrich *et al.* (1969), though the latter have admitted that when interpreting the Charter since the responsibility for interpretation is vested in organs and members alike, the process is more likely to be political than judicial . . . Decisions tend to reflect the common interests of members in achieving certain results.

(Goodrich *et al.* 1969: 15)

Other legal commentators have placed emphasis on the role of international organizations in the development of particular aspects of international law and again have seen the development of the rules and norms of international society – however imperfect – in these cases. Examples are Kratochwil (1989) who has written generally on the subject, Jackson (1997) and Thomas and Meyer (1997) on the world trading system, Kiss and Shelton (1991) and Hunter (2014) on international environmental law, and Human Rights Watch (1992, 2013) and Bianchi (1997) on human rights issue. The growing importance of the rule at law at the international level can be seen in the publications of the UN, such as the report of the Secretary-General on this issue (UN General Assembly 2011).

### *International government/governance*

Another American legal authority, Clyde Eagleton, gave the United Nations a critical, though somewhat understanding, appreciation, summing up its dilemma thus: 'If the United Nations cannot do more than it has, the fault lies with the Members who made it and operate it, and who, it seems, still prefer the tooth and the fang to international law and order' (Eagleton 1948: 552).

Eagleton placed the record of the United Nations in the context of its predecessors in the history of the growth of international government, and of its legal and political background. He examined proposals to achieve the 'international government' that the UN failed to reach but concluded that a change in the attitudes of states and their peoples is needed first (Eagleton 1948: 583). Eagleton's work underlined the point made by Evan Luard in his *International Agencies* (1977): that with the existence of the UN and its associated agencies, many of the world's problems are not without institutions exercising authority over them. The powers of this range of organization can be questioned, as can their standing in relation to their sovereign state members, but their existence in the post-war world – and their growth from their nineteenth-century beginnings – is a reality.

This interest in the growth of 'international government' is neither new nor restricted to the legal profession. One of the earlier publications on the subject was by the writer Leonard Woolf who was a founder of the Fabian Society, the reformist discussion group within the British Labour Party. Writing in 1916, he outlined the extent to which 'international government' had been accepted through diplomatic gatherings, the use of public and private international unions and the increase in commodity agreements, and he put forward plans for the further regulation of international activity. 'If war is to be prevented', he claimed, 'states must submit to some international control and government in their political and administrative relations' (Woolf 1916: 228). He advanced a Fabian Committee plan for 'The Supranational Authority that will Prevent War', elements of which found their way into the League Covenant and which, inter alia, recommended 'the establishment of an International High Court, an International Council of states' representatives and an International Secretariat'. Woolf and his Fabian colleagues hoped that with this machinery, legal, justiciable disputes would be submitted to the Court or a similar tribunal and other disputes to the Council for settlement, with the parties to the dispute constrained from warlike action for a period of a year. Provision was to be made for sanctions which all states should put into operation and all agreed 'to make common cause, even to the extent of war, against any constituent State which violates this fundamental agreement' (Woolf 1916: 233).

Woolf, together with jurists such as Hersch Lauterpacht and Alfred Zimmern and British political writers such as Philip Noel-Baker, Lord Cecil and Gilbert Murray, represented both the practical and the intellectual supporters of the League of Nations in the interwar period who were often classified as 'idealists' or neo-Grotians. Hedley Bull (1966: 52–5) described the central Grotian assumption (named after the seventeenth-century legal writer Hugo Grotius) as being 'that of the solidarity, or potential solidarity, of the states comprising international society, with respect to the enforcement of the law' and Grotius's basic criterion of just war being fought in order to enforce rights – a notion clearly echoed in the Fabian Committee's 'The Supranational Authority that will Prevent War'. Bull criticized the way this group lost sight of international politics in their preoccupation with international law, international organization and international society:

> In dealing with international morality, which they were inclined to confuse with international law, they contributed only a narrow and uncritical rectitude which exalted the international interest over national interests (but without asking how the former was to be determined), constitutional reform over revolution as the means of transcending the society of sovereign states (but without considering whether states could become the agents of their own extinction), and respect for legality over the need for change (but without facing up to the fact that the international legal system, as they construed it, could not accommodate change).
>
> (Bull 1972: 36)

This is a telling enough assessment of the idealists' views, including their writings on international organizations. However, the background of the group should be remembered – they represented a generation devastated by the First World War and which was used to a national society (early twentieth century Britain) that had benefited through institutional change and in which the rule of law had not precluded reform. The League of Nations, the Permanent Court of International Justice (PCIJ) and the ILO were for them part of 'a Great Experiment', to use Lord Cecil's phrase.

More modern writers picked up and developed many of the notions current in the above literature and stressed how international intercourse has been governed by a body of laws, rules and regulations and by institutions, including international organizations. Though they have kept the analogy with the domestic government of citizens, they have preferred the term 'international governance', demonstrating that such a system does not have the sort of enforcement powers expected of national governments. Notions of global governance are covered below, where reference is made to the idea of an international regime. This concept helped bring international organizations into the wider literature about international co-operation and governance in a state of anarchy, meaning an absence of international government with significant enforcement powers.

By the early and mid-1990s attention was again turned to the management of the international environment in the wake of the UN Conference on Environment and Development (UNCED) at Rio de Janeiro, Brazil. The environment seemed to be a classic candidate for global governance, partly because it was global and partly because of the range of institutions involved in its management. In the words of Joseph Nye '(e)ffective international environmental institutions thus helped to overcome some of the typical national bottlenecks that hinder co-ordinated measures to reverse the frightening trends of global environmental degradation and improve the possibility of sustainable development of our planet' (Nye 1995: x). The assumption of Keohane *et al.* was that while states may have difficulty addressing international environmental problems, co-operation between governments could bring dividends. Effective international institutions were needed which may take the form of international organizations, regimes or informal conventions. They were seen, in the words of Maurice Strong (Secretary-General of UNCED) as 'the basic framework for a world system of governance which is imperative to the effective functioning of our global society' (1990: 211–12). The aim was pragmatic – to see whether the international institutions covering the environment had made a positive difference, especially in the political field.

Case studies were presented that explored the impact of international institutions with three conditions essential for effective action on the environment: 'high levels of *government concern*, a hospitable *contractual environment* . . . sufficient *political and administrative capacity* in national governments' (Keohane *et al.* 1995: 11). The case studies were seen in terms of agenda setting, international policies and national policy responses (Keohane *et al.* 1995). The three authors were aware of the strong influence of state powers in international institutions and of their meagre results in some areas. Nevertheless, they set down three conditions under which 'international institutions can alter the behavior of state actors, and in turn improve environmental quality' (Keohane *et al.* 1995: 19). These are (Keohane *et al.* 1995: 19–20):

- governmental concern has to be high enough to prompt the use of scarce resources to tackle the problem;
- there has to be a contractual environment where states make credible commitments and make and keep agreements that 'incorporate jointly enacted rules, without debilitating fear of free-riding or cheating by others';
- states should have the political and administrative capacity to make the domestic adjustments necessary to implement international norms, principles and rules.

The emphasis in this view of global governance is on the relationship between the international and the national. Others have identified wider elements such as the importance attached to the process of collective action that supports the global governance model and a stress on the growth of internationally agreed rules and norms (Rittberger and Zangl 2006: 214–15).

Part of global governance – as noted in Chapter 4 – is international regimes. These are 'sets of implicit or explicit principles, norms, rules and decision-making procedures around which actors' expectations converge in a given area of international relations' (Krasner 1983: 2). They are subsets of international society and its institutions. International regimes, which are often specialized arrangements limited by function or geographical area, are arrangements that govern co-operative behaviour internationally. They are thus more widely drawn than international organizations. International organizations, according to one of the most prolific writers on the subject, Oran Young (1989, 1994), can both stimulate the process of regime formation and can help implement their provisions (Young 1994: 164).

### Functionalists

An early break with the traditional view of international organizations based on the state-centric model can be seen in Leonard Woolf's book *International Government*. Although still primarily concerned with interstate relations and the questions of peace and security, a sizeable section of his writings covers governmental technical and economic co-operation and INGOs:

> We are accustomed to regard the world as neatly divided into compartments called states or nations . . . But this vision of the world divided into isolated compartments is not a true reflection of facts as they exist in a large portion of the earth today.
>
> (Woolf 1916: 216–17)

Such a step placing greater emphasis on non-state international relations was taken further in the writings of the Romanian-born author David Mitrany. Mitrany's ideas, known as the functionalist approach to international politics, were inspired by his early life in the Balkans. He found much intellectual stimulation after coming to London in 1912 and working together with Leonard Woolf, among others, in the League of Nations Society, the Labour Party's Advisory Committee on International Affairs, and the Fabian Society. His two major early works were *The Progress of International Government* (first published in 1932, reprinted in Mitrany (1975a)) and *A Working Peace System* (first published in 1943, republished in 1966), though he also made a substantial contribution in articles until his death in 1975. Many of his writings together with an autobiographical piece and an introduction are gathered together in *The Functional Theory of Politics* (Mitrany 1975a). In his 1932 work he outlined the nineteenth-century growth in international government along similar lines as Woolf:

> The nineteenth century produced that amazing growth in the material equipment of civilization, which welded the world together into one organic whole, making each people a partner in the fate of all. The outward expression of that change was the appearance of world-wide popular movements and the making of innumerable private and public international agreements.
>
> (Mitrany 1975a: 89)

Mitrany was concerned that the rise of the nation state and the insistence of new states on the doctrine of sovereign equality when they were clearly weaker and smaller than the Great Powers hindered international co-operation in, for example, the economic sphere. However, he saw that the force of events was working against 'statism':

> No matter what the size and shape of the particular community, its functions are such that they have to be organized; and the forces and factors now at work no longer have any true relation to the old political divisions, within or without the state. The new functions imposed upon our political institutions are compelling

a complete reconstruction of the technique of government, on a purely practical basis. I reach that conclusion by asking at the outset not, 'what is the ideal form for an international society?'; but rather, 'what are its essential functions?'

(Mitrany 1975a: 99)

He claimed that essentially the aims of international government were no different from those of municipal government: to create equality before the law for all members of the community and to promote social justice. To expect to achieve the first aim in international society where states were neither equal nor unchanging units would be unreasonable. It would be far more practical to compromise this aim and establish a League of Nations in which Great Powers would be directly represented. Secondary states would have group representation and smaller states would have 'panel representation'. At the same time, secondary bodies would be set up in various parts of the world as organs of regional groupings of states and these bodies would be connected with, and subordinate to, the new central League organs. They would also be able to deal with problems more readily, especially as the unanimity of all states would not be needed for a settlement.

These suggestions are not the novel aspects of Mitrany's work. They are important in changing the emphasis away from the rights of states towards the duties, or at least the activities, of states. Still the concern was with arranging relations between states. In a paper submitted to the British Foreign Office in 1941 and in his study *A Working Peace System* (1966), Mitrany concentrated on how the functions of government might be carried out more expeditiously. He recognized that within liberal democratic states the line between which functions are carried out by public and by private action was shifting and that this line 'under the pressure of fresh social needs and demands . . . must be left free to move with them'. A similar demarcation existed in the territorial sphere internationally: some functions (e.g. railway systems) could best be organized continentally, some intercontinentally (e.g. shipping) and some universally (e.g. aviation). However, there would be no need for rigid patterns except perhaps in the exercise of negative functions – those related to security where more formal, static institutions would be needed. In the field of positive functions (those related to economic, cultural and social affairs), the dimensions, organs and powers of any organization would be determined by the nature of the function and would be fairly flexible. Mitrany foresaw the establishment of functional bodies 'with autonomous tasks and powers' which would 'do things jointly'. This would link 'authority to a specific activity' thus breaking away 'from the traditional link between authority and a definite territory' (Mitrany 1966: 125). This move would avoid the sterility of many of the wartime suggestions for post-war federations or constitutional innovations in the United Nations, which foundered on the opposition of sovereign state resistance. Mitrany hoped that the number of international agencies that had existed before the Second World War, augmented by the Allied boards during the war itself, would serve as the basis for the network of international government. He quoted with obvious approval the words of an American scholar, J. Payson Wild, Jr, on the various wartime experiments:

The lines between domestic and international activity are blurred, and national administrative agencies of the Powers concerned sometimes engage in domestic business, and at other times extend their functions into the international sphere.

The result is a conglomeration of international board and domestic staff whose duties intermingle. Administrative officers of national units deal directly with their opposite numbers in other states without benefit of diplomatic intermediaries, and simultaneously perform both national and international tasks. So far no attempt has been made to establish a super-state.

(Mitrany 1966: 167)

Mitrany's vision is of a world in which the functions of everyday social life – transport, health care, communications, agriculture, industrial development, scientific development and so on – are no longer assiduously carried on within the confines of each sovereign state but are undertaken across frontiers on a regional, continental, or universal basis. These activities would be overseen by international organizations which would be more like boards of management. The functional agencies of the UN (the ILO, WHO, FAO) already undertake such co-operative tasks, as do some non-governmental groupings of specialists (International Federation of Red Cross and Red Crescent Societies, World Organization of the Scout Movement). However, the line between what has been done internationally and domestically has been drawn very much to the benefit of the latter; and international activities have been riddled with political disputes, many of which have little to do with the good management of the function involved. Mitrany's scheme would gradually lower the line to allow more functions to be carried out at the level where they work more efficiently and would provide management of these functions rather than political interference. Not only would this development benefit the general social welfare of the world, it would also help to solve the problem of peace and security. The Lilliputian ties of international functional co-operation would pin down the giant of conflict, weakening the urge to destruction and warfare by the promise of construction and co-existence.

The functional approach does not focus solely on intergovernmental organization but allows for a network of specialized agencies, many of which could be non-governmental. It differs in emphasis from the mainstream traditionalist writings, and Mitrany's work presaged a move away from interstate relations to world politics. While 'the functional approach does not offend against the sentiment of nationality or the pride of sovereignty' (Mitrany 1965: 139), there is no doubt that it is meant to weaken the importance and power of the 'middle man' between the individual and a world community – the sovereign state. The feeling of solidarity encouraged by functional links is not between states but between people or associations of individuals: 'Each of us is in fact a "bundle" of functional loyalties; so that to build a world community upon such a conception is merely to extend and consolidate it also between societies and groups' (Mitrany 1965: 143).

Such an imaginative approach to world problems and the mundane, hard-working, apolitical role it implies for international organizations has its faults. To criticize Mitrany's functionalism as being impractical is unfair both because international functional links have grown, especially since the Second World War, and because Mitrany's approach is a gradual one – he did not expect it to be adopted overnight. Even so, it does have certain ambitious aspects, which should be critically examined.

First, despite the reference to possible regional functional arrangements, Mitrany's plans run counter to the notion of all-embracing regional organizations such as the European Communities, now European Union (Mitrany 1975b: 53–78). While these organizations may link their 'authority to a specific activity' such as the conditions for running the coal and steel industries or the agriculture of the EU's member states, they still hold to 'the traditional link between authority and a definite territory'. The coal and steel policies or the Common Agricultural Policy of the EU are not extended to the industries and farmers of other non-member countries who may wish to participate in their schemes. Yet it can be argued that it is precisely in these limited geographical blocs that functional arrangements are best executed, with limitations on membership. To work properly, schemes must encompass defined areas with a good deal in common – the flexibility of Mitrany's proposal would soon break down or the members would have so little in common in, for example, the running of agriculture that co-operation would be difficult or non-productive. Furthermore, these regional arrangements overcome the problems of deciding 'the meaning, boundaries, and consequences of any particular function' (McLaren 1985: 142).

Second, Mitrany did not really envisage any political control of the functional ties between countries, thus distinguishing him from the more traditionalist approach to international organizations. He was hopeful that the problems of co-ordination between functional agencies could be worked out as they arose:

> To prescribe for the sake of traditional neatness something more definite than the guidance and supervision of, e.g., the Economic and Social Council, would be to distort the whole conception from the start. . . . To impose upon them [functional bodies] a 'co-ordination' authority, with anything like controlling status, would be to move again towards that accumulation of power at the centre.
>
> (Mitrany 1965: 143)

Thus the institutions of the then European Communities – the Council of Ministers, the Commission, the Court of Justice, the European Parliament, the Economic and Social Committee – were an anathema for Mitrany. They were just mirroring the political controls of the nation state at a part-continental level and, according to Mitrany, 'Continental unions would have a more real chance than individual states to practise the autarky that makes for division' (Mitrany 1966: 27). This may offend against the functionalists' hope for a universal approach to problems, but the abhorrence of political institutions is strange when the functional agencies will, after all, be making political decisions – decisions concerning the authoritative allocation of resources. Not only will international functional transport organizations, established according to Mitrany, have to decide that certain areas will be well served by railways and roads, others not; some ports built up, others left to decay; some airlines expanded while others are allowed to contract; but decisions will also have to be made on how to distribute scarce resources between, for example, investment in transport or building more hospitals, or restructuring the steel industry throughout the area covered by the organizations. These are political decisions. In a period of economic growth and plenty, their political nature may be less obvious as resources are available for almost every plan advanced by world or regional shipping, aviation, health or steel organizations. Otherwise there must surely be a system by which scarce resources are allocated. This problem was faced squarely by Mitrany's successors in the neo-functionalist school (dealt with in the section that follows), but it does seem from Mitrany's writings that 'the world of functionalism is a world of unlimited resources' (McLaren 1985: 146).

A third problem in Mitrany's approach is brought out in a comment by Inis Claude: 'The functional theory of international organizations . . . is ultimately concerned with the issue of political and military struggle; functionalism treats the promotion of welfare as an indirect approach to the prevention of warfare' (Claude 1968: 34–5). Mitrany quoted Claude with approval, implying that functionalism would indeed make a positive contribution (albeit indirectly) to the prevention of war. This proposition is open to several criticisms. Given the level of armaments in the world and the potential for conflict, the contribution to peace made by functional activities may come too late. A youth group exchange between Israel and Iran may bode well for the future, but will be of little use if the respective parties are beaten to their destinations by missiles. Furthermore the promotion of welfare may increase international conflict by increasing expectations. Especially if social and economic changes are brought about by international functional agencies, developing countries' political leaderships may find it increasingly difficult to meet their populations' demands for more economic benefits, for a fairer distribution of benefits or, in some cases, for control of the social consequences of economic growth. Internal strife and unrest may then spill over into international conflict. Finally Mitrany claims that 'the functional approach circumvents ideological and racial divisions, as it does territorial frontiers' (Mitrany 1975a: 226). There is good evidence that the opposite has been happening: that the existing functional organizations such as UNESCO, WHO and ILO have been riddled with ideological and racial (or at least North–South) divisions which have reflected political arguments outside the organizations but have nevertheless adversely affected their basic work (Imber 1989; Ghebali 1986: 118–36).

## Neo-functionalists

The move away from the state-centric view of international organization started by Woolf and Mitrany was continued in the immediate post-war period by social scientists applying aspects of functionalist theory to European and Atlantic institutions. This new functionalist approach showed particular interest in the European Communities (EC, later European Union, EU) which arose in the wake of the Schuman Plan. In May 1950, Robert Schuman, the French Foreign Minister, advanced the idea that West European states should establish a 'High Authority' with powers to administer their coal and steel industries. Negotiations on the details of this plan led to the signing of the Treaty of Paris in April 1951 by France, West Germany, Italy, the Netherlands, Belgium and Luxembourg ('the Six'). This gave substance to the idea that functional activity could be managed across frontiers by an organization over and above the governments of the member states, a supranational authority. The idea was widened to cover an expanded range of economic activity when the Six established the European Economic Community (EEC) with the Treaty of Rome in March 1957. An Atomic Energy Community (Euratom) was established at the same time. However, the element of supranationality was diluted in the High Authority's successor (the Commission of the EEC) having only limited decision-making powers and having mostly the task of proposing action to the representatives of the member states sitting in the Council of Ministers. Despite this, other Community institutions contained the germ of supranationality: the Court of Justice employing Community rather than national laws; a European Parliament which was eventually elected by direct elections among a Community-wide electorate voting for Community-based parties; and interest groups representing farmers, consumers, trade unions and business on a Community rather than a national basis.

These innovations in Western Europe triggered a spate of literature, primarily in the United States, which examined the nature and purpose of the Community institutions. The dominant strand among this writing was that of the neo-functionalists, specifically Ernst Haas, Leon Lindberg and Joseph Nye, whose works are of importance in the study of international organizations. In contrast to Mitrany, the new functionalists tended at first to limit their study to developments in Western Europe (Haas's *Beyond the Nation State* (1964) being a noticeable exception), especially the EC, although later comparisons were made with the growth of common markets in Africa, East Europe and Latin America. On the whole, the neo-functionalists had retreated from Mitrany's world view.

The neo-functionalists also realized the dilemma faced by Mitrany in dealing with political decisions and did not flinch in introducing a method of making necessary choices at the international level. Indeed, this was the kernel of their ideas: that not only specific functions would be carried out at the subcontinental rather than the national level, but also the decisions concerning these functions would be made at that level – with important consequences. It would have consequences for those groups interested in the decisions and would also affect other areas of policy. For example, suppose the Economic Coal and Steel Community (ECSC) required that the steel industry be organized as a West European entity instead of a number of national industries all controlled by different regulations, and that a supranational authority be created to decide on the policy for the running of the West European steel industries. In consequence those involved in, say, the French steel industry would switch their attention away from Paris, where policy was previously made, to Brussels where ECSC policy is made. Furthermore a Community, rather than national, policy on steel could spill over into creating a Community policy for coal, transport and other associated activities. As the number of functional policies decided at a Community rather than a national level expanded, so the need for political action at this higher level would grow, and the political systems of the countries involved would become inexorably intertwined. This was the logic of the innovator of the Schuman Plan idea, Jean Monnet, who considered that the establishment of a coal and steel community followed by similar organizations dealing with other functional areas – agriculture, transport, trade, defence – would be steps on the way to 'building Europe'. The end would be an economically and politically integrated Europe: in Monnet's scheme, a federal West European state. The means would be functional but with a political content.

In his study of the ECSC, Ernst Haas examined this strategy and also defined political integration in its ideal type as being 'the process whereby political actors in several distinct national settings are persuaded to shift their loyalties, expectations and political activities toward a new centre, whose institutions possess or demand jurisdiction over the pre-existing national states' (Haas 1958: 16). This 'new centre' would be the power-house managing the political problems of functional co-operation, the High Authority of the ECSC and the institutions of the EEC. The 'political actors' involved would be those elites leading the political groups habitually concerned with public decision-making and would include trade union officials, business and trade repre- sentatives, higher civil servants, and active politicians. As these elites turned their attention to the new political centre, they would find that Community policy in one area 'can be made real only if the task itself is expanded' (Haas 1961: 368) by way of a 'spillover' of activity into another policy area. Eventually, Community policy-making would take over from state policy-making in all the crucial areas, and the new centre would emerge as being potentially more powerful than the member states' governments, which had been drained of their most meaningful political activities.

At this stage it can be queried whether Haas was describing an international organization or a potential federal state. In discussing this question in his book on the ECSC, Haas concluded that: 'The balance of "federal" as against "intergovernmental" powers seems to point to the conclusion that in all matters relating to the routine regulation of the common market, the High Authority is independent of government' (Haas 1958: 55). He also voiced the opinion that: 'Supranationality in structural terms, therefore, means the existence of governmental authorities closer to the archetype of federation than any past international organization, but not yet identical with it' (Haas 1958: 59). However, this supranationality 'in practice has developed into a hybrid in which neither the federal nor the intergovernmental tendency has clearly triumphed' (Haas 1958: 527). It is also clear that the original Coal and Steel Community was much more functional-federal than the later Economic Community, and, until the mid-1980s, the unified and expanded Community seemed to play down the elements of supranationality in favour of its intergovernmental institution, the Council of Ministers. This and other developments led Haas to reconsider his original view of Community institutions.

In the 1968 preface to *The Uniting of Europe* (which was written in 1958), Haas already identified factors that had changed the nature of the Economic Community experiment in the previous ten years. He observed that during this period 'various spill-over and adaptive processes still had not resulted in a politically united Europe' and in answering the question 'What went wrong?', he outlined four considerations. First, the new functionalists had failed to distinguish between background variables, conditions prevailing at the time when the Community was established, and new aspirations and expectations that had developed after establishment that had run counter to the Community spirit. Second, the impact of nationalism had been underestimated. Third, factors within the Community had been stressed to the detriment of those coming from the outside world. Finally, the massive transformation of Western society taking place independent of European integration also had been underestimated (Haas 1968: xiv–xv).

Haas's definition of integration also became somewhat more negative, more state-centric than his original 1958 emphasis on national actors shifting 'their loyalties, expectations and political activities toward a new centre'. By 1970 Haas considered the study of regional integration to be concerned

> with explaining how and why states cease to be wholly sovereign, how and why they voluntarily mingle, merge, and mix with their neighbours so as to lose the factual attributes of sovereignty while acquiring new techniques for resolving conflict between themselves.
>
> (Haas 1970: 610)

By 1975, Haas considered regional integration theory 'obsolete in Western Europe and obsolescent – though still useful – in the rest of the world' (Haas 1975: 1). By 1976 he had carried out a major reinterpretation of new-functionalist theory as it applied to the EC. The definable outcome of integration in Western Europe was seen either in traditional federalist terms – a West European federal state created out of years of functional activity which had led to a transfer of political activity away from the old nation states towards a new structure – or as the institutionalizing of some intermediate stage such as the present status quo, whereby authority is distributed unequally between several centres with the old nation states losing their previous authority but with no new federal government in prospect. While the original aspects of the EC – the customs union and the Common Agricultural Policy – have become entrenched, the 'spillover' into other policy areas had not occurred by the mid-1970s as the neo-functionalists had predicted. Also, common policies had been developed in different organizations – the OECD, the summit of industrialized countries, the Group of Seven – rather than within the EC. The problem, according to Haas, was turbulence whereby those involved in politics had found themselves 'in a setting of great social complexity' where the 'number of actors is very large' and each 'pursues a variety of objectives which are mutually incompatible; but each is also unsure of the trade-offs between the objectives'. He continued: 'This condition implies the erosion of such interorganizational patterns of consensus, reciprocity, and normative regularity as may have existed earlier . . . Everything is "up for grabs"' (Haas 1976: 179). Haas suggested that in the EC, 'policies and the institutions devised to implement them *illustrate the attempt to deal with the turbulence rather than achieve regional political integration*' (Haas 1976: 180, original emphasis).

A similar shift away from the earlier aspirations is seen in the works of Lindberg and Nye. Lindberg, whose book *The Political Dynamics of European Economic Integration* (1963) had followed on closely from Haas's work, was by 1966 showing that moves towards integration within the EC could cause stress within the system and increase the barriers to further integration (Lindberg 1966: 254). Together with Scheingold in 1970, he described an EC which had not developed into a federal structure, had different levels of integration for different functions, and was still susceptible to crisis. It was 'an unprecedented, but curiously ambiguous "pluralistic" system . . . there seem to be no satisfactory models or concepts in the social science vocabulary to adequately define it' (Lindberg and Scheingold 1970: 306). In a 1970 article, Joseph Nye considered that despite these and other revisions, 'the neo-functional approach still embodies a number of faults that reflect its origins in the 1950s' (Nye 1970: 797). He proposed various changes, stating the dependent variable less ambiguously, adding more political actors, reformulating the list of integration conditions and, perhaps most significantly, dropping 'the ideas of a single path from quasi-functional tasks to political union by means of spillover' (Nye 1970: 797). He concluded that, short of dramatic change, 'the prospects for common markets or microregional economic organizations leading in the short run (of decades) to federation or some sort of political union capable of an independent defence and foreign policy do not seem very high' (Nye 1970: 829).

There has been a long journey from the functionalist-federal hopes of Jean Monnet back in 1950, but it has seen the evolution of not only the Community institutions and policies but also neo-functionalist thinking. The 'logic of integration' gave way to coping with the crises; institutions mixing federalist and intergovernmental elements were replaced by a Western Europe in which 'institutional tidiness is best forgotten' (Haas 1976: 211); and the federal elements seemed, at most, dormant. The hopes of the 1950s had been replaced by the uncertainties of the 1970s and the early 1980s.

With the launching in 1985 of the idea of creating a Single European Market within the EC by the end of 1992, the signing of the Single European Act in 1986 (which extended EC competence and changed its institutional balance), and the settlement of a number of Common Agricultural Policy problems in February 1988, the 'logic of integration' seemed to be revived.

Writing in 1990, Keohane and Hoffmann restored and refined the neo-functionalist notion of spillover advanced by Ernst Haas. They were sceptical that the 'theory of spillover' could explain the EC's institutional developments of the late 1980s but saw it acting positively in other ways; for example, through the incentives to institutional change given by enlargement of EC membership in the early 1980s (Keohane and Hoffmann 1990: 289–90). They saw the process continuing and, barring catastrophic external factors, were 'moderately optimistic about the Community's future prospects' (Keohane and Hoffmann 1990: 296).

This view was taken up by Tranholm-Mikkelsen (1991) and Holland (1993) both of whom saw the revival of the Community agenda in the Maastricht Treaty – with its blueprint for a move to economic and monetary union – as being a revival of neo-functionalism. Other writers on European integration at this time adapted the basic notions of neo-functionalism but brought in extra factors. Majone (1994) agreed that the EU had seen an 'upgrading of common interests' but placed an emphasis on public choice policy to explain particular outcomes. Marks *et al.* (1996) saw a much more complex relationship between the Community and domestic decision-making level. Though the state was still very important, it 'no longer monopolizes European level policy-making or the aggregation of domestic interests' (1996: 346). Instead they identified the growth of multilevel governance within the EU. By the late 2000s it was clear that the EU was again in crisis both after a failed attempt to create 'a Constitution for Europe' from 2004 to 2007 and with the economic crisis in the region after 2008. Nevertheless, the process of functional integration continued and membership increased to twenty-eight states, and neo-functionalism remained as a means of explaining developments in the EU. In the words of Sandholz and Stone Sweet (2010: 28, 34), '[v]ery few extant theories of integration share Neofunctionalism's goal of explaining the broad course of institutional development in the EU' and that neo-functionalism 'offers a causal explanation of the development of EU institutions and the expansion of their authority'.

Indeed, these developments in neo-functionalist writings on international organizations point up some of the criticisms of the school.

First, despite the best efforts of Haas, Schmitter and Nye, it remains a theory overwhelmingly dominated by an interest in the EC, and later the European Union. In 1964, Haas and Schmitter tried to extend some of the lessons of economic union in Western Europe to Latin America. Drawing on Haas's 1968 preface to *The Uniting of Europe*, they discerned nine variables: four related to background conditions (similarity in power of members, rates of transaction, pluralism in member states, complementing elites); two referring to conditions at the time of economic union (similarity of governmental purpose, powers of the economic union); and three to process conditions (decision-making style, transactions rate, the adaptability of governments) (Haas and Schmitter 1964: 711–19). They looked at the 'chances of politicization', that is the possibility 'that the actors seek to resolve their problems so as to upgrade common interests and, in the process, delegate more authority to the centre' (Haas and Schmitter

1964: 707). Nye in his article 'Comparing common markets' (Nye 1970) tried to modify the 'Europo-centric' nature of the neo-functionalist approach and drew on a wide range of cases of economic integration – Latin America, Central America, the Caribbean, Eastern Europe and East Africa as well as EFTA and the EC. He concluded that:

> The original neo-functionalist model was close to its origins in the strategies of European integrationists in the 1950s and thus might be seen as a tempting and misleading guide for policy in other areas. The revised neo-functionalist model is not something to be imitated but is simply a tool for making comparisons. We want to know what difference it makes if a group of states form a common market.
>
> (Nye 1970: 830)

Though by the end of the 1980s there were few places to be found outside Europe that were forming common markets, the formation of the North American Free Trade Area (NAFTA) and the renewal of economic co-operation in Latin America and South-East Asia during the 1990s provided different models from the more politicized EU. By the 2000s, the Association of South East Asian Nations (ASEAN) had established itself as an alternative integration model to that of the EU, one that was more interstate in nature and which reflected the extensive differences between the member states (Hew 2007). These examples seemed to challenge some of the basic assumptions of the neo-functionalists and perhaps give some weight to Nye's 1970's scepticism cited above.

Second, it is clear that the neo-functionalists have had trouble with the institutional formats. They have retreated from being 'functional federalist' almost back to Mitrany's eclectic approach towards institutions. They have also accepted the durability of the nation state in resisting 'the logic of integration' and have sought compromise formulas which at least continued to place emphasis on non-state activities, even if institutions above the state (supranational) were seen to be susceptible to state interference.

A third criticism concerns the sort of non-state actors favoured by the neo-functionalists. They have constantly emphasized the importance of political activists, the elites of interest groups and technocrats. This may have partially blinded them to a weakness in the EC/EU that could have affected neo-functionalism's earlier prognostications from being fulfilled: its institutions cannot draw on the day-to-day political resources available to the national political actors. This has led to a gap, most noticeable in the newer members, between perceptions of the EU by the representational elite and those of the ordinary voter or consumer. While some earlier studies of opinion in the EC did include opinion polls, these often dealt with easy questions (showing one's European identity) or soft options (whether there should be, say, a more active EC industrial policy). With the first expansion of the EC in 1973 and the first major oil price increase which coincidentally happened a year later, European voters were faced increasingly with much harder options – inflation versus employment, trade union rights against consumer interests. The possibility was that 'being a good European' might mean allowing some other country's nationals to exploit one's fish or oil. The creation of a Single European Market within the EC by the end of 1992 and the move towards a single currency from 1999 by eleven, rising to eighteen by 2014, of the EU member states brought the activities of the Union closer to the world of the consumer or worker. However, this seems, if anything, to have increased the alienation of voters from the institutions and activities of the EU. The 2009 election for the European Parliament showed the lowest turnout yet in such direct elections (43%) and 'Euro-barometer' opinion polls have demonstrated a negative trend in public opinion on the EU (ec.europa.eu/public_opinion/archives/eb/eb76/eb76_first_en.pdf). It may be that a number of interest groups have switched their 'expectations and political activities' towards the EU, but many of the ordinary European voters seemed to have failed to transfer their 'loyalties' to the Union.

In summary, the neo-functionalists took up Mitrany's study of the relations between groups and individuals in different states as well as the states' representatives. They tried to grapple with the question of political control of such institutionalized functional relationships and to understand how it would affect the nature of the nation state. They attempted to define the status of these newly created institutions, though they were not always helped by developments in the EC/EU, which was the focus of their studies. Their works have demonstrated that the EU institutions are by no means just ordinary intergovernmental ones. They have also provided a mirror of the history of events in Western Europe in particular – moving from 'uniting' and 'political dynamics', through 'stress', 'joys and anguish', to 'obsolescence', 'turbulent fields' and back to 'moderate optimism' and a 'new dynamism'.

### Transactionalists

Another American writer whose work dealt with the question of integration is Karl Deutsch. Although not a neo-functionalist, his transactional approach has dealt with some common themes. He has been concerned with more than intergovernmental relations and indeed has stressed relations between peoples rather than just the elites favoured by many neo-functionalists. Deutsch concerned himself with 'the absence or presence of significant organized preparations for war or large-scale violence' between international political communities. It was the 'security communities' that had eliminated 'war and the expectation of war within their boundaries' which Deutsch and his Princeton colleagues examined in *Political Community and the North Atlantic Area* (1957). A security community was defined as 'a group of people which has become "integrated"' in the sense that 'there is real assurance that the members of that community will not fight each other physically, but will settle their disputes in some other way' (Deutsch 1957: 5). Integration does not necessarily mean 'the merging of peoples or governmental units into a single unit', an idea explicit in federalist thinking and implicit in much functionalist writing. Instead, two sorts of integrated security communities are identified: the amalgamated, where previously independent units have been formally merged into a larger unit with a common government (e.g. the United States) and the pluralistic, where separate governments maintain their legal independence (e.g. Canada and the United States). In studying a number of cases of attempted or actual integration in the North American and West European area, Deutsch concluded that there were twelve conditions essential for the success of an amalgamated security community and that three were necessary for its pluralistic counterpart. These three consisted of 'the compatibility of major values relevant to political decision-making', 'the capacity of the participating political units or governments to respond to each other's needs, messages and actions quickly, adequately, and without resort to violence', and the 'mutual predictability of behavior' (Deutsch 1957: 66–7). In Deutsch's work, emphasis was placed on communication between political units: increased transactions between them (such as political exchanges, tourism, trade and transport) brought increases in mutual dependence. For a community to be created, this high level of transactions must be accompanied by mutual responsiveness, so that the demands of each side on the other can receive adequate and sympathetic treatment. This would not only preclude the need for aggressive action to achieve ends but would also build up a feeling of trust and security in the relationship.

Deutsch does not have an obsession with international organizations; although his 1957 book is in the end concerned with the creation of a security community in the NATO area, there are few references to international organizations. Many of the case studies are set in the period before the post-war expansion of such organizations, and almost all deal with bilateral relationships. Deutsch's work has consequences for the study of international organizations: governmental and non-governmental international organizations can be created as a result of a pluralistic security community, the integration of which may eventually become institutionalized, as happened when the Scandinavian states created the Nordic Council. There can also be forms of institutionalized communications between societies which provide the transactions and understanding that help create a security community. Deutsch wrote:

> If the way to integration, domestic or international, is through the achievement of a sense of community that undergirds institutions, then it seems likely that an increased sense of community would help to strengthen whatever institutions – supranational or international – are already operating.
>
> (Deutsch 1957: 7–8)

Deutsch's work was taken further in a volume edited in 1998 by Adler and Barnett (1998) that does pay some attention to international organizations. Indeed their volume contains chapters that refer to the OSCE, NATO, the EU, the UN, the Gulf Cooperation Council (GCC) and the Association of South East Asian Nations (ASEAN). They claim that '[i]nternational organizations and institutions played an important role in encouraging more intensive and extensive interactions between states through their trust-building properties' (Barnett and Adler 1998: 418). They list six conclusions of this statement:

- By monitoring states' agreements, international organizations give them the confidence to co-operate in the absence of trust.
- International organizations allow states 'to discover new areas of mutual interests'. In particular they tend to link particular areas.
- International organizations can help shape state practices by setting down norms that define what is acceptable.
- The increasing number of international organizations encourages multi-lateralism.
- They also encourage states and societies to see themselves as part of a region.
- They can also shape the identity of their members.

(Barnett and Adler 1998: 418–20)

The authors claim that their studies demonstrate 'the extent to which social communications becomes institutionalized and embedded in international organizations, and, in turn, how these organizations express an intent to develop trust and mutual identification' (Barnett and Adler 1998: 418). The work on security communities is perhaps at its strongest when dealing with the established Western democracies, though Adler and Barnett's work shows that it may have a wider utility and subsequent work has shown how the growth of social communications in other regions is being reflected in strengthened international organizations (Webber 2006: 289–311).

## *Interdependence*

Further emphasis on the growth in transactions between societies can be seen in the works of Keohane and Nye, who were in the forefront of the interdependence school in the United States. They pointed out the consequences of the increase in transnational actions to the study of international relations. Their starting point was summarized thus:

> Transnational relations are not 'new', although . . . the growth of transnational organization in the twentieth century has been spectacular. Yet, our contention is not only that the state-centric paradigm is inadequate . . . but also that it is becoming progressively more inadequate as changes in international relations take place.
>
> (Keohane and Nye 1971: xxv)

They listed five consequences of this growth of international interactions and organizations for interstate politics: (1) the promotion of attitude changes among citizens; (2) an increase in international pluralism, 'the linking of national interest groups in transnational structures, usually involving transnational organizations for the purpose of co-ordination' (Keohane and Nye 1971: xviii) which has been the basis for much neo-functionalist writing; (3) 'the creation of dependence and interdependence, is often associated with international transportation and finance' (Keohane and Nye 1971: xix); (4) 'creating new instruments for influence for use by some governments over others' (Keohane and Nye 1971: xx); and (5) 'the emergence of autonomous actors with private foreign policies that may deliberately oppose or impinge on state policies' (Keohane and Nye 1971: xvii).

In a later book (1977), Keohane and Nye dealt with the question of interdependence in world politics in greater depth. Interdependence since the Second World War has often resulted from increased transnational activities and is divided into two sorts: sensitivity interdependence (the costly effects of changes in transactions or societies or governments) and vulnerability interdependence, where the actors' liability to suffer costs imposed by external events is taken into account (Keohane and Nye 1977: 12–13). In contrast to the realist view of world politics, Keohane and Nye put forward the ideal type of complex interdependence which, they claimed, 'sometimes comes closer to reality than does realism' (Keohane and Nye 1977: 23) and which has three main characteristics: it allows for multiple channels – interstate, transgovernmental and transnational – connecting societies; there is an absence of hierarchy among the many questions at issue between states, with military security no longer dominating any agenda; and 'Military force is not used by governments toward other governments within the region, or on the issues, where complex interdependence prevails' (Keohane and Nye 1977: 25).

These three conditions are said by Keohane and Nye to typify fairly well some issues of global economic and ecological interdependence and 'come close to characterizing the entire relationship between some countries' (Keohane and Nye 1977: 25). Complex interdependence gives rise to distinctive political processes: a state's goals will vary by issue area with transgovernmental politics, making goals difficult to define as transgovernmental actors (e.g. ministers of agriculture, intelligence agencies, national weather bureaux) pursue their own aims. The following factors are relevant in each issue area:

- the resources of a state for that particular area are most relevant rather than the state's overall military strength;
- international organizations and transnational actors will be manipulated as major instruments of state policy;
- the agenda of issues will be formulated by changes in the power distribution within the issue areas, by the position of international regimes, by changes in the importance of transnational actors, and by linkage from other issues;
- linkage between issues will be more difficult for strong states to undertake if force is downgraded;
- linkage by weak states through international organizations sets agendas, helps coalition-forming and provides arenas for the political activity of such states which can use the choice of organizational forum for an issue and the mobilization of votes as a political resource.

(Keohane and Nye 1977: 37)

Thus Keohane and Nye gave international organizations an important role in their complex interdependence model of world politics, a model which, while not used to explain all world politics, was one which they claimed to have increasing relevance in a large and growing area. They used an international organization model as one of the explanations for international regime change, that is the change in the sets of governing arrangements affecting relationships of interdependence. In this case, international organizations referred to 'multilevel linkage norms and institutions' (Keohane and Nye 1977: 54) which, once established, are hard to eradicate. Because of this, they may stand in the way of states using their capabilities in order to change regimes. Instead, power outcomes will be more affected by voting power (in the UN General Assembly for example) and the ability to form coalitions and to control elite networks (such as that found in the institutions of the European Communities, later the European Union). While the complex international organization model was only one of four advanced by Keohane and Nye to explain regime change, they did expect it to contribute to such change in a world where complex interdependence conditions pertain.

The contributions by Keohane and Nye demonstrate both the concern of American writers in international relations in the 1970s with alternatives to the state-centric model and their willingness to draw from more than one approach, bringing together elements from the more traditional approaches with economic models and non-state-centric elements. Their work does, however, have certain weaknesses. Perhaps the most serious is the use of the term 'interdependence' and its division into sensitivity and vulnerability interdependence. Accepting that interdependence means 'mutual dependence' (and this leads to discussion as to how mutual many relationships are), the phrase 'sensitivity-interdependence' scarcely warrants the use of the term 'interdependence'. The fault lies with the authors' loose definition of dependence as 'a state of being determined or significantly affected by external forces'. The inclusion of 'significantly affected' weakens the utility of the term, so that the notion of sensitivity interdependence seems to refer to any noticeable effect of one state and society on another. A person may be significantly affected by taking drugs without being dependent on them. David Baldwin showed that this use of the term 'interdependence' ran contrary to the stricter understandings of the concept found in Machiavelli, Montesquieu and Rousseau as well as in the works of twentieth-century writers such as Norman Angell, Francis Delaisi and Ramsay Muir (Baldwin 1980: 7–8). He suggested the use of the terms 'mutual influence', 'mutual responsiveness', or 'mutual sensitivity' instead of 'sensitivity interdependence' (Baldwin 1980: 19).

A second criticism of Keohane and Nye's books also concerns their terminology. In dealing with transnational influences, 'They lump together . . . all types of relations in which non-governmental actors participate', thus making the components of their new paradigm 'shifting and poorly defined' (Wagner 1974: 440–1). Wagner questioned whether their work simply demonstrated a shift in interest to new areas of international politics – especially economic ones – and whether the world had really changed, 'or whether we have just overlooked some things all along' (Wagner 1974: 441). The extent of interdependence was also challenged by Waltz (1970) and Rosecrance *et al.* (1977) in the United States and by Little and McKinlay (1978) and Sullivan (1978) in the British literature.

Finally, realists such as Gilpin (1975), have criticized seeing the basis of inter-dependence – the growth of transnational relations – as undermining state power. He has pointed out the fused nature of the interests of multinationals and those of the state (especially the United States) and the more recent attachment of Russian and Chinese multinationals to their governments underlines his critique.

Since the 1970s, Keohane in particular has extended and refined the coverage of interdependence. Keohane wrote in 1998 that to analyse world politics in the 1990s 'is to discuss international institutions', showing their growing importance for maintaining world order (Keohane 1998: 82). Keohane also admitted that what Nye and he 'called complex interdependence is now conceptualized in much more sophisti-cated ways in terms of networks' (Keohane 2009: 37) and he asked colleagues to pay attention to five big questions facing the world economy (and, by implication, its institutions): (1) that economic development is taking place for most of the world's population; (2) China's role as a player in international trade and finance; (3) the extreme volatility of the financial and energy markets; (4) the importance of truly global actors – such as corporations and NGOs – in world politics; (5) electronic communications becoming the basis of world communications (Keohane 2009: 40–2). All these developments have consequences for international organizations, not least by placing an increased load on the existing trade and economic organizations.

Despite any shortcomings, Keohane and Nye provided insights into transnational politics; they shifted attention away from purely governmental actors in interstate relations; and they pointed out the importance of international organizations in the interdependence or, at least, mutual responsiveness of states.

The reformist view of both international relations and international organizations has always provided an alternative to the more conservative realist approach. It tended to be dominated in the pre-war period by international lawyers and idealists but since the Second World War has latched on to the changes in world politics first in the economic field and then in Europe that have been more difficult to explain in realist terms. It has seen international organizations not only as a means to manage trends such as increased economic interdependence but has also accepted that these organizations may become important actors on the world stage themselves and can certainly become involved in changing the preferences of governments.

## Radicals

Writers covered in this section see the international system not so much as being dominated by states but more by different divisions of its peoples. This is not to say that they ignore states. They consider them either to be less important than the divisions of class or wealth or merely to reflect these other factors or to be roadblocks to unity in the face of more important challenges. Power is seen as being exercised by the wealthy and privileged and open to challenge. Change in the system is possible but only through struggle or by an awakening of peoples to their 'real' situation. Most international organizations are thus regarded as reflections of the current unsatisfactory state of affairs, though some more activist organizations may have potential as vehicles of change.

This section has been subdivided into three. The first are the economic structuralists and include Marxists and Global South (previously the Third World) writers critical of the current international system. They have in common a belief that the political structures of the world have been fashioned mainly by economic factors and that there has been an inequality built into the present system. The second are the critical approaches whose radicalism is more of the intellectual sort. They reject – or at least question – many of the assumptions underlying the views of the world represented by the realists and reformers. Finally, there are the globalists. Their perspective is planetary and their main concern is for the survival of Earth. Again, they challenge the more state-based approaches of both realists and reformers.

### Structuralist views

The structuralist approach to the study of international relations differs in important ways to those of the realists and reformists, though it has some elements in common with strands of both schools. As many of the neo-realists emphasize the power structure of world politics, this section will limit itself to those writers concerned with the impact on the political system of the world's economic structure. Unlike the realist approach, the economic structuralists are concerned not just with states in world politics and their economic and political differences, but also with the divisions within and between societies (Willetts 1990: 263). They are therefore concerned with the rift between rich and poor within states and that between rich and poor globally. This leads to an interest in transnational relations as well as in intergovernmental links. They have this in common with reformist views, but differ from them in the emphasis placed on the structures of world politics being formulated by economic factors. In this section, attention will be given to Marxist writers, and some Global South views – particularly those of the dependency school and the developmentalists – who have made a contribution quite separate from that of the Marxist tradition.

## Marxist views

There is no one Marxist interpretation of the role of international organizations in world politics. But Marxist approaches have certain elements in common and form a distinctive school of thought about international relations generally and therefore about international organizations. These approaches are based on the writings of Karl Marx (1818–83) in co-operation with Friedrich Engels (1820–95) with perhaps the greatest later contribution being made by V.I. Lenin, leader of the 1917 Bolshevik revolution in Russia. They are of importance partly because they form the basis for communist thinking and thus they have an attachment to the Soviet Union, which was the strongest communist state until 1991, and to the People's Republic of China, communist since 1949. Apart from this, Marxist beliefs had a strong input into Western intellectual thinking and continue to inform some views about world politics in the Global South.

Neither Marx nor Marxists took the state to be the 'currency' of international relations. Unlike the realist viewpoints, they did not consider interactions between sovereign states to be of overriding importance. Unlike the functionalists and other modern Western views that stress non-state actors, Marxists in particular emphasized class relationships, both within states and across state boundaries. Indeed, it is difficult to talk only of a Marxist view of international relations, let alone of international organizations, as this separates one particular aspect of human behaviour for Marxist treatment, divorcing it from the underlying tenets of Marxist beliefs. Marxism provides a framework of understanding by which, it is claimed, society past and present can be explained and the future development of mankind determined.

According to Marx, relationships between people, and the forms that institutionalized those relationships, depended on the 'economic structure of society', the way that production was organized. He traced the history of civilized mankind through five historical stages – Asiatic, ancient, feudal, capitalist and socialist – which have different dominant methods of production leading to 'a complicated arrangement of society into various orders, a manifold graduation of social rank' (Marx and Engels 1965: 40). Each form of society has contained the conflictual divisions which help to transform the nature of that society: contradictions in the mode of production placed strain on the existing social order, sharpening the divide between economic foundation of society and leading to a rapid transformation of its superstructure, its legal, political and religious institutions. Thus by a confrontation of class contradictions, one historical form of society was transformed into a higher stage of social development: 'the history of all hitherto existing society is the history of class struggles' (Marx and Engels 1965: 39). Marx and Engels were particularly concerned with capitalist society – at its heyday during their lives – and its transformation into socialist society. Within this form of society there would be no division of labour, and no classes and no states; no expropriation of labour's surplus value, and thus no private property; no exploitation of one class by another, with no need for war.

For Marx and Engels, 'Class then, and not nations or states, are the basic units in history, and the struggle between classes, instead of interstate conflict, occupies the centre of attention' (Berki 1971: 81). From the nineteenth century onwards this struggle, seen in Marxist terms, has been primarily between this capitalist class (the bourgeoisie) and the labouring class (the proletariat). As the transformation from capitalist society to socialism to communism took place, the superstructure of bourgeois society – religion, national division, bourgeois political institutions, the state – would be swept away and, in Engels's phrase, 'the government of persons is replaced by the administration of things' (Feuer 1969: 147) with the state relegated to the museum together with 'the spinning wheel and the bronze axe' (Feuer 1969: 433).

Marx saw the European states of his own time as being means by which the ruling class could oppress the working class by using the agents of the state such as the judiciary, the police, the army and the church. The external activities of the state were also determined by its class nature. Meanwhile transnational relations of a more meaningful kind would be created by trade, the movement of capital, and increased contact and solidarity between the proletariat of various nations. Indeed, the international organizations of which Marx and Engels had direct experience were the First International and, for Engels, the Second International, both of which attempted to organize the representatives of working people across frontiers. Once again this stresses the Marxist emphasis on transnational class relations rather than on interstate relationships.

While Soviet writings on international organizations were fairly desultory in Stalin's control of the USSR (1924–53), they did latterly herald the move towards peaceful co-existence and foreshadowed the later rather restrictive view of such organizations by Soviet commentators.

In the post-Second World War period and in particular in the post-Stalin era, Soviet literature on international organizations blossomed. This reflected Soviet membership of many post-1945 organizations, the emergence of a socialist bloc of states, and the increase in the number of sovereign states: all factors demanding a more sophisticated Soviet view of interstate relations than the survivalism of Stalin's period. During the late 1980s, it also reflected the 'new thinking' introduced by Gorbachev, the last ruler of the Soviet Union.

Stalin's successor, Krushchev, developed a revised view of international relations which gave a position to the emerging Third World. (The Third World – now called the Global South – was then taken to mean those states that had emerged from colonialism. In effect, the term later included the states of Latin America, Africa – excluding the then apartheid state of South Africa – the Middle East, Oceania and South Asia.) Peaceful co-existence between socialist and capitalist states was still considered necessary but this did not preclude the ideological struggle between the two camps: indeed, the Soviet international lawyer G.I. Tunkin wrote: 'peaceful coexistence of states representing the two different social systems is a specific form of class struggle between socialism and capitalism' (Osakwe 1972: 37). The Soviet Union also developed relations with the newly emerging ex-colonial countries, and Soviet writings had to take account of this development. There was a recognition of a third group of states between the capitalist and the communist – that of potentially friendly independent states in Europe and Asia such as India, Egypt, Indonesia and Yugoslavia, which would form a zone of peace. Although the relations with the capitalist states still remained embedded in peaceful co-existence, there was an emphasis by post-Stalinist Soviet writers on the class element in the relationship – that is, the contact with 'progressive' elements in Western society such as the labour movement. Neither did peaceful co-existence rule out support of 'just wars of national liberation'; indeed, it was seen as a strategy for world revolution. Finally, the relationships between the Soviet Union and East European countries were deemed to be based on socialist internationalism, postulating a harmony of national and community interests and concluding that 'independence and sovereignty of a socialist state means above all independence from capitalism' (*Red Star*, 1 December 1968).

Tunkin underlined traditional Soviet thinking that the constituent instrument of an international organization (e.g. the Charter of the UN) was all-important in determining the extent that the organization had an international legal personality, that is, a standing in international law similar to that of a sovereign state. Examining the question of the autonomous will of international organizations, Tunkin allowed that they need not just act as agents for member states:

> In international practice treaties concluded by international organizations take their special place as treaties by which international organizations acquire rights and take upon themselves certain obligations. International organizations are created by states; they are brought into being by states but the actions of international organizations are not in any way, de facto, or de jure, to be equated to the actions of states.
>
> (Osakwe 1972: 23)

This did not mean that an international organization was 'an entity independent of its member states', as any powers that they had were delegated by the members. In line with the Soviet doctrine of peaceful co-existence, Tunkin placed stress on the nature and the membership of an international organization; those which drew their membership from communist, capitalist and Third World states could expect to be generally recognized as having an international personality. He wrote:

> The nature of contemporary international organizations is to a very great extent determined by the existence of states belonging to different socio-economic systems and the inevitable struggle between them. That is why peaceful coexistence is now the basic condition of the development of general international organization.
>
> (Osakwe 1972: 289)

Morozov contributed some extra points. First, he included INGOs in his study. He wrote that 'International organizations have, as a rule, at least three member countries. These may be governments, official organizations or non-governmental organizations' (Morozov 1977: 30). In a later section on NGOs, they were identified as the largest group of international organizations, with two aspects that concerned socialist commentators: the NGOs' attitude towards the preservation of peace, with the World Federation of Trade Unions, the World Federation of Democratic Youth and other members of the Soviet-backed World Peace Council gaining special mention, and the specialized character of some NGOs, such as the International Council of Scientific Unions and the Scientific Committee on Antarctic Research. Morozov mentioned how NGOs can help establish a social climate, citing their contribution to the settlement of a number of international conflicts such as that in Vietnam. He also dealt with the role of the NGOs in the UN and the consultative status they have with IGOs, saying that 'students of international affairs in the socialist countries are critical of many aspects of this system, for the consultative status arrangements still fall short of what the development of modern international relations in fact calls for' (Morozov 1977: 43). The 'specialized nature' of NGOs was attributed by Morozov (1977: 42) to the public's increased influence on foreign policy and international relations and the greater importance of the ideological factor in such relations.

Second, Morozov, writing in the late 1970s, made more positive references to the role of Third World states in international organizations. He noted that 'the emergence of a large number of young national states have led to the emergence of international organizations among developing countries' (Morozov 1977: 29) and claimed that 'participation in these organizations is part of the process of consolidating their sovereignty and national independence and of solving their pressing economic and other problems' (Morozov 1977: 31).

Finally, Morozov developed the point made by Tunkin about the limited nature of international organizations – 'second-class members' of the international system as opposed to the first-class members, sovereign states – by reference to their decisions which result from the interaction of political forces within the organizations.

After the coming to power of Mr Gorbachev in the Soviet Union in 1985, a change took place in Soviet policies towards international relations, including international organizations, and this was reflected in new Soviet writings on the subject.

Gorbachev introduced a major review of the foreign policy of the Soviet Union that matched the intensity of his domestic reforms. He encouraged 'new thinking' based on a revised view of the world situation. Peaceful co-existence with the capitalist states was no longer seen as being 'a specific form of class struggle', as Tunkin had written, but as being in the common interests of all countries. It was predicated on the need for survival of the human race which, in Shakhnazarov's words, 'must, of course, take first place' (Light 1988: 297). This meant that a new concept of security had to be adopted by the Soviets, that of 'common security' which was based on some of the ideas of the Palme Commission (see below). Greater emphasis was given to arms control and disarmament agreements with the West and to co-operation in international affairs, while Soviet intervention in the Third World ebbed and military support for the East European communist governments was withdrawn.

Soviet writings on international relations, both official and academic, came to mirror Gorbachev's new thinking, with ideas drawn from the West and from Moscow 'think-tanks' such as IMEMO (the Institute of World Economy and International Relations) (Light 1988: 295). Gorbachev and his foreign minister, Eduard Shevardnadze, gave the academics a green-light for further discussion and debate (Shevardnadze 1990: 23). As a result, studies examined the role of the United Nations as an agent for peace (Kozyrev 1990: 12–19) and the role of international organizations in environmental matters and disarmament questions (Chossudovsky 1988; Roginko 1989: 133–43) and international law was reassessed (Butler 1989: 363–75).

Once the Soviet Union collapsed, many of the writers lost their main point of political reference. A number left academe, others adapted their ideas to Western ones and a few remained as policy advisers to the new Russian government. However, communism as an intellectually dominant organizing force with political clout had disappeared in Russia, together with much of the perspective it provided – when seen through the often distorting lens of the Soviet Union – of international relations and international organizations.

Chinese Marxist writers have largely reflected the views of the leadership in China since the coming to power of the Communist Party in 1949. Until the 1970s, communist China was excluded from almost all international organizations, and it is not surprising that what little writing there was on the subject was fairly dismissive, usually consisting of condemnations of the UN for its action in Korea and the security alliances for their 'hegemonic' nature. Chinese Marxist thinking divided the modern world into three groups. The First World, consisted of the two imperialist superpowers, namely the United States and the USSR. The Second World was made up of other areas of advanced industrialized countries, primarily Europe and Japan, which were open to domination by the superpowers but which could start a dialogue with the Third World. Then there was the Third World itself, consisting of the Afro-Asian-Latin American states supported in their struggle against First World imperialism by China. This view of the world coloured past Chinese writings on international organizations. The superpowers were seen as cynical manipulators of international institutions. Mao Tse-tung, the Chinese communist leader, wrote of US policy towards such institutions: 'It makes use of them when it needs them, and kicks them away when it does not' (Society for Anglo-Chinese Understanding (SACU) 1979: 42). US-dominated pacts such as SEATO and 'imperialist groupings' such as the Alliance for Progress were derided. Special vitriol was saved for the Warsaw Treaty Organization, which in one article was described as 'Soviet social-imperialism's tool for aggression' (Ming Sung, cited in Chen 1979: 194). The Soviet Union was accused of trying to manipulate the Pact and negotiate with Western countries through the European Security Conference to consolidate its hegemonic status in Eastern Europe at the same time as dividing Western Europe, squeezing out the United States 'so as to make way for its expansion and infiltration into Western Europe' (Ming Sung, cited in Chen 1979: 197).

Chinese writers regarded the Second World, especially Western Europe, as being a spent force in terms of imperialism, which responded to the Third World with dialogue as in the Lomé Convention between the European Communities and African, Caribbean and Pacific states. Furthermore, the defensive aspects of NATO were stressed and 'with growing European cohesion the trend is likely to be towards a force in which the American element is seen as a temporary necessity, eventually to be phased out' (Society for Anglo-Chinese Understanding 1979: 90).

The countries of the Third World were seen as constituting 'the main force combating imperialism, colonialism and hegemonism', referring not only to the vestiges of West European colonialism but also to US imperialism and growing Soviet 'social-imperialism'. The Third World could help to exclude the great powers by banding together in such organizations as the OAU, and they could work to correct unequal trade and economic relations with the superpowers through UN agencies and conferences such as UNCTAD and UNCLOS. Also raw material and exporting organizations such as OPEC, the International Bauxite Association and the Union of Banana Exporting Countries were praised as changing the old international economic order and 'battering the biggest material plunderers in the world, the United States and the Soviet Union' (*Peking Review*, 26 September 1975, cited in Chen 1979: 309).

The poverty of Chinese study of international organizations, no doubt caused by the lack of Chinese membership of such organizations until the 1970s and the turmoil of the Cultural Revolution, came to an end by the 1980s. Instead there was a more realist view of the world, if one sometimes couched in Marxist terms. In a major study of China and international organizations, Ann Kent (2007) has little need in her introduction to mention Marxism as a controlling factor in this relationship. In Chinese universities there has been a growth in detailed studies of international organizations and the European Union (Lisbonne-de Vergeron 2007).

*Global South (Third World) views*

Many writers on international organizations from the Global South (formerly known as the Third World and covering Africa, Asia and Latin America) have adopted a structuralist framework and are particularly concerned about how institutions can be used as tools of exploitation of the Global South and how some can be used as agents of liberation. They have not been included in the section on Marxist views for three reasons: not all of them are Marxist; those who are Marxist place particular stress on the position of the Global South; and as Global South citizens they have, through their own experience, another perspective than that of writers from industrialized states.

Yash Tandon (1978: 377) identified three then Third World perspectives on international organizations. First there was that of the bourgeois or petty nationalists, who were in power in most Third World states and who were progressive in terms of anti-imperialism but were 'reactionary to the extent that they would sooner make their peace with imperialism than surrender power to the masses and peasants'. This group used international organizations to put pressure on imperialist states in order to extract concessions from them and appease the masses in their own countries. They saw the UN as 'an opportunity to parley with their erstwhile imperial masters at a presumed level of equality' (Tandon 1978: 365). The second perspective was that of the 'really backward regimes' of the Third World, such as Taiwan and Jordan, 'for whom international organizations are of marginal significance for they prefer to deal with imperialism directly'. The third perspective identified by Tandon was that 'of the masses of the Third World', for whom international organizations were peripheral for as long as 'they continue to reflect the existing balance of class forces in favour of imperialism' (Tandon 1978: 378). From the end of the 1960s, forces representing this third group became more prominent in world politics in the form of liberation groups such as the ANC and PLO, and while these were interested in gaining recognition for themselves at the UN and the specialized agencies, they were not dependent on these organizations. Indeed, Tandon considered that, for the revolutionary struggles in South-East Asia and Africa, 'international organizations are too peripheral to be of much significance' (Tandon 1978: 377).

Tandon provided an interesting history of the development of the anti-colonialist forces in the Third World since 1945 but his division into the three perspectives is too stark. Leaving aside the less important 'backward regimes', he basically grouped the Third World leadership into the revolutionaries, who had little need for international organizations, and those who slipped into reformism and were duped into believing that they could change their dependence on industrialized nations through international organizations. This seems to understate the use of such organizations by revolutionary groups – especially the PLO and the Southern African liberation organizations – which made substantial use of the UN, the Arab League and the OAU to sustain the political aspects of their efforts. It also overestimates the extent to which the Third World countries had any illusions about international organizations such as UNCTAD. Furthermore, the identification of 'good' revolutionaries and 'fallen' reformists is rather simplistic: the major sponsor of the UN's 'New Economic Order' which Tandon condemned as the 'Old Economic Order, with a different rhetoric' was the Algerian radical government of Boumedienne; the PLO itself was dependent on a number of 'bourgeois' Arab governments for financial and diplomatic support; and to Tandon's assertion that 'For national liberation movements guided by a proletarian ideology, such as those in China and Vietnam, international organizations were of no use' can be added the reservation 'until they came to power'. While it took some twenty years before communist China made use of such organizations, the unified communist state of Vietnam was quick to take up its position in the UN, to ask for aid through UN agencies, as well as to become a member of the CMEA (Comecon).

Global South commentators on world politics have emphasized the nature of their area's political, economic and cultural relationship with the industrialized North. This is most often typified as being one of neo-colonialism – control of the Global South by the North by indirect means rather than by direct colonial rule – and of *economic dependency* (or *dependencia*). International relations between states are subsumed to relations between classes worldwide: between, on the one hand, the exploiting imperialist capitalists in the northern industrialized countries and their middle-class collaborators in the southern states and, on the other hand, the exploited masses, the proletariat, of the southern continents. The latter groups have been made economically dependent on the former so that they are, in the words of the Brazilian T. Dos Santos 'in a situation in which the economy of a certain group of countries is conditioned by the development and expansion, of another economy to which their own is subjected' (Bodenheimer 1971: 327).

The underdeveloped countries depend on the developed for their capital and expertise; they find key sectors of their economy controlled from outside; they act as a source of raw materials, as a cheap source of labour and as a market for manufacturers from Europe, Japan and North America. As their living standards were determined by the vicissitudes of the Northern-dominated 'world' market, the relationship was one of unequal exchange, the result of which was a world experiencing 'unequal development' with a developed, rich industrialized capitalist northern centre and a poor, underdeveloped, agriculturally backward, exploited periphery in the South. The dependent South has been divided between the predominant underdeveloped areas and a few centres of development with their trade, cultural, traffic and political links to the developed North – the 'dependent development' outlined by F.H. Cardosa (1974), another Brazilian. Samir Amin (1977) rejected the prospect of an autonomous capitalist development in the Third World: the new bourgeoisie of Latin America, Africa and Asia were in alliance with capitalists from the North and the main source of finance for imported equipment was from the export of raw materials to the industrialized states. Amin (1977: 1–21) saw the call made for a New International Economic Order (NIEO) by then Third World leaders at the UN, UNCTAD and the various North–South dialogues as an attempt to increase the price of their raw material exports, obtain more imported technology and thus finance a new stage of development. He saw this as just placing the Third World more in the grip of the neo-colonialist system and instead recommended a more self-reliant development with mutual assistance between Third World states, a reduction in trade with the industrialized world, and thus a loosening of dependence. Amin, like Tandon, had little faith in international organizations as tools for fashioning a more independent Third World. His suggestion of greater mutual assistance between Third World states implied something more sophisticated than a number of bilateral arrangements. As the present organizations used for intra-Global South co-operation (the AU, the Arab League, ASEAN) are dominated by just those governments that accept the course condemned by Amin – the greater integration into the world economic system – then Amin's solution involves like-minded developing countries, or more likely, political changes leading to more indigenous international organizations.

Other Third World/Global South writers have placed emphasis on greater use of existing institutions and can broadly be described as *developmentalists*. Raul Prebisch, an Argentinian economist, not only studied the question of economic dependency, but his ideas were used as the basis for the work of two major international organizations – the UN Economic Commission for Latin America and the Caribbean (ECLAC) and UNCTAD. In his study of British-Argentinian trading relations, Prebisch identified the unequal terms of trade between the favoured industrialized state of the 'centre' and the less privileged, non-industrialized 'periphery'. Prebisch, unlike the dependencia school of Amin, Dos Santos and Cardosa, believed that this inequality could be overcome by political action: by trade preferences favouring the periphery, by commodity agreements, by international aid and by more foreign investment in the periphery. It was these remedies that Prebisch encouraged when he was Executive Secretary of ECLAC from 1955 to 1963 and Secretary-General of UNCTAD from 1964 to 1968. Indeed, the amount of aid the periphery needed in order to overcome their unfavourable trade balance became known in UNCTAD circles as the Prebisch Gap.

Dependency theory was later criticized on empirical bases, especially as the Global South, particularly East Asia and Latin America, started to develop, though often in an uneven fashion, and the theoretical underpinning became less Marxist after the end of the Cold War (Katzenstein *et al.* 1998: 665–6). It had, however, helped to shift institutional concerns towards Global South organizations such as ASEAN. The distinguished African academic, Ali Mazrui, wrote on the plight of that continent and its role in international affairs. He sought to answer the question: 'Now the Imperial Order is coming to an end, who is going to keep the peace in Africa?' and to examine the concept of Pax Africana – the Africans' ambition to be their own policeman. The policing and self-government of Africa depended on the notion of an African 'self' which Mazrui discussed in detail. He considered how this independence might be threatened by the political and cultural fragmentation of the continent, and economically by dependence on Europe. He quoted Kwame Nkrumah, first President of Ghana, on the European Economic Community: 'The Treaty of Rome . . . marks the advent of neo-colonialism in Africa . . . and bears unquestionably the marks of French neo-colonialism' (Mazrui 1967: 93). He concluded from this that 'What Africans therefore needed was a central authority of their own to co-ordinate their economic and political defence against this threat' (Mazrui 1967: 93).

Given this theme, it is not surprising that Mazrui set store by the OAU (later AU), but he was realistic in his judgement:

> In relations between African states a modest step towards Pax Africana was taken when the Organization of African Unity set up its Commission of Mediation, Conciliation and Arbitration.
>
> . . .
>
> Another OAU Commission of relevance for Pax Africana is the Defence Commission. But the Defence Commission has so far been among the least effective of Pan-African institutions. Africa may indeed aspire to be her own policeman, but she does not seem ready as yet to pay the price for it.
>
> (Mazrui 1967: 213)

Mazrui outlined the varied backgrounds of the leaders of newly independent Africa and their radical and revolutionary ideas, and it is perhaps surprising that the institutions they created for the continent were so conservative, with the possible exception of the OAU's National Liberation Committee. Mazrui noted that Africa still had the problem of how other powers responded to its behaviour and that foreign intrusion in Africa continued. Indeed, this intrusion has continued in the 1990s and 2000s. The debt burden continued while some states collapsed into civil war and others took to intervention in their neighbour's affairs. Outside interference from both Europe and North America continued. One of the few bright spots was the end of apartheid in South Africa and the peaceful transition to majority rule. In all this, to quote Julius Nyerere, the former president of Tanzania, 'The OAU exists only for the protection of the African Heads of State' (cited in Alagappa 1998: 15). The relative optimism of Mazrui has given way to African writers examining some of the disturbing details of inaction by the OAU and regional organizations such as ECOWAS being used as cloaks for the machinations of regional hegemons such as Nigeria (Adibe 1998: 67–90). The transformation of the OAU into the AU in 2000 has led to a more active organization that has attempted to limit conflicts in the continent (African Union 2014).

In all, Global South commentators have provided a varied and lively approach towards the problems of international organizations. Their emphasis has naturally been on the use of world institutions to change the economic condition of the southern continents. Should these conditions not improve in the near future, further, more radical contributions on the role of international organizations in North–South relations might be expected from the Global South. Alternatively writers from that area may just despair that intergovernmental organizations offer them so little.

## Critical approaches

Critical approaches to the study of international relations are those that reject the dominant views represented by the realist and reformists as outlined above. In particular, they regard realists as apologists for the current configuration of power in the world system, and consider that the reformists are either unable to understand the true nature of that system or are unwilling to accept that it needs more than modest reforms. Though they may sympathize with the agenda of some Marxists and Global South writers, they do not have the historical certainty of the former nor rarely do they have the experience and perspective of the latter. They view international organizations with a jaundiced eye, as these are mainly the instruments of those who dominate the system. This section contains an account of three approaches, that of the critical theorists, of feminist writings and postmodernism.

### Critical theory

The approach of critical theory to international organizations is determined by their wider world-view, which in itself is explained by their name. One of the leading exponents, Robert Cox, said that it is 'critical in the sense that it stands apart from the prevailing order of the world and asks how that order came about'. It does not take existing institutions and power relations for granted but calls 'them into question'. It is directed to 'the social and political complex as a whole rather than the separate parts'. Instead of subdividing and limiting an examination of a problem, it looks at the larger picture of which the problem is just one part and tries 'to understand the processes of change in which both parts and whole are involved' (1993: 277–8). Rather than focusing on 'a problem-solving preoccupation with social power relationships, critical theorists, and especially those focusing on notions of hegemony, direct attention to the prevailing order of the world'. From the perspective of international organizations, critical theory 'does not take institutions and social and power relations for granted but calls them into question by concerning itself with their origins and where they might be in the process of changing' (Cox 1981: 129). Indeed, although Cox's work is largely identified with the Frankfurt School of Critical Theory, the term 'critical theory' has come to encompass a wide range of approaches. This section will only address those that have particular explicit ramifications for the study of international organizations.

As a theory, critical theory rejects the claims of positivism of an external reality and being value-free. For critical theorists, knowledge is not morally neutral, it is more the result of the social background of those that hold it. Given this, 'critical theory allows for a normative choice in favour of a social and political order different from the prevailing order, but it limits the range of choice to alternative orders which are feasible transformations of the existing world . . . It must reject improbable alternatives just as it rejects the permanency of the existing order' (Cox and Sinclair 1996: 90).

Critical theory differs from Marxist approaches because of its rejection of any claim to hold the objective truth and because of its avoidance of the pursuit of a utopia. Nevertheless its analysis of international relations is one that has a number of similarities with the Marxist perspective. It regards the existing structures of world politics as being oppressive, not least because of the dominance of the capitalism of the United States. For many, the United States is seen as a hegemonic power – the prevailing order – in terms that reflect the writings of the Italian Marxist writer Antonio Gramsci (1891–1932). Gramsci advanced the notion of 'an historic bloc' which in itself reflects the social relations of production. The dominant class in a country – or indeed any social grouping – 'maintains cohesion and identity within the bloc through the propagation of a common culture'. A new bloc can be formed when a subordinate class can establish its hegemony over other subordinate groups (Cox 1993: 56–7). The move towards hegemony comes with the 'passing from the specific interests of a group or class to the building of institutions and elaboration of ideologies' (Cox 1993: 57–8). It is that process that embeds the interests of the dominant class in an institutional form that has an appeal wider than that class itself. It therefore represents more than just the dominance of one state over another, but implies a certain acceptance of the rules and institutions patronized by the hegemonic power. In other words it is 'an order which most other states (or at least those within reach of the hegemony) could find compatible with their interests' (Cox 1993: 61). It also involves not just interstate activities but those of civil society (non-state societal institutions), thereby encouraging links between social classes in the countries covered by the hegemony.

What does Cox have to say about international organizations? They are seen in the context of the wider understanding of international relations, mentioned above. He is direct about them: 'One mechanism through which the universal norms of a world hegemony are expressed is the international organisation' (Cox 1993: 62). Why is this so? Cox (1993: 62) gives five reasons:

- They embody rules that help the expansion of a hegemonic world order. These institutions reflect the interests of the dominant social and economic force but allow a certain amount of adjustment to accommodate other subordinated interests. Thus the United States was prepared to make concessions to bring in the EU states, Japan and even China and Russia to the World Trade Organization.
- They are products of that order. Though the institutions and rules are normally initiated by the hegemonic power, it takes care to involve and consult a number of second-rank states and gain their support. The World Bank and International Monetary Fund were very much part of the world order that emerged after the Second World War and which was dominated by the United States.
- They legitimate its norms by providing guidance for states and by legitimizing certain activities at the national level. The OECD and the international financial institutions have spread an acceptance of market conditions and strict monetary policies.
- They co-opt elites from peripheral countries. Talented staff coming from the Third World are expected to accept the script written by the dominant power. Boutros Boutros-Ghali, as Secretary-General of the United Nations, strayed too far from the grip of Washington and his second term was vetoed by the United States. His successors, Kofi Annan and Ban Ki-Moon, brought the concerns of other states to the UN but not in a way that threatened the United States.
- 'They absorb counter-hegemonic ideas'. Ideas such as sustainable development and even debt forgiveness are taken on board by the international financial institutions but are transformed into policies that suit them.

What is to be done? Cox thinks that the problem of changing the world order should be shifted 'back from international institutions to national societies' where the socio-political base for a new historic bloc might be created (Cox 1993: 64). Failing the creation of a new historic bloc of the new working class and rural and urban marginal groups, there might be transformation of the current 'monopoly-liberal hegemony' by adjusting to the demands of local elites for policies such as nationalization (Cox 1993: 65). He also advocates re-regulation of economies and a re-composition of civil society. International institutions, including organizations, can become contact points for new social forces (Cox 1994: 111).

Bieler and Morton (2004) have developed Cox's neo-Gramscian arguments by employing ideas of 'supremacy'. This seeks to demonstrate that new historic blocs of elites may achieve a position of supremacy but not complete hegemony in an international world order dominated by neo-liberal thinking. For Bieler and Morton (2004: 96–9) supremacy defines the position of a leading class of transnational elites that has enabled such 'supreme' elites to lead and shape the development of various international economic organizations that underpin the continuation of a neo-liberal economic world order. This explains the development of the IMF, G7 and G20. However, critical theory has in more recent times offered two useful dimensions in relation to international organizations. First, neo-Gramscian theorists explain why there remains some resistance to globalization and the uses of international organizations to solve international economic problems, embodied in anti-globalization movements. Critical theory also highlights notions of resistance towards the utilization of inter-national organizations, such as the IMF, G7, and G20, towards regulating the global world economy through neo-liberal ideas. Bieler and Morton (2004) challenge the way that the discipline of market forces and the advance of neo-liberal economic policies is leading to a narrowing of the social basis of popular participation. Second, Gill shows how, partly in reaction to the constraints of popular resistance, the development of international organizations has continued in which there is a 'move towards construction of legal and constitutional devices to remove or insulate substantially the new economic institutions from popular scrutiny or democratic accountability' (Gill 1992: 165). The creation of the EU's Economic and Monetary Union (EMU) is regarded as a good example of this process (Bieler and Morton 2004: 97).

Critical theorists such as Cox offer a refreshing exposition of the position of international organizations in a world where the main revolutionary powers have either collapsed (the Soviet Union) or settled into a cautious conservatism (China). It provides a sceptical and realistic world-view without accepting the inevitability of a future dominated by monopoly-capitalism and the United States. However, its application to international organizations is somewhat limited to the main global institutions and the financial and economic organizations. It has less to say about regional organizations or about NGOs. Furthermore, its alternative future rests on outcomes that are far from certain. Revolutions in the Global South are more likely to be inspired by nationalism or by Islamic fundamentalism, scarcely the solid bases for new historic blocs.

*Feminist approaches*

Feminist perspectives on international relations have in common with the critical theorists a rejection of the dominance in the subject of the realist and reformists. Although feminist writers cover a wide scope, the general basis of their argument is that in international relations, as in most political and economic activity, women are disadvantaged. Petersen and Runyan (1993: 6) cite figures claiming to show that women's share of the world's property and take-home pay is very low whereas their burden of working hours is high. This is a demonstration of gender inequalities, the 'socially learned behavior and expectations that distinguish between masculinity and femininity' (Peterson and Runyan 1993: 5). Feminist approaches often go beyond the statistics and examine the mind-set of those engaged in the practice of international relations, which they see as gendered. In other words, the world is seen in a masculine way that favours the position of males in the hierarchy and devalues the contribution of women (Sylvester 1994). War, in particular, is gendered in a way that 'keeps women and men from questioning the essential purpose and the negative effects of war, militarization, and violence on their own and other's lives' (Petersen and Runyan 1993: 91).

What of feminist views of international organizations? It is not possible to present a collective view that encompasses the works of radical feminists and, say, liberal feminists. Instead the work of one author, Sandra Whitworth (1997), will be used as she pays some attention to international organizations. After introductions to feminist theory and international relations and gender and international relations, Whitworth examines gender and international organizations. She accepts Cox's view of international organizations that they reflect the dominant power relations in the international system and that '[i]nternational organization is the process of institutionalizing and regulating conflict – either that which may arise among states or that which has its roots in trans-national society' (Cox 1980: 375). The way in which people organize themselves within international institutions reflects a variety of power relations, 'including, of course, gender relations' (Whitworth 1997: 74). The triad of institutions, ideas and material conditions help to locate assumptions about gender within international relations. Whitworth uses these to examine the understanding of gender in an INGO, the International Planned Parenthood Federation (IPPF), and an intergovernmental organization (albeit one with some non-governmental representation) the International Labour Organization (ILO).

Whitworth's studies show that the IPPF tended to accept the de-emphasizing of the gendered nature of reproduction and to ignore the importance of birth control for women's reproductive freedom. Instead, in an effort to popularize birth control, stress was placed on parenthood rather than just the woman's choice. However, IPPF policy became more radical in the 1990s with links being made between birth control and women's sexuality (Whitworth 1997: ch. 4, *passim*).

The ILO concerned itself with women as workers. It considered that they needed special attention and promoted protective legislation. This reinforced the view that the male worker was the norm, with women workers not deserving the same rights, remuneration and conditions. Latterly, however, the ILO has reflected views that proclaim women's equality in the workforce and has started to assess the importance of policies on women's role in the workplace as well as in society more widely (Whitworth 1997: ch. 5, *passim*). Whitworth comes to the conclusion that an 'analysis of gender in the IPPF and ILO shows how these relationships and definitions of what it is to be a woman or man are structured relationships, and historically have been structured to disadvantage women' (Whitworth 1997: 157).

In common with the critical theorists, Whitworth has used an examination of two international organizations to demonstrate a point about international relations, indeed social relations, more widely. The point is about power and its use, not to balance one state against another but for one group to dominate another. In this case it is not the domination of one class, race or culture over another (though Whitworth recognizes those relationships as well) but of men over women.

Other writers have pointed up the dual nature of international organizations and the role of women. Berkovitch (1999) points to the evidence of such organizations mainstreaming gender issues while others such as Prügl, while accepting this, have remarked that '[i]nternational institutions are implicated in the reproduction of hegemonic masculinity while constructing various femininities as subordinate' (2004: 77). Prügl (2004: 70–1) sums up the dilemma for feminist writers considering inter-national organizations: 'Defenders of international institutions find in global rules and international bureaucracies a potential source of women's equality. Detractors distrust global visions of gender equality and gender-mainstreamed institutions. Seeing in them mechanisms to co-opt feminist agendas while cementing gender hegemonies.' International organizations are thus seen as reflecting the difficult choices to be made in wider political life.

*Postmodernism*

The postmodernist approach to international relations is one that has come to the fore in the period since the end of the Cold War. It is based on a wider intellectual viewpoint instigated by French intellectuals of the 1960s generation – Barthes, Derrida, Foucault and Lyotard – and which suggested that the modern era had been overcome. It rejects 'meta-narratives', grand accounts of history and other subjects, as having no independent substance. Scientific beliefs, including those of the social sciences, are rooted in culture, politics and mores of a society and are therefore subjective. As there is no objective reality, empirical claims have no special standing in the realms of knowledge. Indeed, power and knowledge are intimately intertwined. Postmodernism stands against the belief of the 'modern' period which is seen as beginning with the Enlightenment of mid-eighteenth century Europe and America. It therefore rejects the concepts of rationality and progress associated with the Enlightenment and the modern age. The unity of mankind and ideas such as the universality of human rights are rejected. Instead, local action in small groups is advocated.

Postmodernist ideas have affected the study of international relations, as they have other social sciences. Postmodern international relations theorists have used their views on objectivity 'to examine the "truths" of international relations to see how the concepts and knowledge-claims that dominate the discipline in fact are highly contingent on specific power relations' (Smith 1997: 181). Postmodernists have attacked the 'meta-narratives' of the realists and reformists alike. The 'objective' analyses of the realists and neo-realists are seen as being dependent on the subjective standpoints of their mainly American and European authors. Richard Ashley (1986: 258) claimed the works of Kenneth Waltz, then the leading neo-realist, 'treats the given order as the natural order, limits rather than expands political discourse, negates or trivializes the significance of variety across time and place ... What emerges is an ideology that anticipates, legitimizes, and orients a totalitarian project of global proportions; the rationalization of global politics.' The reformists are likewise tainted and have a mistaken belief in progress. The postmodernists point to the Holocaust as the height of modernism – a combination of science and political organization. It was scarcely progress.

Given an antipathy towards the sovereign state both as a centre of power and as a creation often imbued with a concepts of progress, postmodernists can scarcely be expected to view intergovernmental organizations with sympathy. The preferred forms of international organizations, when mentioned, are those that display differences and diversity in global politics, that are regionally based or that reflect individual action. Indeed, it seems that Michel Foucault was involved with an alliance of two INGOs (Médecins du Monde and Terres des Hommes) in protesting against international inaction over the 'boat people' who fled Vietnam in the late 1970s and early 1980s. He is quoted as saying that 'Amnesty International, Terres des Hommes, Médecins du Monde are initiatives which have created a new right: the right of private individuals to intervene in the order of politics and international strategies' (cited in Campbell 1998: 516).

Another researcher has examined the European Communities, at the point when it was transforming into the European Union, and asked whether it was a postmodern configuration (Nørgaard 1994). His conclusions were that it was 'qualitatively a new organization of human collectivities which might usher the coming of post-modernity' (Nørgaard 1994: 275). The basis for this judgement was that the EC did not approximate any modern form of political organization, it did not command the means of violence, its authority derives not from the people and it appeared to be a region trying to protect itself against globalization (Nørgaard 1994: 274–5). Events since then, in particular the EU's response to the financial crisis after 2008, suggest that this evaluation may have been presumptive as the EU's institutions were increasingly dominated by state interests.

Generally the critical approaches to international relations have provided some innovative insights into the study of international organizations. The critical theorists have been sharpest in their understanding of international organizations as servants of a dominant power configuration, though they have perhaps limited their scope when viewing international organizations. Feminist writers have given voice to what is, after all, the semi-silent majority in the world, and are only starting to question the male dominance not just of the running of IGOs but also of their agenda. The postmodernists are the least concerned of the three groups with international organizations as such, but their intellectual approach is the most radical and can lead to a form of nihilism.

## *Globalist views*

A globalist perspective does not view world politics as being predominantly about intergovernmental relations, as would realists, or about interstate and intersocietal relations, as a number of reformists may consider. Instead it takes a more holistic view. Problems are confronted at a global level; solutions have to be sought there as well. This is not to neglect the local or the state level, it is more a recognition of the limitations of activities there. The 'world-view', like the reformists, places emphasis on what unites people and has little time for the demands of power politics and state-centric organizations. It goes further by not limiting its view either to parts of the world or to relations between particular politics or indeed just to the economic, social and political demands of mankind. Paradoxically, it can be seen as an approach as the very opposite of the functionalist, with whom there is much in common. In contrast to the functionalist (or neo-functionalist or interdependence school) and certainly in contrast to the power politics and Marxist writers, the 'whole world' approach places emphasis not on the discrete requirements of groups, states or individuals, but on the well-being of the ecosystem in which these function – the planet Earth. The concern of this approach, which is reflected in its treatment of international organizations, is for the survival of the planet, for its efficient functioning in its widest sense, and for the survival of the myriad of species – only one of which is homo sapiens – that inhabit the globe.

Since the 1960s, a number of writers on international affairs have expounded on this view and have consequently considered the implications for international organizations. John Burton in his *World Society* considered interstate relations to be only a part of world politics and wrote:

> If we employ the term 'world society' instead of 'international relations', if we approach our study in this global way instead of the more traditional 'national way', we will tend to have a wider focus, to ask questions that are more fundamental and important to civilization, and be able to assess better the relevance of our own national behaviour to the wider world environment.
>
> (Burton 1972: 21)

Richard Sterling posed the problem more specifically:

> Nuclear escalation, the population explosion, the pollution of the environment, the communications revolution, the world-wide concentration of wealth and world-wide expansion of poverty are all essentially global and not local phenomena. They

have given rise, in turn, to earth-spanning and revolutionary demands for mass education, mass health, mass welfare, and mass participation in the decisions affecting man's fate.

(Sterling 1974: 322)

This world-view of the problems of 'the spaceship Earth' begged for global solutions. It suggested that not only is the system of sovereign states as yet unable, or unwilling, to come to grips with the above-mentioned problems but that a network of inter-governmental organizations based on the rights of state sovereignty will also be hamstrung. Global problems needed global solutions based on institutions that can take a global perspective. Thus Sterling considered that 'it is not unreasonable to antici-pate that the member states will be moved to consider equipping the United Nations with more comprehensive powers as global pressures build' (1974: 323).

A more compelling call was issued by Barbara Ward and Rene Dubos in their book prepared for the UN Conference of the Human Environment, *Only One Earth: The Care and Maintenance of a Small Planet* (1972). They stressed the unity of the Earth and its environment and the problems faced by its inhabitants, essentially those outlined by Sterling. The authors pointed out that the environmental question had, by 1972, already had some impact on governments and international organization but the effect was somewhat uncoordinated and unfocused. In three particular areas – the global atmosphere, the oceans, the world's weather systems – they saw the immediate need for common policy and co-ordinated actions 'where pretensions to national sovereignty have no relevance to perceived problems'. But there was a need to go further and deal with other global problems: disease, starvation, illiteracy, unemployment, overcrowding. International policies were at the stage reached within the developing states of the nineteenth century: 'Either they will move on to a community based upon a more systematic sharing of wealth . . . or they will break down in revolt and anarchy' (Ward and Dubos 1972: 295–6). They looked forward to a sense of global community based on the hope of protection (from war and disaster) and the hope of enhancement (ecological as well as economic). The 'practices and institutions with which we are familiar inside our domestic societies would become, suitably modified, the basis of planetary order' (Ward and Dubos 1972: 297–8). This would include 'non-violent settlement of disputes with legal arbitration and policing procedures on an international basis'; it would mean the transfer of resources from rich to poor and increased co-operation in areas such as health and education, farming, urban planning and pollution control. As there has been a shift of loyalty from family to clan, from clan to nation, and from nation to federation, there was hope, claimed Ward and Dubos, for 'an ultimate loyalty to our single, beautiful and vulnerable Planet Earth' (Ward and Dubos 1972: 298).

While the institutional framework and organizational structures remain, of necessity, vague in *Only One Earth*, it is clear that the authors were aiming at a network of worldwide, functionally based organizations (both IGOs and INGOs) that could take on much of the work presently done by governments – or rather, which ought to be done by governments.

Later writings have attempted to deal with the policy implications of dealing with problems globally. Soroos (1986) has pointed to what has already been achieved in global problem-solving and has sought to build on this. His critics have pointed out that what has already been undertaken has been done more along traditional intergovernmental lines (Donnelly 1990: 221–30). Other writers have tied achievement in addressing the global agenda more to renewed activity in the UN (Rochester 1990: 141–54) or to greater grass roots and INGO activism (Alger 1990: 155–68) or to wider historical factors that have favoured a decline in violence (Pinker 2011: xxv–xxvi).

The new millennium brought a fresh emphasis on global problems, if not always a willingness to pursue solutions. Chase-Dunn and Inoue (2012: 166) have pointed to the factors that could lead to global state formation such as population pressure, and that 'major organizational changes tend to emerge after huge catastrophes' (2012: 167) and mapped out how global governance might emerge from existing institutions. Barnett and Finnemore (2004: 172–3) have pointed out that increasingly bureaucratized institutions established to solve the world's problems could come at a cost. While beneficial, these institutions could be undemocratic and unresponsive and the very source of their ability to do good 'might also be the source of their power to do harm' (Barnett and Finnemore 2004: 173).

Nye (2002) has defined globalism as 'networks of connections that span multi-continental distances' with globalization as the process that makes globalism more intense. An expanded literature has described this process (see, e.g. Reinalda 2013) and the authors cited above consider the implications less of some worldwide state and more of global governance – making rules and laws without necessarily having a government – and its evolving institutional form. The inspiration for globalists has been a fear of what may happen if humanity does not tackle the worldwide problems facing it in the twenty-first century.

The globalist approach is open to the criticism of being too idealistic in a cynical world and too impractical in its institutional suggestions. But the dismissal of these words as 'globaloney' does not rid the world of the problems which they have so effectively publicized. They have tried to add another dimension to what is possible, by showing that it is necessary for the survival of the planet.

The radical approach to the study of international organizations reflects world-views that normally go beyond those dominated by the activities of states or of the organizations themselves. There is a sceptical view of what is happening at any one time in international relations and of the ability of more traditional writers on international relations to explain, let alone understand what is happening. It is the feeling that approaches such as the Marxist, the critical theorists' and some of the globalists' are coming closer to understanding humanity's wider dilemmas that makes them so attractive. They are less likely to apply themselves to the details and workings of particular international organizations but, nevertheless, provide intriguing insights on this phenomenon by seeing them through more panoptic philosophical lenses.

## Summary

The three major schools dealt with in this chapter – the realist, the reformists and the radicals – and the variations they contain, did not, and do not, exist in a historical vacuum. Ideas were formulated within the context of particular societies and in response to particular problems: the communications revolution of the nineteenth century; the First World War; the rise of Nazi Germany; the spreading of nuclear weapons; the development of post-Second World War Europe; the processes of decolonization and détente; the end of the Cold War and the advance of the information revolution. In some cases, the views of those writings on international organizations have had an effect on events themselves, particularly on the attitudes of governments towards international organizations. An example is the work of Leonard Woolf, whose suggestions concerning a world organization contributed to the detailed preparation of the League of Nations by the British government. Likewise, Hans Morgenthau, Joseph Nye and E.H. Carr provided stimuli for informed United States and British governmental thinking about international relations from the 1940s onwards. In other cases the general writings of persons such as Marx, Lenin, Mao Tse-tung and the dependencia school have affected the political climate within which governments conduct their policy, including that towards international organizations.

Other factors, apart from their historical context, have affected the views of the schools mentioned. They have different backgrounds in their ideology (Western, communist, Global South radical, environmentalist) and in their level of analysis of international relations (state-centric, interest and transnational groups, class dominant, global). This affects the type of international organization dominant in their studies (IGOs, INGOs) and their geographical area of interest (the North Atlantic, Europe, Global South or global).

The range of writings about international organizations has, on the whole, reflected wider understandings of international relations and world politics. These in themselves have fed on the wider intellectual ferment and on developments in world affairs. Views about international organizations will continue to take account of the intellectual debate in the studies of politics, international relations, philosophy, economics, international law, sociology, history and geography. They will also reflect, among other factors, the strategic balance in the world, the relative power of the United States, China and other states, the state of world markets, the process of European integration, the relative position of the developing world, the level of conflict throughout the world, the state of the environment and the ability of large states to withstand centrifugal forces. The way that international organizations reflect these developments and their capability to deal with some of them will provide the raw material for future studies.

# 4 Role and function of international organizations

Chapter 1 placed international organizations in a historical context by demonstrating that this phenomenon had evolved during a definite period of international history starting in the mid-nineteenth century and flourishing in the period after the Second World War.

In Chapter 2 the aims and activities of international organizations were used as one way of classifying them. These aims and activities were primarily internal to the organizations, that is, they represented what their founders considered their tasks to be and what the organizations attempted to achieve during their existence.

Chapter 3 covered some of the main writings about international organizations, dividing them into realist, reformists and radicals. It showed how these commentators reflected the wider understandings of both international relations and events in world politics.

This chapter examines international organizations in the contemporary world. International organizations take their place in a sort of political marketplace where the relationships between peoples, groups, business, nations, states and blocs can be observed. Here we seek to find out what role they play in this 'global marketplace': are they one of the many participants jostling in transactions with other groups, with political leaders and states' representatives? Are they the mere instruments of the other players, being used as tools to gain advantages or as means of communication between interlocutors? Or are they part of the scenery itself, plinths for speeches, forums for meetings, common grounds for gatherings?

Second, the functions of international organizations in international relations will be examined. How do they affect the functioning of the global political marketplace? Do they allow those who frequent it to organize themselves more efficiently, to express their desires more forcefully or more clearly? Do they influence the running of the marketplace, or behaviour there? Can they determine who shall do business there, even to set standards for behaviour and perhaps enforce rules and regulations? Or can they affect the functioning of the global political marketplace by themselves trading in it or indirectly by providing information to those who 'buy and sell'? Do they function as a form of global governance?

Clearly, some organizations will fulfil limited roles and functions while others may cover a wide range. Naturally, the role played by an international organization will affect the functions it performs in international relations. A mute messenger boy may have a less overt, seemingly less important function in the running of the marketplace than an armed policeman. This is not to say that one day the messenger boy's duties may not include providing the crucial information for a life-and-death decision, or that the work of the policeman might not be hamstrung by the actions of armed brigands or just by lack of public support.

Likening contemporary international relations to a global political marketplace begs certain questions. What is the nature of the marketplace? Is it open with free contact between all who use it, person and beast, large and small, whatever their background or intention? Or is it regulated with certain discrete areas having only carefully controlled relationships with others? Are the activities of individuals curtailed and just certain traders allowed to approach one another's territory? Or has it a loose structure with fairly random activities performed between groups who have little to do with one another outside their formal dealings?

Are, then, international relations part of the world system or a network? Those who identify a global political system consider that it consists of 'numerous more or less autonomous actors interacting in patterned ways to influence one another. Their independent decisions and policies serve as stimuli for one another and induce or constrain the behavior of others' (Mansbach *et al.* 1976: 5). The emphasis here is placed on an overall pattern of interaction and response, whereas a network suggests something more modest: contact and interconnections between individual entities which may not be used in a patterned fashion to influence one another. A network is less organized, less active and reactive, less enclosed than a system. The structure of world politics is clearly enclosed on the planet Earth (though this is beginning to change) but its level of organization and interaction depends on whether one sees the glass half full or half empty. Russett and Starr define a system as a 'complexity of interactions . . . When we speak of a global or regional system, we imply that the major elements or influences at different levels of analysis affect each other' (Russett and Starr 1992: 19). The crucial word here is 'major'. The two authors go on to identify a good analyst as one who can 'simplify a complex reality in a way that concentrates on the most important relationships and at least temporarily ignores the others' (Russett and Starr 1992: 19). Following this advice, the term 'international system' – within which international organizations function – will be used in its fairly simple meaning suggesting that contemporary international relations take place within a defined area (which nevertheless is diffuse), wherein activities in one area are clearly seen to affect those elsewhere and the whole structure is seen to be interconnected, though to what extent may be disputed. It is clear this set-up has no central authority, no directing power, no imposed pattern of behaviour.

It is perhaps the nebulous nature of the international political system that makes the task of assessing the role and function of international organizations within it so difficult. A number of warnings should be sounded.

The classification of international organizations in Chapter 2 showed that they range from those with general aims and activities and a wide membership to those with specific aims and a limited membership. It is therefore likely that a number of roles will be fulfilled by international organizations, some overlapping, some conflicting, making their function in international relations difficult to discern. International organizations cover such a broad spectrum that evidence about the activities of individual organizations, especially the more specific non-governmental organizations, is not readily available and the overall effect of their existence has to be estimated or summarized from the larger, better-known institutions.

Second, the functional use of international organizations may be deduced from their aims and activities and from the response of the membership to their existence. It is assumed that organizations are playing a role of some note in international relations, and importance is consequently attached to the work of the organizations. However, being short of laboratory conditions in international relations, it is not possible to compare 'reality' with a 'control' in which international affairs might be replicated in the absence of international organizations. While it is possible to observe certain phenomena, such as war, trading and tourism both before and after the creation of organizations affecting those activities, it is difficult to establish what factors have caused any changes. This is not to rule out such studies. Indeed, events over an extended period and studies with a large number of cases may suggest interesting associations between international organizations and certain behaviour in international relations; individual studies may demonstrate connections through 'detective work' – for example, a particular settlement of a dispute may have the 'fingerprints' of a UN mediator on it; and often negative evidence can be used to call in question common assumptions or to suggest further research.

Finally, an assessment of the role and function of international organizations in the international system is bound to be affected by the view of the nature of the system. It is generally accepted that the present international system has no controlling overall authority and is anarchic in the sense of being without government. How the present set-up may develop is disputed. Each interpretation can produce a different evaluation of international organizations' roles and functions. If the present system is seen as a necessary and continuing result of power politics, then any international institutions will have a somewhat limited aspect and will only be able to ameliorate unwanted consequences of relations between sovereign states. If the contemporary system is interpreted as an international society (Bull 1977), then the role of international organizations will be seen as part of the institutions that support such an order. If, however, it is felt that the international system is developing very much in the way that political systems within states have, then present-day organizations can be seen in the role of potential instruments of world government.

Indeed, another element of this point is that of change. If one views the international system as being fairly static, then there will be little expectation of a growth in the role and function of international organizations. Indeed, a pessimistic view of the system would see their decline. However, a more sanguine view of the system that stresses progress – the reformists covered in the last chapter have taken mainly that approach – is likely to predict a growth in the role and function of international organizations. Studies that point to less conflict in the system (Human Security Report Project 2012) and those that see an improving economic and social world scene (Higgins 2014) also include descriptions of a growing network of international organizations, both IGOs and INGOs.

International relations operate within an international system – 'a set of interacting elements' – where a bullet ringing out in Sarajevo can have major consequences for those living in South Africa, Siberia or Sydney; and the activities of diplomats in New York or Geneva affect the future of a regime in Syria, the survival of the state of Sierra Leone, the lives of political prisoners in South America or the use of the world's oceans, outer space or the Antarctic. In this system, rather as in a town's marketplace, relationships can cover a wide range of activities such as personal travel, trade, business, diplomacy, the exchange of information, propaganda, police actions, crime and conflict.

It is clear that international organizations' role and function have a part to play in the international system. Quantitative studies have demonstrated their presence and

Chapter 2 showed their range. The *Yearbook of International Organizations* (www.uia.org/yearbook) and works by Angell (1965), Feld (1971), Feld, Jordan with Hurwitz (1994), Reinalda (2009, 2013), Sheets and Maarer (2000), Singer and Wallace (1970), Skjelsbaek (1971), Speeckaert (1957), Tallberg *et al.* (2013) have produced a welter of information on the growth of both IGOs and INGOs. As shown in Chapter 1, there was an exponential growth in the number of intergovernmental organizations in the 170 years after the 1815 Congress of Vienna, somewhat reflecting the expansion of the international system itself. From the end of the 1980s, the cost-benefit of some IGOs was questioned and the number of existing conventional IGOs began to fall from 378 in 1985 to 251 in 1999 (Union of International Associations 1999). Jacobson (1979: 52) shows that of the 289 IGOs accounted for in 1970, 276 had a specific purpose, covering a field of activity such as health (WHO), education (UNESCO), agriculture (FAO), finance (IMF), trade (GATT) and fisheries (NEAFC). The number of INGOs has seen an exponential rate of growth since 1815, to such an extent that they soon outstripped IGOs in quantity. At the end of the twentieth century there were some 5,800, most of which had fairly specific aims (Union of International Associations 1999) and this number continued to grow to some 8,000 in 2010 when a small decrease was experienced (Tallberg *et al.* 2013: 6). A more expansive definition (Turner 2010: 83) places the number of INGOs in 2010 at 27,000.

## Roles of international organizations

What roles do these considerable number of international organizations play in the montage of exchanges in the international system? Three major roles can be identified: those of instrument, arena and actor.

### Instrument

Perhaps the most usual image of the role of international organizations is that of an instrument being used by its members for specific ends. This is particularly the case with IGOs, where the members are sovereign states with power to limit independent action by international organizations. The former Executive Secretary of the UN's Economic Commission for Europe, Gunnar Myrdal, has outlined this role in a lecture from which it is worth quoting at some length:

> The basic fictitious notion about inter-governmental organizations, as conveyed by their constitutions, is that they are something more than their component parts: something above the national states. . . . In the typical case international organizations are nothing else than instruments for the policies of individual governments, means for the diplomacy of a number of disparate and sovereign national states. When an intergovernmental organization is set up, this implies nothing more than that between the states a limited agreement has been reached upon an institutional form for multilateral conduct of state activity in a certain field. The organization becomes important for the pursuance of national policies precisely to the extent that such a multilateral co-ordination is the real and continuous aim of national governments.
>
> (Myrdal 1955: 4–5)

Myrdal's intuition was supported by the empirical findings of a databased study of IGOs used by McCormick and Kihl who showed that 'IGOs are used by nations primarily as selective instruments for gaining foreign policy objectives' (McCormick and Kihl 1979: 502). This view squarely relegates IGOs to the role of convenient tools for use by their member states. INGOs in an analogous position would merely reflect the requirements of the various trade unions, business organizations, political parties or church groups that were members. The consequences for the international organization are that it is likely to become fought over by the most powerful members eager to utilize it, and thus its chances of independent action are limited.

The United Nations in its first eight years of existence is often characterized as being an instrument of US diplomacy. The US government could count on a majority consisting of West European, Old Commonwealth and Latin American states in the General Assembly (thirty-four out of the original fifty-one members), on a majority in the Security Council only attenuated by the Soviet veto, and a Secretary-General with clear pro-Western sympathies. During this period the United States used the United Nations to pillory the USSR over its activities in Eastern Europe; to help prevent Soviet incursions in Northern Iran; as a midwife for the birth of the two new states of Indonesia and Israel against, respectively, Dutch and Arab protests; to establish a multilateral force led by the United States to fight on behalf of South Korea against North Korea and communist China; to extend the term of office of Secretary-General Trygve Lie against Soviet opposition; to exclude the new communist government in Beijing from taking the China seat, and to have that government condemned as an aggressor over the Korean War. The United States did not obtain all it wished at the UN during this period: the Soviet Union vetoed a number of Security Council resolutions ranging from the admittance of Italy as a UN member to attempts to interfere in events in the Balkans. As Inis Claude (1964: 145) pointed out: 'From the Soviet standpoint, the veto power is an essential but regrettably limited and indecisive instrument of defense against Western utilization of the organization for anti-Communist purposes.' Indeed, in 1950 when Soviet absence from the Security Council allowed the United States to mobilize United Nations support for action in South Korea, the Soviet government realized its mistake and sent back its representative to veto further Security Council action.

As well as these limitations experienced by the United States during the early period of the UN's existence, it soon became clear that the organization could not be used indefinitely as an appendage to US foreign policy machinery. The political shape of the world was changing with the emergence of the Soviet Union as a nuclear power and of the Third World (later called the Global South) non-aligned movement. Membership of the UN changed and by the mid-1950s the United States had lost its automatic majority in the General Assembly. The second Secretary-General, Dag Hammarskjold, was more his own man and was also aware of the fate of his predecessor. Even in the Security Council it was no longer only the Soviets who were defending themselves with the veto; in November 1956 Britain and France cast their first ones against resolutions concerning the Suez operation against Egypt.

An organization cannot continue to be the instrument of policy of one dominant member when the membership is as varied as that of the UN. As long as a large majority was satisfied with US activities in the UN – as seemed the case from 1945 to 1953 – then the United States government could use this organization as a Cold War implement. This role of the UN could no longer be sustained once the membership of the General Assembly and the nature of the Cold War began to change. The United States did not cease its attempts to utilize the organization to further its foreign policy ends, but it found that it was not alone in doing this successfully. The USSR, which up until the mid-1960s had merely defended its interest at the UN, began to take a more active approach. Furthermore, the Third World countries started to use the UN as an instrument for implementing their foreign policies, made more necessary by their not having a traditional network of diplomacy at their disposal. Indeed, as early as 1956 Dag Hammarskjold described how through the machinery of the UN and other international organizations, 'regularized multilateral negotiation had been added as a new tool for politicians, a new instrument for governments, a new technique of diplomacy' (Cordier and Foote 1972: 661).

The use of international organizations as adjuncts to their members' policies affects their constitutions and development. The possibility of IGOs developing their own decision-making powers becomes, in Myrdal's words, 'a fictitious notion'. The UN's Economic Commission for Europe, of which Myrdal was Executive Secretary, was a classic example of an organization which only had modest institutions because of member states' unwillingness to lose control over their economic policies. Co-operative arrangements on specific research, co-ordination of national policies, multilateral agreements and limited delegated powers were accepted as they were 'nothing else and nothing more than a set of mutual promises of co-ordinated and synchronized national policy action' (Myrdal 1955: 8). These limitations are reflected in the powers of the secretariat and in the decision-taking mechanisms.

The secretariat of an organization such as ECE represented the 'collective aspirations of the member governments' and herein lies both its strengths and its limitations. By earning the respect of member states, the secretariat can influence their thinking, act as honest broker, and even find some matters increasingly delegated to them; for example, the Secretariat of the ECE Coal Committee could prescribe changes, when conditions demanded, in the agreed quarterly allocations of coal (Myrdal 1955: 23). Such powers are normally only 'technical', willingly delegated by governments and open to review by the members. The secretariat has to watch that it neither strays from its remit nor undermines the aims of member states, particularly powerful ones, as it will inevitably lose in a confrontation. Examples of individuals being ousted from secretariat posts of international organizations after having alienated one or a number of member states are Trygve Lie in the United Nations in 1953 (and Dag Hammarskjold had he not died in 1961), Etienne Hirsch of Euratom in 1962, Theo Van Boven of the UN's Human Rights Committee in 1982, Mary Robinson as the High Commissioner for Human Rights in 2002 and Boutros Boutros-Ghali as the Secretary-General of the UN in 1996.

This sort of political interference of a secretariat should not be confused with the question of an international civil service. The League of Nations' first Secretary-General, Sir Eric Drummond, wrote that such a service would be one:

> in which men and women of various nationalities might unite in preparing and presenting to the members of the League an objective and common basis of discussion . . . the Secretary-General would not only be the co-ordinating centre of the activities of the Secretariat, but its members would be responsible to him alone, and not to the Governments of the countries of which they were nationals.
>
> (cited in Jordan 1971: 43)

But such a secretariat would be entrusted 'with the execution of any decisions taken by the Governments' (Jordan 1971: 44). A secretariat based on those seconded from national missions is more open to direct interference and there is good evidence that since the 1960s the UN Secretariat has been increasingly subject to such pressures (Weiss 1982: 294–305; Spillius and Waterfield 2010). Furthermore, the hierarchical structure of the UN Secretariat has meant that the Secretaries-General can often make appointment to top posts with little regard to competence or competition. Ban Ki-Moon, the eighth Secretary-General, was accused of appointing people to executive posts in order to satisfy major donor nations (Deen 2012). All this can affect the efficiency of the organization and can also interfere with its ability to carry out policy agreed by the collectivity of members and thus represents an attempt by some states to have 'two bites at the cherry': having not quite obtained all they want in plenary meetings they can then direct 'their' members of the Secretariat to implement (or not implement) policy in such a way as to favour their interests. It seems that a growing number of states agree with the statement of the Soviet leader in the early 1960s, Mr Krushchev, cited by Walter Lippman, 'that there can be no such thing as an impartial civil servant in this deeply divided world' and that, therefore, members of an international civil service can legitimately be used to further the demands of their home state. Governments of such states do not seem to be diverted from such action by it being contrary, in the case of the UN, to the requirements in Article 100 of the Charter that:

> In the performance of their duties the Secretary-General and the staff will not seek or receive instructions from any government.
> . . . Each Member of the United Nations undertaking to respect the exclusively international character of the responsibilities of Secretary-General and the staff and not to seek to influence them in the discharge of their responsibilities.

The way that decisions are taken in many international organizations can also demonstrate their use 'for the pursuance of national policies'. It is noticeable that, as well as limiting the powers of any secretariat, the constitutions of most international organizations do not allow for decisions, at least major ones, to be taken that may bind members that have voted against them. This is not the case in the United Nations but is the rule in most IGOs. In the case of the UN General Assembly, resolutions only have the strength of recommendations; while Security Council resolutions, which can be passed by a majority of nine out of fifteen members and can be mandatory, are subject to veto by any one of the permanent members. The use of the veto has severely limited the number of cases where states have found that the UN, far from helping in the pursuance of their national policies, has overridden their wishes and even acted against them. In these rare cases – white-ruled South Africa and Israel come to mind – these states still have used the UN machinery to persuade Western states, especially the United States, to prevent really effective action against them by use of the veto. Thus the UN has produced verbally strong resolutions but little harmful action against Israel and pre-1992 South Africa in addition to that already organized by the Arab League and the then OAU.

Organizations with a more limited membership often have decision-taking mechanisms which reflect their being at the service of the membership. While the unanimity principle is the best assurance for a member that its interest will not be jeopardized by the decisions of the organization, it has its limitations. A vote at every stage of a complicated process of decision-taking would soon paralyse an institution if complete unanimity were needed at all times. Myrdal claimed that in the ECE's technical agencies, votes were not taken: non-substantive issues were cleared in advance by the secretariat for unanimous decisions 'while the efforts in deliberations on substantive questions were directed towards reaching a maximum agreement between a maximum number of Governments' (Myrdal 1955: 19). Furthermore it was not necessary for all to agree on a programme: 'one or several governments should not hinder two or more other governments for using the organization to reach a settlement among themselves'. This has also been the case in the Organization for Economic Co-operation and Development, where those voting for decisions are bound by them while those abstaining are not. The Treaty of Lisbon, 2007, allows for a certain flexibility in greater co-operation among some, though not all, EU members. These arrangements only apply to the participating member states, though other members can join them later on (Europa summaries of EU legislation 2010).

These apparent deviations from the rule of unanimity do not undermine a member's ability to use an international organization as an instrument of policy. Instead they demonstrate that in any political process the participants have to calculate the extent to which they are in a 'zero-sum game'. If they believe that gains made by any other member are going to be to their detriment, then they will insist on tight constitutional control of the international organization, exercising their right of veto over any move that does not benefit them. If they believe that co-operation can produce new benefits which would otherwise remain unexploited and that all, or most, members can take advantage of these, then it is logical to allow the institutions of the organization some scope for action. Likewise, a long-term view may persuade a member to suffer apparent losses by not preventing decisions detrimental to its interests in the expectation that larger gains will be made when other decisions are taken. To describe international organizations as functioning as instruments of their membership does not mean that each and every decision made must be explicable in terms of serving the interests of each and every member. An instrument demonstrates its purpose if it shows its utility over a period of time to those that have brought it into service. Their satisfaction should not be jaded when another makes use of the instrument, provided it is not turned into a weapon against them.

## Arena

A second image of the role of international organizations is that of their being arenas or forums within which actions take place. In this case, the organizations provide meeting places for members to come together to discuss, argue, co-operate or disagree. Arenas in themselves are neutral – they can be used for a play, a circus or a fight. Stanley Hoffmann, examining the various roles of the UN, wrote of this aspect:

> As an arena and a stake it has been useful to each of the competing groups eager to get not only a forum for their views but also diplomatic reinforcement for their policies, in the Cold War as well as in the wars for decolonization.
>
> (Hoffmann 1970: 398–9)

Conor Cruise O'Brien's view of the UN is that 'Its Council Chambers and Assembly Hall are stages set for a continuous dramatisation of world history' (O'Brien and

Topolski 1968: 9). A more down-to-earth approach is advanced by Yeselson and Gaglione in a book whose title suggests that the UN plays more the role of an instrument: *A Dangerous Place – The United Nations as a Weapon in World Politics* (1974). Despite this, the UN is described as 'an arena for combat' (Yeselson and Gaglione 1974: 3). More traditionally, international organizations have provided their members with the opportunity of advancing their own viewpoints and suggestions in a more open and public forum than that provided by bilateral diplomacy. It is not surprising to find that a study of forty-one academic publications written during the 1970–77 period showed that 78 per cent portrayed the UN as an arena (Dixon 1981: 51). Even by 2009, one writer was describing the UN as 'an exceptional forum' and 'an essential arena in which states actually codify norms' but admitted that it was also 'a maddening forum because dissent by powerful states or mischief by large coalitions of even less powerful ones means either no action occurs, or agreement is possible only on a lowest-common denominator' (Weiss 2009: 3).

During the 1970s, the United Nations and its agencies were used by Third World countries to air their views on the subject of a New International Economic Order (NIEO). The old order had been based on the negotiations carried out at Bretton Woods (1944–46), when the victorious Allies – though with opposition from the Soviet bloc – created a multilateral structure for the post-Second World War economy. This system was based on American economic strength, the dollar as the lynchpin currency, and an agreement to liberalize markets and the exchange of currencies, so that eventually a free market could be created for the Western world and its dependencies. By the start of the 1970s this system was collapsing. A large number of newly dependent countries found the Bretton Woods system and its associated organizations (the IBRD, IMF and GATT) unsympathetic to their economic aspirations and they resented the dominance of OECD countries in these institutions and in the world economy generally. The United States was no longer in the superior position it had been in 1945: other economic centres had emerged in West Europe and Asia which, while not as powerful as the United States, sapped some of its economic strength. The dollar had been severely weakened by constant US balance of trade deficits, inflation and growing fears about its link to gold. From 1971 to 1973 the dollar-based currency system of Bretton Woods gave way: the US dollar ceased to be backed by gold and was devalued in price. At the end of 1973, after the Arab–Israel Yom Kippur War, the Middle Eastern oil producers persuaded their colleagues in OPEC to increase petroleum prices substantially – fourfold from October 1973 to the summer of 1974 – thereby delivering another blow to the already reeling Western industrialized states. The West still held control of the world's financial and trading institutions and the rules of the economic game were those drawn up largely by the United States and Britain at Bretton Woods.

The new Third World states had already been calling for a fresh set of economic priorities; by 1964 they had established the UN Conference on Trade and Development (UNCTAD) as a forum at which they could articulate their trade and economic demands outside the predefined discussion of the Bretton Woods organizations. As a result of UNCTAD meetings, the Third World had formed the Group of 77 (G77), a bloc whose interests were those of the African, Asian and Latin American developing states. On political questions, G77 was mirrored by the meeting of ministers from the non-aligned countries which again were most of the states of the Southern continents. By the end of the 1960s, the Third World had enough forums within which to put forward their ideas and demands, but when the richer industrialized states were present – at the Bretton Woods institutions, in ECOSOC, at UNCTAD meetings – the poorer states could exercise little or no bargaining power, only persuasion. As Sidney Weintraub (1977: 97) commented: 'Each group of countries will wish to negotiate issues of importance to it in the institutions that it dominates.' The difference is outlined by Robert Gregg (1981: 54–5): the South preferred the UN General Assembly, and to some extent UNCTAD, because of its 'universality, its egalitarian/majoritarian decision-making rules and practices, and its political character'; the North, the developed economies, preferred a more pluralistic system of forums with regard for the specialized institutions such as IMF, IBRD and GATT.

The search by the developing states for a New International Economic Order (NIEO) surfaced in the 1970s at the Third United Conference on Trade and Development (UNCTAD III) in 1972, the 1973 Algiers summit of non-aligned states and a preparatory committee of the developing countries which produced a draft declaration and programme of action for the establishment of a NIEO ready for the UN General Assembly's Sixth Special Session on raw materials and development. The four basic points advanced were:

1   Permanent sovereignty over natural resources.
2   The right to establish commodity producers' associations by developing states.
3   The indexation of commodity export prices linking them to the cost of imports from industrialized countries.
4   International control of multinational corporations.

The Sixth Special Session was not a noticeable success. Its product, the Charter of Economic Rights and Duties of States, was adopted at the following regular General Assembly session, much against the opposition of the developed countries, sixteen of which either abstained or voted against. Later in 1974 the French government called for a meeting of a small number of states representative of developed and developing countries, and in early 1975 both the OPEC ministerial meeting at Algiers and the Dakar Conference of Developing Countries accepted the idea. During 1975, a preparatory conference for the 'North–South' Paris meeting showed that, despite any reservations, the OPEC states were willing to back Third World demands against the developed world. Further preparations for dealing with economic questions in a wider framework were made at the meetings of the UN Industrial Development Organization (UNIDO) and of the non-aligned countries, both held in Lima, Peru, in March 1975; at the Commonwealth ministerial gathering at Kingston, Jamaica, in May 1975; and at an OECD meeting and an ECOSOC preparatory session in the summer of that year.

The Seventh Special Session of the UN General Assembly (summer 1975) dealt with development and international economic co-operation and produced, by unanimity, what the US Ambassador to the United Nations described as 'the broadest development program in the history of the United Nations and, for that matter, in the history of the world' (Moynihan 1979: 139).

The agreement reached between developed and underdeveloped states at the Seventh Special Session provided some solid achievements and guidelines for further negotiations. The United States agreed to a system of compensatory financing in the world commodity market which was intended to safeguard against the economic effects of market disruption of the developing states; the Generalized System of Preferences allowed by the Western countries for goods exported from the less-developed states was to be continued; aid targets were confirmed and promises made to expand the resources and the flexibility of the World Bank Group and the UN Development Programme; the transfer of technology to the Third World was to be made easier. Many of the more difficult problems – the future market structure for raw materials and commodities, indexation schemes, the removal of trade barriers to developing states' exports, an international investment trust scheme, the problem of the debt burden of the Third World, a code of conduct for technology transfers – were postponed to be discussed at UNCTAD IV in Nairobi, 1976. Progress in these later discussions was laborious and somewhat uncertain. Furthermore, the gathering of a number of developed, developing and OPEC states in Paris in 1975–77 at the Conference on International Economic Co-operation proved less than successful, and by the end of the decade much of the initiative created at the Seventh Special Session had been dissipated. The independent commission of 'wise men', which produced the Brandt Report in 1980, helped to raise expectations that rich and poor could find common interest in a new economic world plan, but the Reagan administration's hard line at the subsequent North–South summit in Cancun (1981) put an end to any speculation that the United States would support a rescue programme for the economically beleaguered Third World.

The NIEO has been dealt with in a number of international organizations acting as forums at which proponents, detractors and the half-convinced could propose, discuss and formulate solutions. Some of these organizations, such as the World Bank Group, were also used as means to implement some of the solutions, but most were primarily arenas for debate and negotiation. The influence of the collapse of the Western-based Bretton Woods monetary system, the political uncertainty of US leadership after the Watergate scandal and withdrawal from Vietnam, the increased desperation of indebted underdeveloped states, and the growth in the bargaining power of the oil-producing countries, presented the chance in the mid-1970s for serious negotiations over a wide range of socio-economic issues. The Seventh Special Session of the UN General Assembly demonstrated that the UN could provide the right context for such a massive task.

This second image of the role of an international organization can also be seen reflected in the working of its institutions. In the case of the negotiations for an NIEO, it was essential that the process should be inclusive of as many states as possible, that any new rules should be agreed by the widest range of states, that both principle and detail should be open to informed discussion and negotiation, and that the process should have a time limit, though unfinished business might be delegated to associated bodies. A Special Session of the United Nations General Assembly fitted these requirements well. It had to finish before the new plenary session of the General Assembly met, but matters could be handed on to other UN agencies and associated institutions such as the World Bank and UNCTAD IV. The preparatory work of UNCTAD III, of the non-aligned states, of the OECD countries and at ECOSOC meant that a variety of topics ranging from the general principles of world trade down to the details of patent law could be compassed. The Secretariat of the UN was needed in this case to fulfil the vital role of servicing the meetings, preparing documents, advising and conciliating. Although the UNCTAD Secretariat had done much to prepare material on trade and development issues, it was 'never able to perform for the Group of 77 the functions which the OECD Secretariat has performed for Group B [the Western States] (not to mention the superior resources which many of the Western market economy states have at their disposal back in their capitals)' (Gregg 1981: 63). However, 'The trade-union mentality of the UNCTAD Secretariat has seriously compromised its ability to play the role of honest broker in the NIEO negotiations, and has contributed to the weakening of UNCTAD's role in these negotiations relative to the UN in New York' (Gregg 1981: 63).

The aim of the Seventh Special Session was not to force through radical resolutions against the wishes of the richer industrialized states but to gain acceptance of the process of revising the existing economic order – something that could only be done with the rich countries' consent or, at least, their lack of resistance. With this in mind, the negotiations at the Session tended to be between the OECD states (led by the United States) and G77 (led by the Algerian Foreign Minister who was also President of the General Assembly, Abdelazziz Bouteflika). The European Communities (forerunner of the European Union) and the industrialized countries sympathizing with the developing states (Sweden, Norway, Finland and the Netherlands) formed two other groups actively participating in the debate (Dolman 1979: 62). On the whole, the then Soviet bloc tended to remain on the sidelines, claiming that the socialist countries were not responsible for the plight of the Group of 77 and could not be expected to make recompense, as should the West. These groupings and the desire not to cause the breakdown of the Session led to its relatively successful conclusion despite the wide range of topics and the participation of some 140 delegations. The process was facilitated by the absence of voting. Rather than rely on the weight of majority votes, G77 accepted that consensus with the West had to be sought. In the words of the first Secretary-General of UNCTAD, Raul Prebisch: 'There is obviously no immediate practical purpose in adopting recommendations by a simple majority of the developing countries but without the favourable votes of the developed countries, when the execution of those recommendations depends on their acceptance by the latter' (Cassan 1974: 456). This tactic meant not only giving way on certain important issues – at least for the time being – but also formulating resolutions acceptable to all. The US delegation helped in this by using the G77 working paper as the basis for negotiation (Gosovic and Ruggie 1976: 322).

The system of blocs, formalized in UNCTAD and seen in the Seventh Special Session, together with the use of consensus, meant that on this occasion the General Assembly could offer an effective forum for a wide range of states to discuss the process of revising the world economic order. The forum itself was neutral: the previous year the Sixth Special Session had ended in failure as the major contenders were not ready for mutual compromise. The forum of the UN may have added authority to the agreement but did not guarantee its future sanctity, indeed political events conspired against continuing success. Indeed, many of the gains made on paper by the poorer states have been eroded as their solidarity has cracked and global economic forces have undermined notions such as sovereignty over resources. The arenas for creating a world economic order have shifted from UNCTAD to institutions such as the G20, which has notably excluded the poorest of states (G20 2013).

Nevertheless, in its role as a forum, the UN General Assembly has fulfilled a requirement often sought of international organizations. When members of organizations want to negotiate, agree or publicly disagree, they can of course do so on a bi- or multilateral basis. They can arrange an ad hoc meeting for their purpose. First they would have to agree on the time, place, the protocol, even the shape of the table around which all would sit. They would have to agree the agenda, the method of voting, the rules of conduct of the negotiations. What better than having an acceptable meeting place, a set of rules and conventions, together with ancillary services? Whether it be the members of the International Olympic Committee planning the next Olympics, delegates of the Médecins Sans Frontières discussing activities in war zones, the Council of the European Union airing their views on a trade agreement, or the 190-plus members of the UN General Assembly gathering in New York to discuss a new world economic order, all have decided that an existing international organization provides them with a forum which otherwise would have to be created from the start.

### Actor

The third role attributed to international organizations in the international system is that of independent actor. The crucial word here is 'independent'. If it means that international organizations – or at least some of them – can act on the world scene without being significantly affected by outside forces, then very few, if any, fulfil that criterion; neither do many 'independent' sovereign states. If it is used to mean autonomous in the sense Karl Deutsch uses it, that the organization's 'responses are not predicated, even from the most thorough knowledge of the environment' and that 'it possesses a stable and coherent decision-making machinery within its boundaries' (Deutsch 1966: 7), then a number of international organizations clearly fit this description. Arnold Wolfers considered that there was ample evidence, even in the early 1960s, to show that a number of non-state entities, including international organizations, were able to affect the course of world events:

> When this happens, these entities become actors in the international arena and competitors of the nation-state. Their ability to operate as international or transnational actors may be traced to the fact that men identify themselves and their interests with corporate bodies other than nation-states.
>
> (Wolfers 1962: 23)

Wolfers goes on to claim that the 'actor capacity' of an international institution depends on 'the resolutions, recommendations, or orders emanating from its organs' compelling 'some or all member governments to act differently from the way in which they would otherwise act' (Wolfers 1962: 22). This leads to Inis Claude's dictum that 'an international organization is most clearly an actor when it is most distinctly an "it", an entity distinguishable from its member states' (Claude 1971: 13). Thus the oft-asserted contentions that 'the UN should do something' or that 'OPEC has increased petroleum prices' show the popular form of attributing to an organization the flesh and bones of an existence somewhat apart from that of its membership.

How far can this be taken? Clearly, almost all organizations are dependent for their existence on their membership: this is as true for the UN as for a trade union, a religious order or a scout troop. Some have such a weak institutional form that they are little more than the collective wills and activities of the members; for example, the Southern African Customs Union with its five member states (Botswana, Lesotho, Namibia, South Africa and Swaziland). Even this has a secretariat and tribunal operating separate from the Council of Ministers and Commission of senior officials (Southern African Customs Union 2014). However, many international organizations have institutional frameworks that allow them to achieve more than would be the case if their members acted separately or only co-operated on an ad hoc basis. It can be claimed that this shows up these organizations as instruments, being used by the members to obtain their requirements on the international scene. That is undeniable, but the very existence of an organization and, in some cases, the strength of their institutions mean that those representing the institution can make their own decisions, can act contrary to the wishes of some members and can affect the actions of other members. Also the presence of these international organizations collectively and individually has an effect on the international system, and some of them are more active than some of the weaker sovereign states.

Many well-know INGOs display a strong corporate identity, showing the organization to be stronger than the sum of its membership, and many also act effectively on the world stage. The International Federation of Red Cross and Red Crescent Societies together with the Swiss-run International Committee of the Red Cross have provided relief assistance in war and disaster zones, have generally cared for many suffering people whom governments have been unable or unwilling to help, and have also provided discreet mediation services in international disputes; for example, in Lebanon, Syria and Korea. On a more limited scale, Amnesty International has organized extensive pressure to help prisoners of conscience of whatever political hue and has sometimes been more effective than individual governments or the UN's Human Rights Committee. Other INGOs such as the International Trade Union Confederation, the International Organization of Standardization, the International Chamber of Commerce, the International Co-operative Alliance and the World Federation of United Nations Associations have pursued their aims through national contacts and by a network of relationships with the leading IGOs in their functional areas, such as ECOSOC, ILO, UNESCO and FAO (Union of International Associations 1974: S25). Many of these organizations posses 'stable and coherent machinery' within their own institutions and their activities compel governments to act differently than they would otherwise. The extent to which they themselves are significantly affected by outside forces depends on organization and circumstances but it is safe to say that, in the international system of the 2010s, the International Federation of Red Cross and Red Crescent Societies is more of an independent actor than, say, Nauru or Swaziland.

Estimating the degree of independent actor capacity of IGOs in the international system presents a further problem. As these organizations are established by intergovernmental agreement, can they be anything more than instruments of or forums for those member states?

It can be justifiably claimed that certain international organizations, by the sovereign will of their founders, have been given a separate capacity to act on the international scene and that this is reflected in their institutions. The International Court of Justice and the European Court of Human Rights are two examples. The structure of the ICJ prevents any interference in its work by the signatories to its articles and the judges appointed by the members of the UN may be representative of certain streams of law throughout the world but they are not the delegates of their state of origin. Their decisions are taken independently, not after instructions from their home, and each case is adjudged by the standards of international law, not by an amalgam of national laws. At the start of 2014 the International Court of Justice had ten cases before it (www.icj-cij.org/docket/index.php?p1=3&p2=1).

The Council of Europe, set up by the democracies of Western Europe in 1949, advanced the European Convention on Human Rights in 1950 which then established the European Court of Human Rights (ECHR) in 1959. This court hears applications that the member states – now forty-seven European countries including Russia and

Turkey – have breached the human rights provisions of the Convention. These cases can be brought not only by member states but also by individuals or groups of individuals. Signatory states of the Convention are obliged to implement the Court's decision and the Council of Europe has a committee of ministers that supervises the execution of the Court's decisions. Thus in human rights' matters, the Court has authority above that of the national courts or authorities (European Court of Human Rights 2014). This has sometimes caused criticism in member states. A British legal expert, Lord Hoffmann (2009), complained that the European Court of Human Rights 'has been unable to resist the temptation to aggrandise its jurisdiction . . . It considers itself the equivalent of the Supreme Court of the United States, laying down a federal law of Europe'. This perceived exercise of 'actorness' has not gone unchallenged, in particular in the United Kingdom and Russia.

In the case of both the ICJ and the ECHR it can be claimed that not only is any 'independent' actor capacity dependent for its existence on the desires of the member governments, but also the very substance of that capacity – implementation – is reliant on the authorities and agencies of the members. President Jackson of the United States reportedly said in 1832 of the Chief Justice of the Supreme Court who had ruled against his policy: 'John Marshall has made his decision: now let him enforce it.' If the presidents and prime ministers of the signatory states of the ICJ or ECHR ever say likewise, those institutions would face an even greater task, especially as their authority has not the standing that the US Supreme Court had after some four decades of existence.

Once life has been breathed into an intergovernmental organization and once it has started to build up a bureaucracy, a way of operating and a role not totally dependent on the acceptance of its every act by all its membership, then it becomes politically more difficult for a member state effectively to stop that IGO's activities. Any attempt to prevent unwanted action by the international organization risks alienating other states as well as ending any benefits that the IGO may provide. This gives organizations with a wide range of members and activities and well-developed central services a certain degree of autonomy in their actions. The United Nations offers the greatest possibility here, even in the crucial area of the search for peace.

UN peacekeeping operations demonstrate the ability of an international organization to perform on the world stage with a certain degree of independence and with an effectiveness not always matched by state actors. They also show the limitations on international organizations – even the UN – as actors. The UN's peacekeeping role is not mentioned in the Charter by which the original member states established the organization, neither has it been the subject of any amendment to that Charter. What can be found in the UN Charter is Chapter VI (Articles 33–38) on the Pacific Settlement of Disputes, and Chapter VII (Articles 39–51) on Action with Respect to Threats to the Peace, Breaches of the Peace, and Acts of Aggression. Chapter VI first of all requires states party to a dispute to settle it 'by negotiation, enquiry, mediation, conciliation, arbitration, judicial settlement, resort to regional agencies or arrangements, or other peaceful means of their own choice', with a possibility that the Security Council may call upon the parties to end their differences by such means (Article 33). Indeed, the Security Council may investigate disputes to see whether they threaten international peace and security (Article 34). It can recommend solutions to the dispute (Article 36), and states can bring disputes to the Security Council or the General Assembly for peaceful settlement (Articles 35, 37 and 38).

Chapter VII is quite distinct from the pacific settlement of disputes covered by Chapter VI. Article 39 states:

> The Security Council shall determine the existence of any threat to the peace, breach of the peace, or act of aggression and shall make recommendations, or decide what measures shall be taken in accordance with Articles 41 and 42, to maintain or restore international peace and security.

Article 41 covers a number of non-warlike sanctions that the Security Council can ask UN members to employ 'to give effect to its decisions'. If these prove inadequate, then Article 42 provides for 'such action by air, sea, or land forces as may be necessary to maintain or restore international peace and security'. These actions could include 'demonstrations, blockade, and other operations by air, sea, or land forces of Members of the United Nations'. Furthermore Article 47 created a Military Staff Committee consisting of the Chiefs of Staff of the permanent members of the Security Council (or their representatives) meeting together to decide how best to provide the military requirements for the maintenance of international peace and security – forces, armaments, strategic plans, command and control. The committee was soon plagued with Great Power disagreement and became practically defunct in 1947.

In the case of the North Korean invasion of South Korea in June 1950, it was possible to utilize Chapter VII because the Soviet delegation withdrew from the Security Council in protest against the exclusion of the communist Chinese from that body. The subsequent military operation by UN troops in Korea was scarcely of the sort that could be envisaged from a reading of Chapter VII – it was an American-led and American-dominated force given UN legitimacy by the Security Council in the Soviet's absence. A similar situation arose in August 1990 when Iraq invaded and swallowed up Kuwait. Once again the Security Council was able to utilize Chapter VII, but not because the Soviets were away or the communist Chinese were not represented. The change in real power relations brought about in the late 1980s meant that both the Soviet Union and China agreed to, or at least accepted, the need for condemnation by the Security Council of Iraqi action and the provision, by the Council, of the basis for action against Iraq first by the international community under UN supervision (in the form of economic sanctions) and then by the coalition of forces, this time under US leadership, that finally defeated the Iraqis in February 1991 (Freedman 1991: 195–209).

In 1999 NATO took action against the Serb-dominated Federal Republic of Yugoslavia (FRY) presence in the Yugoslav province of Kosovo, on the grounds of the seeming ethnic cleansing by the FRY forces and local Serb militia against the Albanian population who formed a majority in Kosovo. This action was not authorized by a Chapter VII resolution from the Security Council, though NATO members – especially the United States which supplied 70 per cent of the aircraft that attacked Kosovo – claimed a wider justification in international humanitarian law. Subsequently the UN Security Council in Resolution 1244 (1999) authorized a UN Interim Administration Mission in Kosovo (UNMIK) from June 1999 (see Table 4.2). This is headed by a Special Representative of the UN Secretary-General who has civilian executive powers (see www.unmikonline.org/Pages/about.aspx).

During the early years of the twenty-first century, the UN Security Council has used the articles of Chapter VII more regularly than before, not least in Africa. Coverage of Security Council activities during 2008–09 reports on action under Article 41

*Table 4.1* Past major UN peacekeeping operations

*Africa*

Congo (ONUC, 1960–64; MONUC, 1999–2010), Angola (UNAVEM I, II, III, 1989–97; MONUA, 1997–99), Namibia (UNTAG, 1989–90), Mozambique (ONUMOZ, 1992–94), Somalia (UNOSOM I, II, 1992–95), Liberia (UNOMIL, 1993–97), Rwanda (UNAMIR, 1993–96), Uganda-Rwanda (UNOMUR, 1993–94), Aouzou strip (UNASOG, 1994), Sierra Leone (UNOMSIL, 1998–99; UNAMSIL, 1999–2005), Central African Republic (MINURCA, 1998–2000), Ivory Coast (MINUCI, 2003–4), Burundi (ONUB, 2004–6), Central African Republic and Chad (MINURCAT, 2007–10), Ethiopia and Eritrea (UNMEE, 2000–2008); Sudan (UNMIS, 2011).

*Americas*

Dominican Republic (DOMREP, 1965–66), Central America (ONUCA, 1989–92), El Salvador (ONUSAL, 1991–95), Haiti (UNMIH, 1993–96; UNSMIH, 1996–97; UNTMIH, 1997; MIPONUH, 1999–2000), Guatemala (MINUGUA 1997).

*Asia and the Pacific*

West New Guinea (UNSF, 1962–63), India-Pakistan (UNIPOM, 1965–66), Afghanistan-Pakistan (UNGOMAP, 1988–90), Cambodia (UNAMIC, 1991–92; UNTAC, 1992–93); Tajikistan (UNMOT, 1994–2000), East Timor (UNTAET, 1999–2002; UNMISET, 2002–5; UNMIT, 2006–12)

*Europe*

Croatia (UNCRO, 1995–96; UNTAES, 1996–98; UNMOP, 1996–2002; UNPSG, 1998), Former Yugoslavia (UNPROFOR, 1992–95), Macedonia (UNPREDEP, 1995–99), Bosnia and Herzegovina (UNMIBH, 1995–2002), Georgia (UNOMIG, 1993–2009).

*Middle East*

Sinai, between Israel and Egypt (UNEF I, 1956–67; UNEF II, 1973–79), Lebanon (UNOGIL, 1958), Yemen (UNYOM, 1963–64), the Iran–Iraq war (UNIIMOG, 1988–91), Iraq–Kuwait (UNIKOM, 1991–2003), Syria (UNSMIS, 2012).

Source: 'Past Peacekeeping Operations' on UN website at www.un.org/en/peacekeeping/operations/past.shtml.

(action not involving armed force) in more than a hundred pages. It includes that against Eritrea, North Korea, Iran, Ivory Coast, Democratic Republic of the Congo and Liberia, thematic decisions such as that on children in armed conflict, and action against Al Qaida and the Taliban (United Nations Department of Political Affairs 2009: 29–30, 60). Measures taken involve arms embargoes, freezing of assets, seizing of arms, travel bans, action against transport and aviation, border and customs control, non-proliferation measures, a diamond embargo and a luxury goods embargo (United Nations Department of Political Affairs 2009: 31–134). Action under Article 42, which includes the threat of armed force, involve peacekeeping missions and multi-national forces in Afghanistan, Bosnia and Herzegovina, Central African Republic and its subregion, Chad, Democratic Republic of the Congo, Ivory Coast, the Middle East, Somalia and Sudan (including Darfur) (United Nations Department of Political Affairs 2009: 153). Indeed the resort to Chapter VII actions brought criticism from some states that such action should only be undertaken as a last resort and that the Security Council had used these actions too readily (United Nations Department of Political Affairs 2009: 167).

It was during the Cold War in the 1950s that the peacekeeping operations of the UN emerged. In the late 1940s the UN Security Council and General Assembly had

*Table 4.2* UN peacekeeping operations current in 2014

---

*Africa*

   Western Sahara (MINURSO, Mission for referendum from April 1991)
   Democratic Republic of the Congo (MONUSCO, Mission from July 2010)
   Liberia (UNMIL, Mission from September 2003)
   Ivory Coast (UNOCI, Operation from April 2004)
   Sudan (UNISFA, June 2011)
   South Sudan (UNAMID, July 2007, UNMISS, July 2011)
   Mali (MINUSMA, Mission from April 2013)

*Asia*

   India/Pakistan (UNMOGIP, Military Observer Group from January 1949)
   Afghanistan (UNAMA, Assistance Mission from 2002)

*Europe*

   Cyprus (UNFICYP, peacekeeping force from March 1964)
   Kosovo (UNMIK, Interim Administration from June 1999)

*Middle East*

   Israel/Palestine (UNTSO, Truce Supervision from June 1948)
   Golan Heights between Israel and Syria (UNDOF, Disengagement Observers from June 1974)
   Lebanon (UNIFIL from March 1978)

*Americas*

   Haiti (MINUSTAH, Stabilization Mission since June 2004)

---

Source: 'Current Peacekeeping Operations' on UN website at www.un.org/en/peacekeeping/operations/current.shtml.

authorized peace-observation missions in Greece (UNSCOB), Palestine (UNTSO), Kashmir (UNMOGIP) and Indonesia (UNCI), and the League of Nations even carried out a type of peacekeeping operation in the Saar referendum of 1935 (Fabian 1971: 136–40). The first major military operation was that of the UN Emergency Force interposed between Egypt and Israel to allow the withdrawal of British and French troops that had supported Israeli action against Egypt in the Suez Crisis of November 1956. Past major UN peacekeeping operations are listed in Table 4.1 with current ones in 2014 shown in Table 4.2.

These activities, undertaken in different parts of the world and in varying political circumstances, have some basic elements in common. Peacekeeping did not start out as peace enforcement envisaged under Chapter VII of the Charter. The original idea was that forces were present with the consent of host governments; were not supposed to interfere in domestic politics; on the whole were lightly armed and for self-defence purposes only; were made up of troops mainly from small or non-aligned states; and were assembled on an ad hoc basis for each operation. Their task was not to enforce a particular settlement but to prevent the spread of an already existing conflict. Thus they were not necessarily part of a peaceful settlement under Article VI: they existed to supervise or observe a ceasefire, though their presence may eventually contribute to the peaceful solution of a dispute. It is noticeable that when peacekeeping operations have attempted to enforce particular political solutions they have run into trouble. This was the case in the Congo operation of 1960–64; while with UNEF II, a peaceful settlement process – the Camp David Agreement between Egypt and Israel – led to the disbanding of the force as the process was not approved of by a substantial majority of the UN members. The UN peacekeeping operation in Bosnia and Herzegovina (UNPROFOR) was replaced in 1995 by a NATO-led 'peace enforcement' force (IFOR and then SFOR).

The whole concept of peacekeeping was originally tied up with the 'preventive diplomacy' ideas of the UN's second Secretary-General, Dag Hammarskjold (see Table 4.3). Hammarskjold considered it part of the task of the UN Secretariat to help stabilize areas of conflict so that parties might be brought together (Cordier and Foote 1972: 694). This was particularly necessary in those parts of the world from which the European colonial powers were withdrawing, lest the United States and USSR be drawn into a simmering dispute. Thus peacekeeping emerged in the peculiar historic conditions of the period from the end of the Second World War up to the late 1980s, when East–West confrontation cast a shadow over the process of decolonization.

As the context for peacekeeping changed after the end of the Cold War, so did the nature of the operations. In his report 'An Agenda for Peace', the Secretary-General in 1992, Boutros Boutros-Ghali, added to the notions of peacemaking (under Chapter VI), preventive diplomacy and peacekeeping, the concept of peacebuilding. This involved 'rebuilding the institutions and infrastructures of nations torn by civil war and strife; and building bonds of peaceful mutual benefit among nations formerly at war' (Boutros-Ghali 1992: 3). Thus the UN remit was stretched into post-conflict situations and into those specifically involving civil wars. Subsequent operations – such as those in Sierra Leone and Somalia – involved civil wars or the breakdown of states and it was thus difficult for forces not to be involved in internal politics. Indeed, in many cases the forces were there because of the state of domestic politics. Furthermore it was often hard to identify parties to any dispute, let alone to obtain the consent from all for the presence of the UN force. These UN troops therefore often had to use force to defend themselves. They needed the resources of the larger powers to reach some trouble spots and the permanent members of the Security Council were willing to contribute forces as this was no longer seen as an attempt by one side in the now-defunct Cold War to gain an upper hand.

However, the hopes implicit in 'An Agenda for Peace' were not fulfilled by the end of the 1990s. UN forces were unable to prevent genocide in Rwanda in 1994 or to protect the occupants of UN 'safe havens' in Bosnia and Herzegovina in 1995. The use of UN operations in Somalia, Liberia and Sierra Leone was at best questionable. More often regional organizations such as the Economic Community of West African States (ECOWAS) and collective defence bodies such as NATO undertook peace operations. The Brahimi Report, produced on UN Peace Operations for the Secreatary-General in August 2000, recommended far-reaching changes in the running of UN peace operations, including the reform of the UN department involved in peace and security, more resources for peacekeeping and the need for the Security Council to match the peace activities it authorized with the resources available (www.un.org/en/ga/search/view_doc.asp?symbol = A/55/305). A UN summit in 2005 on peacebuilding – action to address the root causes of violence – almost failed but finally its idea of a Peacebuilding Commission was accepted by UN General Assembly and Security Council, and it was supported by the Peacebuilding Support Office and a Peacebuilding Fund. However, its operation has been clouded by bureaucratic infighting and political disagreement that demonstrate the constraints on the UN system to act independently of its member states (Berdal 2009: 136–69).

The growth of peacekeeping operations allowed the institutions of the UN, particularly the Secretariat, to take an active role. With the establishment of UNEF in 1956–57, the General Assembly gave Hammarskjold a remarkably free hand: 'The Secretary-General made it clear that the composition of the Force was a matter for him to decide' (Higgins 1969: 300). Although he had two advisory committees (one political, one military) of Secretariat members and troop-donor states, Hammarskjold was determined to keep the reins in his hands: 'ultimate decisions rest with the Secretary-General, as the executive in charge of carrying out the operation' (Hammarskjold, cited in Verrier 1981: 21). This was confirmed in a negative way when U Thant, at the behest of President Nasser of Egypt, withdrew UNEF in 1967 without reference to the General Assembly or the Security Council of the UN. Similar independent views were held by the two Secretaries-General on their role in the Congo and ONUC and the outcome was by no means happy (Higgins 1980; O'Brien 1962; Verrier 1981). Since then the control of peacekeeping operations has been exercised more strictly by the Security Council, and the involvement of Secretaries-General has tended to be that of stage managers rather than executive directors (Urquhart 1990: 196–205). Since 1992 the UN Secretariat's Department of Peacekeeping Operations (DPKO) has run the practical side of operations with the management role being taken on by the Special Representative of the Secretary-General (United Nations Department of Peacekeeping Operations 2003: 3, 9).

*Table 4.3* Secretaries-General of the UN and their countries of origin

| | |
|---|---|
| Trygve Lie (Norway) | 1946–52 |
| Dag Hammarskjold (Sweden) | 1953–61 |
| U Thant (Myanmar, formerly Burma) | 1961–71 |
| Kurt Waldheim (Austria) | 1972–81 |
| Javier Perez de Cuellar (Peru) | 1982–91 |
| Boutros Boutros-Ghali (Egypt) | 1992–96 |
| Kofi Annan (Ghana) | 1997–2006 |
| Ban Ki-Moon (Republic of Korea) | 2007– |

Source: www.un.org/sg/formersgs.shtml

To what extent can the United Nations in the form of the Secretariat be said to have displayed the capacity of being an independent actor in its peacekeeping activities? There are *three* touchstones by which this capacity can be gauged: the existence of control of the institution by the UN membership; the ability of the institution to take its own decisions; and the likely outcome had UN peacekeeping facilities not been available.

### Existence of control

In the case of UN peacekeeping, the institution that attempted independent actions was the Secretariat: attempts at control by the membership of the UN being expressed either through the General Assembly or by the Security Council or unilaterally by individual members. In the end, the ultimate control over any Secretary-General is refusal to reappoint him to office – something that the Soviet Union threatened Trygve Lie with because of his support of the UN operation in Korea and the United States carried out with Boutros Boutros-Ghali. Short of that action, refusal to co-operate can be just as deadly as the Secretary-General, in Hammarskjold's words 'commands only the influence that the Member Governments of the United Nations are willing to give his office' (Cordier and Foote 1972: 285). This was said scarcely a year after his taking office to replace Lie who, on having his term extended, found himself faced by a Soviet boycott and decided to resign. Hammarskjold's actions with respect to the establishment of UNEF in 1956 were taken at the behest of the General Assembly after such plans had been vetoed by France and Britain in the Security Council. In the end those two powers were willing to co-operate with the Secretary-General and there was little concern by member states over the initiative and independence of action shown by the Secretary-General in setting up UNEF. Although the United Nations operation in the Congo (ONUC) was created by a Security Council resolution, this was after Hammarskjold had exercised his right under Article 99 to bring to the attention of the Council any matter – in this case the political situation in the Congo – 'which in his opinion may threaten international peace and security' and the whole operation was run more by the inspiration of the Secretary-General than to the letter of Security Council or General Assembly resolution which were anyway often contradictory. This did not stop the USSR from trying to place pressure on Hammarskjold when they felt that his activities in the Congo were working contrary to Soviet interests. The USSR went so far as to suggest abolition of the post of the Secretary-General and its replacement by a 'troika' of three Secretaries-General: one from the West, one from the Soviet bloc and one from the Third World. With Hammarskjold's death, his replacement by U Thant, and the relatively speedy end to ONUC, the pressures on the institution of the Secretary-General were eased. The lesson had been learnt and when the next UN peacekeeping operation was established, in Cyprus, the powers given to the Secretary-General were severely curtailed and a much closer control exercised by the Security Council.

During the 1990s, the Secretary-General was faced by a mounting task with an increasing number of operations and 'turf wars' between the civilian and military wings of the control structure and between the Secretary-General, the Security Council and the lead countries in the peacekeeping operations. After twenty years, the Secretary-General was still looking over his shoulder at the Security Council, though by 2013, there were 97,904 uniformed personnel in UN operations, some 19,000 more than in 1993 (United Nations Peacekeeping 2013).

*Independent decisions*

To what extent has the Secretary-General acted independently over peacekeeping? As suggested above, Hammarskjold exercised a good deal of initiative in both the UNEF and the ONUC. This was in line with his view of the office of Secretary-General and the authority established under Chapter XV of the Charter ('The Secretariat'). Early on in his period of office he told a press gathering:

> The right of initiative given to the Secretary-General in the Charter for situations of emergency is important especially because this right implies a recognition of his responsibility for action for peace . . . irrespective of the views and wishes of the various Member Governments.

> (Cordier and Foote 1972: 285)

Part of the basis for such a role was the assumption that the Secretary-General has at his disposal an international civil service – one which serves the Organization, whose members do not take instructions from the governments of their home states, and which the member governments do not try to control (Article 100). Hammarskjold had to contend with another remnant of Lie's period in office: the attempt by the US government to remove certain American citizens working in the UN Secretariat because of their suspected communist sympathies. While Hammarskjold overcame that crisis, there are indications that since the growth in UN membership in the 1960s, the staff of the Secretariat has become more susceptible to pressure from home, and that many are only seconded from their own civil service (Weiss 1982: 294–305). With an international civil service in the sense established by Article 100; with the philosophy that the institutions should serve 'the Organization', the Charter, or even the spirit of the Charter rather than national views; and with international events requiring non-Great Power activity of a sort that the non-aligned states were not able to carry out, the role of the Secretary-General could indeed be that of a fairly independent actor on the world stage.

Once these conditions changed – the Secretariat's personnel became more partisan, the Hammarskjoldian philosophy of the role of the Secretary-General was challenged and was no longer asserted with such vigour, and international conditions altered – then the independence of the UN institutions, including the Secretariat, was curtailed. By the late 1960s the two superpowers were showing great willingness to become involved in Third World disputes; also the non-aligned countries themselves were organizing their own forms of managing conflict, whether through the UN or through regional agencies such as the Organization of African Unity (later African Union) and the Arab League, so leaving less to the good offices of the Secretary-General of the United Nations. From the mid-1980s, Secretary-General Perez de Cuellar made a number of important initiatives offering his good offices to bring about solutions to such intractable problems as the division of Cyprus, the Soviet presence in Afghanistan, and the future of Western Sahara (Franck 1989: 80–4). Perez de Cuellar himself attempted to regain some of his administrative powers which, he considered, had been 'steadily eroded over the years', not least by member states interfering on the personnel side (de Cuellar 1989: 72). These moves were given substance by the improvement in superpower relations and by the willingness of the Soviet Union (later Russia) and the United States to back UN action on matters of peace and security by the start of the 1990s. However, once the United States started to become the dominant world power after the break-up of the Soviet Union in 1991, the United States started to set its own conditions for co-operation within the UN. As Russia became more assertive and China became more wary of UN action, the Secretariat found the opportunity for independent action more precarious. To this extent the United Nations and its institutions such as the Secretariat, like most sovereign states, could not be said to be actors independent of world events.

## Without peacekeeping facilities

A third test of the extent of the actor capacity of the UN's institutions, especially in the field of peacekeeping, is to estimate whether events would have been substantially different without them. If one imagined a UN with a Secretariat similar to that under Drummond (the first Secretary-General of the League of Nations), then the UNEF and

ONUC operations would certainly have been different. Whether there would have been any international intervention in the Congo is doubtful, though the Western allies might have been induced to take action similar to that by Belgium on the breakdown of law and order in the country. Some form of international operation in the Suez-Sinai area might have been mounted in 1956–57, though the multilateral diplomacy needed to organize it could have postponed its inception. The two models available for copying are those of the Saar referendum of 1935, where Britain played a dominant role as the League's agent – the Secretariat scarcely being of any importance (Fabian 1971: 137–41) – and of Chanak in 1922 when an Allied force kept the Turkish army out of a neutral zone mainly thanks to the determination of the local commander backed up by the diplomacy of the Great Powers (Verrier 1981: xvii). Agents such as the International Committee of the Red Cross, the Swiss, the Swedes or regional organizations could replace the UN in some peacekeeping activities, but the acceptability of such agents would have to be negotiated case by case. This was done when Western observers and military took over the role of UNEF II in Sinai in order to observe the implementation of the last stage of the Camp David Israel–Egypt agreement in 1982 (James 1990: 112–30).

With the use of other agents or joint forces of a small number of states for peacekeeping operations, the independent role of the UN and its Secretariat would decrease. Likewise, a lack of UN involvement in peacekeeping would either have led to further interventions in the Third World/Global South by the superpowers or the continuation of local conflicts or ad hoc and possibly less successful attempts to introduce third-party supervision into trouble spots. In this sense, the UN's peacekeeping operations and the crucial role played in them by the Secretariat have demonstrated the capacity of the organization and its institutions seriously to affect world problems.

It is noticeable that this capacity was less prominent from the 1970s to the late 1980s, with the Western force replacing UNEF II in Sinai; the Syrian (Arab League) peacekeeping force, and later the Israelis and the Western powers, overshadowing the work of UNIFIL in the Lebanon; the Commonwealth and the OAU providing troops and observers in many of Africa's troubled areas from Uganda to Chad to Zimbabwe; and joint forces intervening in Zaire (once the Congo, ONUC's stomping ground) and the New Hebrides (Vanuatu). Only with the second generation of UN operations in the late 1980s – UNGOMAP, UNIIMOG, ONUCA and UNTAG among them – did the pendulum swung back to a greater UN role. At the start of the 1990s it seemed that the UN was not only back again in the business of peacekeeping (see Table 4.2) but, with the action taken in 1991 against Iraq, was also justifying a major international peace enforcement operation. However, a more modest peace enforcement operation failed in Somalia in 1992 and lead countries in the Security Council held back from authorizing enforcement action in former Yugoslavia until 1995 when NATO action against the Serb-dominated forces in Bosnia and Herzegovina (together with Croatian victories on the battlefield) led to the Dayton Peace accords. Further action against Serb forces in Kosovo in 1999 was not sanctioned by the Security Council. Both in 1995 and in 1999 action was taken by NATO forces, though only the former was under a Security Council resolution. Both were followed by a UN presence – UNMIBH in Bosnia and Herzegovina and UNMIK in Kosovo. The invasion of Iraq by the United States and its allies in 2003 was undertaken after the Security Council had split on the issue. Though a UN presence was subsequently established in Baghdad, the destruction of its headquarters and the killing of Sergio Vieira del

Mello, the UN special representative, by rebel forces in August 2003, left the United States as the main external military and political actor in the country.

The notion of the Responsibility to Protect ('R2P'), adopted by the UN World Summit in 2005, potentially provides the basis for further peace operations. The 2005 document and the subsequent Secretary-General's report on the subject in 2009 accepted that the state had the prime responsibility to protect populations against genocide, crimes against humanity and ethnic cleansing, but that the international community had a duty to encourage states to fulfil this role. Furthermore the international community had a responsibility to use 'diplomatic, humanitarian and other means to protect populations from these crimes' and that, should states fail in their duty, then the international community must be able to 'take collective action' in line with the UN Charter (United Nations Office of the Special Advisor on the Prevention of Genocide 2012). However, the potential for Great Power intervention, especially in the Global South, under the 'R2P' heading caused a number of leaders to criticize the concept (Berdal 2009: 167).

In short, the UN is still important in peacekeeping operations by the second decade of the twenty-first century, its activities had increased since the early 1990s. However, there has been greater dependence on regional and other organizations to provide the muscle in peace operations. A distinct UN input into peacekeeping – and other peace operations – was not always clear.

### Overview of the three roles

The three roles that international organizations can perform – instrument, arena and actor – are not mutually exclusive. As can be seen, the United Nations has played, and continues to play, each role in international relations. The importance of each has changed over the years with the instrument element being dominant in the late 1940s and early 1950s, the actor capacity becoming of greater importance in Hammarskjold's term as Secretary-General, and the role as a forum developing since the 1960s with the increase in membership and the new demands of the Third World/Global South.

On a smaller scale, other international organizations, both governmental ones and INGOs, may find themselves taking on two or three roles. The European Communities, for example, were originally instruments by which the French government could regulate the peaceful economic and political development of the Federal Republic of Germany and at the same time obtain German support for French agriculture, while the Federal Republic used them to gain access to the markets of other members and to obtain a place in the comity of nations after the defeat of the Second World War. The Communities and the successor, the EU, also provided a forum within which a number of political problems ranging from aid to the Global South to international terrorism could be discussed by the member governments and, in some cases, common policies adopted. Finally, the institutions of the EU, in particular the European Commission and, before it, the High Authority of the European Coal and Steel Community, have shown a propensity to act independently of the member states.

The World Council of Churches, as an INGO, has also played the three roles, though perhaps in different proportions. It has been used by some members to promote their ideas in certain areas – for example, the African and more radical European churches giving support to liberation movements; it has certainly provided an arena within which a whole range of views has been expressed; and its Secretariat has occasionally acted without first hearing the expressed wishes of the membership, though this has rarely been done in such a way as to annoy the majority of members (World Council of Churches 2014).

Some useful generalizations about the three roles of international organizations can be made.

If the constitutions of the organizations create strong institutions insulated from interference by the membership and with powerful resources – such as the ECSC of the 1950s – then they will more likely perform the role of a relatively independent actor. If the members have constitutional safeguards which allow them to prevent the growth of strong institutions – as had been the case in the European Free Trade Association – then the organization is only likely to function either as a forum for the membership as a whole or as a tool for the furtherance of the policy of some members.

If an international organization has a membership dominated by one powerful member, that organization is susceptible to being used as a hegemonic instrument – rather as the USSR used the Warsaw Treaty Organization in the period before President Gorbachev. Organizations whose members are of about the same weight (EFTA from 1973 to 1995 being an example) will be more egalitarian by nature and thereby act as a meeting place for equals.

Extent of membership may condition the ability of an international organization to accept certain roles. While it would seem that IGOs with a limited membership can play any of the three roles, those organizations with near universal membership will find it increasingly difficult to remain the instrument of a small group of members or to be an active independent actor on the world stage. This is the case with the UN and a number of associated agencies. A wide membership has ruled out domination over a period of time by the United States, USSR or even the Global South cabals. While the growth in membership in the 1950s and 1960s helped the central institutions to take on a more active, independent role, once the new members were organized into their own groupings (G77 and the non-aligned movement), the idea of a Secretariat exercising too wide a discretion of judgement became almost as unacceptable to them as to the Soviet and Western blocs. By their nature, the universal institutions will become forums within which a range of views will be expressed.

## Functions of international organizations

To return to the metaphor of the marketplace with which this chapter opened, it can be seen that international organizations can indeed play the role of instruments for those who bargain in this place – as servants carrying messages; changing money to order; or acting as bodyguards. They can also be likened to that part of the marketplace where the occupants meet to discuss, trade and settle disputes – the forum. Finally, they may also be given the likeness of a participant in the marketplace, perhaps as powerful and as able to mould events as some of the other traders and customers. All these demonstrate possible roles of international organizations in international relations. How then might international organizations, in whatever role, affect the working of the world marketplace, that is, present-day international relations? This section will examine the functions that international organizations may perform in the international system.

To answer such a question, some consideration must be given to the difficult problem of how an international system works. An estimation of how international organizations affect the functioning of this system can then be attempted.

To function, any system needs resources in order to transform inputs into that system into outputs. This is what Almond and Powell call its *conversion function*. It also needs to *maintain* and *adapt* itself. Furthermore its relations with its surroundings have to be considered. This 'behaviour of the system as a unit in its relations to other social systems and the environment' represents its *capabilities* (Almond and Powell 1966: 28–9).

In terms of our world marketplace, how does this work? The marketplace consists 'of numerous more or less autonomous actors interacting in patterned ways to influence one another' – in other words, it is a system (Mansbach *et al.* 1976: 5). The buyers and sellers trade, bargain, do business, threaten, cajole and form associations and groupings. From these people within the marketplace, certain demands are made on and support given to the system that is the marketplace – these are the inputs. These supports and demands are articulated ('the streets should be cleaned', 'no trading on Sunday', 'we need better policing', 'someone should check weights and measures') and aggregated ('the street traders demand . . . ', 'consumers want . . . ', 'money changers request . . . '). The system itself has certain resources which often reflect its ability to maintain and adapt itself and its capabilities. For example, there may be the ethics of the marketplace established over the years – general norms that are commonplace and associated with the system of the marketplace: 'cheating customers is bad for business', 'dirty streets drive away trade', and so on. Furthermore the system, to survive, needs new blood and so there may be an established method of recruiting, say, new stallholders. To live with change, the system may also provide that novices, as well as traditional traders, are well and truly inducted into the ways of the market: they are socialized. A system that had demands made on it (inputs) and which because of its resources is fairly resilient over time, responding to its environment and maintaining and adapting itself, will also produce outputs in the form of authoritative decisions that can be implemented. This can be done by rule-making ('By law: littering the streets is an offence'), rule application ('I arrest you for littering the pavement') and rule adjudication ('You are fined two days' wages for littering the streets'). Outputs may also be in the form of information (a public noticeboard in the marketplace) or certain operations (street cleaning) which are not directly connected to the process of rule-making, application and adjudication.

The international political system functions in a way not unlike our world marketplace imagined above. The participants in the system (governments, MNCs, IGOs, INGOs, individuals) are making constant demands on the set-up – that it should bring peace, redistribute wealth, increase wealth, satisfy religious or cultural requirements – and these demands are aggregated by states, groups and individuals acting together bilaterally, multilaterally, ad hoc, at conferences or in organizations. Despite appearances to the contrary, the system does have resources, however brittle they may be. There are certain generally accepted norms (e.g. agreements should be kept; genocide and slavery are bad); the system has recruited new actors, not only newly independent states but also the growing number of non-state actors that have appeared on the scene in the last hundred years; and a process of socialization exists by which states and non-state actors learn to consider not just their own requirements but also those of the system as well. The international political system produces authoritative decisions that can be implemented, though this is not always done. Decisions may be made by the various actors meeting in small groups or in a large plenary session or they may be arrived at more formally. Efforts are also made to supervise such rules – to apply them and to adjudicate. Furthermore the system has a network of political communications and it offers some other services.

How then do international organizations, in their various roles as instruments, forums and actors, affect this functioning of the international political system? Are they helping to create a form of global governance? The following sections will examine the functions that international organizations perform and will then look at the question of global governance.

## *Articulation and aggregation*

International organizations can perform the task of interest articulation and aggregation in international affairs just as national associations of like-minded people do within a national political system. Within a sovereign state, a national union of miners brings together all those working in the coal-mining industry in order to voice their demands vis-à-vis their employers (e.g. for better wages and working conditions) and vis-à-vis the political system (for a more advanced welfare state, better retirement arrangements and compensation for coal-related illnesses) and to aggregate the interest of each individual miner, each pit, each region, each skill or job into a national voice. Sometimes groups may disagree with what is being said on their behalf by the national organization, and if this disenchantment is consistent enough, they may dissociate themselves from the national leadership and form their own association.

Within a national political system, the authoritative allocation of values – the decision as to who gets what, when and how – is nominally conducted by a central authority, the government, with a number of institutions available through which these decisions may be affected by, say, trade unions, employers' associations, veterans' leagues, youth movements, religious bodies and political parties. The international system is not so structured: it lacks a central body to allocate values, let alone resources. Quite clearly this does not stop values and resources being allocated, and this process is not totally one of states imposing their values (whether economic, political or even religious and cultural) on others and seizing resources for themselves. Much of this allocation is still done by agreement, however reluctantly, and this is usually preceded by a process of discussion and negotiation. International organizations, being one of the institutionalized forms of contact between the active participants in the international system, are forums for such discussion and negotiation. Like the institutions of government on a national level, they provide groups having common interests with a focus of activity. International organizations in fact operate in three ways in this context: they can be instruments for interest articulation and aggregation (rather like the national union of mineworkers in the national example), or they can be forums in which those interests are articulated, or they can articulate interests separate from those of members.

Many INGOs are instruments of interest articulation and aggregation on an international plane. Examples of this are the World Zionist Organization, which brings together the supporters of the state of Israel and Zionism and is used to voice the demands of these groups at the international level; the International Chamber of Shipping, which aggregates shipowners' interests; and the Campaign for a World

Constitution and Parliament Association, which acts as a voice for world govern-mentalists. An example of an INGO acting as a forum for interest articulation would be that of the World Council of Churches, where the participants form groups and temporary coalitions on particular issues such as human rights, world poverty and disarmament. They can also be actors in the articulation and aggregation process: the Salvation Army International is one such INGO which puts forward its own views and demands on the international system – for example, in the World Council of Churches, before it parted ways with that organization in 1978 over the financing of liberation movements (Beigbeder 1992: 66).

Certain IGOs with a tightly knit membership and closely defined aims may act as instruments of interest articulation and aggregation. This was probably the case with OPEC, which behaved rather like an oil exporters' 'trade union' in the middle and end of the 1970s.

On the whole, IGOs tend to be stages for interest articulation and aggregation with the various contending sections forming into 'blocs' or 'groups'. The United Nations Conference on Trade and Development (UNCTAD), which has regular meetings and a permanent Secretariat, has even formalized members into groups which, it is assumed, have aggregate interests to articulate in matters of trade and development: the Western industrialized states; in the past the Soviet bloc countries; the Third World/Global South (G77); and a few independents such as China. The International Labour Organization provides an example of interests being aggregated not just in blocs of countries but also across national divisions. Each member state's delegation to the General Conference is divided into three autonomous sections: two members representing the government, one the employers and one the work people (Article 3(1) of the Constitution of the ILO). The chance arises for representatives of the employees to combine together and those of the employers to unite, with the governmental representatives playing an important intermediary role. However, this threefold division is not always so obvious, as in many states employers' and employees' associations are not free from government direction.

When considering the resources of the domestic political system, it can be seen that various organizations – political parties, trade unions, religious associations, pressure groups – help to maintain and adapt the system. They promote certain norms, recruit new participants into the system and take part in the process of socialization by which others are encouraged to consider the needs of the system as well as their own require-ments. Whether these resources are sufficient to keep a domestic political system functioning, let alone allowing it to adapt to changing conditions, will depend on the various values promoted, the membership recruited and the efficacy of socialization. A deeply divided political system with ideological differences over accepted norms, where new members are not being recruited to take part in the politics of the system and where individual members look after their own concerns to the detriment of any collective need, will not be a strong system.

*Norms*

International organizations have made a considerable contribution as instruments, forums and actors to the normative activities of the international political system. Some of the earlier INGOs in the nineteenth century were concerned with establishing worldwide certain values that were already accepted in the more economically advanced West European and North American states: the rejection of slavery (Anti-Slavery Society), control of the effects of war (the International Committee of the Red Cross), protection of native peoples (Aborigines' Protection Society). The establishment of norms in international relations has now become a complex process to which a wide range of IGOs as well as INGOs contribute.

The UN Charter itself provides a set of values for the international system in its preamble where 'we the people' reaffirmed their 'faith in fundamental human rights', 'in the equal rights of men and women and of nations large and small' and determined 'to promote social progress and better standards of life in larger freedom'. Furthermore Chapter I, 'Purpose and Principles', outlines the concern with the suppression of acts of aggression, the support of the principles of international law, peaceful settlement and international co-operation. A specific proclamation can be found in the Universal Declaration of Human Rights, adopted by the UN General Assembly in December 1948 'as a common standard of achievement for all peoples and all nations' and which includes reference to personal human rights, social and economic rights, as well as 'development of friendly relations between nations'. In the field of justice and social welfare, a network of a number of IGOs under the auspices of the UN family has been established and underpinned by a system of consultation of and support by the NGOs. These have formalized already existing sets of norms (e.g. in the UN Convention for the Suppression of the Traffic in Persons (1949)) or have amended existing conventions (the 1926 Slavery Convention was amended in 1953) or have articulated relatively new normative values in their conventions against genocide and apartheid.

In the field of economic affairs, international organizations have helped establish norms of behaviour. Again the UN and its associated agencies have played a leading role in both encouraging and reflecting the setting of standards for the functioning of the world economy. After the experience of the interwar depression, it was not surprising that the Bretton Woods meeting of 1944 set up institutions which stressed the universality of the economic system and the need to utilize the globe's resources. With the coming to independence of former colonial countries after 1947, emphasis has shifted towards the development of these new states and their right to control their own resources – a right reflected in the 1974 Charter of Economic Rights and Duties of States which proclaimed 'Every state has and shall freely exercise full permanent sovereignty, including possession, use and disposal, over all its wealth, natural resources and economic activities' (Article 2).

Meetings of UNCTAD, the UN Industrial Development Organization (UNIDO) and the UN General Assembly have elaborated on these statements to the extent that UN evocations on the world economy are now quite different from those advanced at Bretton Woods in 1944, the emphasis being less on purely expanding trade and more on the disposal of economic benefits. Another shift over the past decades has been the concern with the qualitative side of the world economy: the framework has been established for population policies at the World Population Conferences, and for ecological policies in the Declaration on the Human Environment. One change at the start of the twenty-first century was an emphasis on transparency, accountability and good service delivery for states requesting economic assistance (World Bank 2013).

In the field of international security, there has been acceptance of standards flowing from the work of the UN and other international organizations. Harold Jacobson

(1979: 168–73) divides the normative activities of international organizations in such areas into five categories: refining principles against the use of force; delegitimizing Western colonialism; pronouncing on specific situations; urging disarmament and arms control; exhorting states to arm.

Examples of the first category include requirements prohibiting intervention in the affairs of independent states, as outlined in the charters of the OAS, the AU and the Arab League as well as the 1965 General Assembly Declaration on the Inadmissibility of Intervention in the Domestic Affairs of States and the protection of their Independence and Sovereignty. Delegitimizing Western colonialism can be found not only in the statements of INGOs such as the Afro-Asian Peoples' Solidarity Organization, but also in the output of the General Assembly following on Resolution 1514 in December 1960 on the Granting of Independence to Colonial Countries and Peoples. International organizations have also been used in the process of 'collective legitimization' to prove or disapprove of specific actions by particular countries – the UN on Portuguese colonialism or Israel's activities; the OAS against Cuba and in support of US action; NATO condemning the USSR action in Hungary, Czechoslovakia, Poland and Afghanistan and, later, the actions of Serbia in the Balkans region and Russia in Crimea. A wide range of INGOs and IGOs have also dealt with the question of armaments: how to abolish them or control them. Ranging from the Quaker (Society of Friends) pacifist groups to the UN Committee on Disarmament and the more specific Organization for the Prohibition of Chemical Weapons, international organizations have been prominent in this question. It is, however, fair to say that on such a problem, dealing as it does with the core area of national security, states have been more willing to negotiate agreements either bilaterally (Strategic Arms Reduction Talks between the United States and the USSR, later Russia) or multilaterally outside the major UN forums (the Treaty Banning Nuclear Weapon Tests in the Atmosphere, in Outer Space, and Under Water, 1963). The exhortation to arm is expressed by organizations that offer selective collective defence, such as NATO, with part of the agreement by the members being an agreement on the norm of a certain level of armed force.

International organizations have played an important part in the world's institutions which have helped create norms in international relations, though it should be noted that a number of these values are fairly weak and many are also contradictory. As Evan Luard (1990: 222) wrote: 'Despite these difficulties every international society has evolved rules of a sort. None has been genuinely anarchic. Most members have observed most of the rules most of the time . . . As communications have improved and contacts developed, ever more complex norms have been established.'

A more recent Canadian study has suggested that the adoption of norms has helped to bring down the level of conflict in the international system, especially after the end of the Cold War:

> The extent of the change in global norms over the past 60-plus years is evident in the universal recognition of the illegitimacy of colonial rule . . . in the proscription on war except in self-defense, or with the sanction of the UN Security Council; and in the near-complete absence in foreign and defense establishments in the developed world of the type of extreme hypernationalism that underpinned German and Japanese aggression leading up to World War II.
>
> (Human Security Report Project 2010: 32)

International organizations have been one of the contributors to such changes both within states and at the global level. IGOs have provided sets of norms and INGOs, in particular, have campaigned for their acceptance and implementation.

### Recruitment

International organizations can have an important function in the recruitment of participants in the international political system. The fact that IGOs consist almost exclusively of representatives of sovereign states gives a further incentive for non-self-governing territories to achieve their independence. This allows them to represent their own interests in a range of IGOs and brings those organizations closer to universality of membership. In theory, membership of an IGO may require little more than that the prospective state be sovereign. For example, the UN Charter allows membership 'to all peace-loving states which accept the obligations contained in the present Charter and, in the judgement of the Organization, are able and willing to carry out these obligations' (Article 3(1)). It may appear that this paragraph and Article 6, which allows for the expulsion from the UN of a state that has persistently violated the Principle of the Charter, encourage states joining the international political system, as manifested in the United Nations, to recognize a certain minimal standard of behaviour. However, exclusion from the UN has almost always been on political grounds through the veto of permanent members of the Security Council; members of the organization have been remarkably lax in excluding or expelling states on the grounds cited under Articles 3(1) and 6. Furthermore, it is generally accepted that it is governments rather than states that are peace-loving or not, and the usual way of condemnation of warlike activities has been the non-seating of governmental representatives. This was the case in the UN with the communist Chinese government after 1949 until 1971 (especially after its involvement in the Korean War) and the Heng Samrin regime established in Kampuchea (later Cambodia) by the Vietnamese in 1979. The irony of the latter case was that a majority of members rejected the Vietnamese-backed regime because it had been established by an invasion of Kampuchea but they were prepared to accept the indigenous Pol Pot government (which the Vietnamese had evicted) despite its genocidal record. This illustrates the tension between making universal organizations such as the UN truly global forums, covering all countries, and the need to uphold certain accepted norms, particularly when this is being done by existing UN members using the organization as an instrument for the furtherance of their policy – the United States in the case of China; South-East Asian states and China in the case of Kampuchea.

INGOs have increasingly recruited new participants to the international political system. By gathering together groups and individuals for a particular purpose, whether supporting world government, promoting trade union activity, furthering commercial interests or spreading religious beliefs, they have mobilized what must be regarded as the fastest-growing and widest-based group of participants in the current international political system. They have brought new actors into the old nineteenth-century, state-centred system. They provide the underpinning for a more close-knit international system and for the intergovernmental organizations. This is recognized by the leading IGOs such as the UN Economic and Social Council, ILO, FAO, UNESCO and UNCTAD (United Nations Department of Economic and Social Affairs NGO Branch 2009).

## Socialization

Socialization is carried out within the nation state by a number of agencies. Its aim is to instil in the individual loyalty to the system within which he or she is living and to gain acceptance of the prevailing values of that system and its institutions. Schools, churches and youth clubs can all be used as agents of socialization. In newly independent states, the armed forces may be the main instrument of socialization, inculcating loyalty to the country, its flag, anthem and president instead of a feeling of identification with a smaller group such as a regional nation, a tribe or the family. While a government may have a number of socialization instruments available to it – compulsory schooling, military service, state-run youth groups, political parties – it is rarely without competition. This may be in the form of more traditional socialization (through the family or the tribe), the values of which clash with those of the government, or they may be organizations such as trade unions preaching workers' solidarity or a church or mosque teaching Christian or Islamic values in opposition to the belief system of the state. The existence of such groups that have undergone their own socialization quite different from that of the ruling elite can have a destabilizing effect as seen from the viewpoint of governments. Communist-ruled Poland provides an example: throughout the 1970s the government there was unable to impose its will on a people who had on the whole resisted the agents of socialization provided by the Polish Communist Party but had accepted those of the Catholic Church.

As there is no world government, the forces of socialization at an international level can be expected to be weaker than those within the state. The process of socialization works at two levels internationally. Agents of socialization may work across frontiers, affecting directly individuals and groups in a number of countries. Multinational corporations have taken a powerful lead here. Barnet and Muller (1975: 13) quote Aureijo Peccei, a Fiat director, as claiming that the global corporation 'is the most powerful agent for the internationalization of human society' and another director as describing such corporations as 'agents of change, socially, economically and culturally' (Barnet and Muller 1975: 31). Popular outlets such as fast-food chains or IT providers – MacDonalds and Microsoft – have created a form of global culture in a short period of time, though it would seem to be fairly shallow in content. INGOs may not have the wealth, expertise and manpower of transnational corporations, but they too can seek to affect peoples' systems of belief and patterns of behaviour by a process of socialization. The International Olympic Committee attempts to further the ideals of Baron de Coubertin among the world's athletes, while the Scout movement spreads similar value to the youth of many countries.

Among the IGOs, the European Union (if it can be judged as an IGO) probably has the most sophisticated instruments of social nation. Through its institutions such as the European Commission, the European Economic and Social Committee, the Committee of the Regions, the European Parliament and the Court of Justice, a 'Community spirit' can be fostered among the various interest groups dealing with the Union and among the citizens of the member countries. These institutions are by no means as strong as the national ones but neither are they necessarily in direct competition with the nation state for citizen loyalty: the idea still exists that one an be a good EU citizen and a good Frenchman, Dane or Irishman. Although many interest groups tend to use Union institutions to further their own ends and are not especially interested in the 'message', the extent of common feeling fostered among the people of the EU differs substantially. Countries where over 70 per cent of respondents in an opinion poll in 2013 felt they were 'citizens of the EU' included Luxembourg, Malta, Finland, Germany, Estonia, Denmark, Slovakia and Belgium, while those giving under a 50 per cent response were Bulgaria, Cyprus, Italy, Greece and the United Kingdom. There seems to be little association between positive feelings and length of involvement in the European integration process, though Italy is the only one of the original six European Communities states that is substantially under the EU average (European Commission Standard Eurobarometer 2013: 35).

Second, the process of socialization can take place between states acting at the international level and between their representatives. In other words, over a period of time, states' governments can become 'socialized' to act in a certain way that is acceptable to the rest of the international community, or to adopt a certain common value system. A classic example was that of the new Bolshevik Russian government, which after renouncing 'bourgeois' diplomacy in 1917 soon found itself an outcast in international society and eventually started to re-adopt most of the norms of accepted diplomacy in order that it might obtain the benefits of international commerce and of the security provided for by bilateral treaties and, eventually, membership of the League of Nations.

Organizations such as the League of Nations and the United Nations are voluntary by nature – states are not compelled to become members or stay members – so the sanctions against asocial behaviour are few. The League attempted to socialize members into following set procedures for the settlement of disputes (as laid down in Articles 12–16) with sanctions against any 'outlaws'. During the 1930s it became clear that states could behave unsocially towards countries outside the European pale in Manchuria or Abyssinia (Ethiopia) for example, with only ineffectual recourse to punishment by other League members. When it suited the others they were prepared to stigmatize the Soviet Union by expulsion from the League for its invasion of Finland in 1939.

The members of the UN seemed even more tolerant than their pre-war predecessors. Both because there was no longer agreement over what constituted social behaviour internationally once the standards of European diplomacy and international were challenged by the Soviet bloc and the Global South countries, and because the UN members rate universal membership so highly, there was a great reluctance to condemn other states, let alone expel them from the UN for asocial activities. Israel after its take-over of Jerusalem and the Golan Heights and its invasion of Lebanon; apartheid South Africa; Idi Amin's Uganda; Pol Pot's Kampuchea; Iran after United States embassy staff had been taken hostage in 1979; the Soviet Union after its invasion of Afghanistan; Argentina after its occupation of the Falkland Islands in April 1982; Iraq after its invasion of Kuwait in 1990; North Korea and Iran with their nuclear programmes; and Syria after using chemical weapons on its citizens in 2013 – all remained UN members. However, the Yugoslav Federation under President Milosovic was not allowed to join the UN because of its warlike activities in the Balkan region after the Socialist Federal Republic of Yugoslavia – a founder UN member – broke up at the end of 1991. The other successor states were admitted in 1992 and 1993 but the Federal Republic of Yugoslavia had to await the downfall of Milosovic in 2000 to gain admittance anew as the 189th member of the UN. It was renamed Serbia and Montenegro in 2003 and in 2006 Montenegro broke away and became a UN member. However, Kosovo, which declared its independence of Serbia in 2008, has not been admitted to the UN as Serbian non-recognition of the new state has been backed by

Russia and China, permanent members of the Security Council that can block new members.

Despite a reluctance to use sanctions – whether moral or material – against asocial members, international organizations have not been totally ineffective in the socialization process. A study by Butterworth in 1978 of the UN, the OAS, the OAU, the Arab League and the Council of Europe concluded that:

> The institutionalization of shared norms and perceptions will enhance the force of national reputation and organizational precedent in effecting inter-state co-operation. . . . Habits of co-operation will enhance the importance of policies that simulate compliant behaviour through consensus, rather than coercion.
>
> (Butterworth 1978)

The organizations contribute by encouraging members to act in a co-operative way and, in particular, not to undermine the norms that they share with other members: the stress is on 'establishing dependable and enduring patterns of behaviour'. The study attributes to the OAS, the UN and the OAU a degree of success in registering and contributing to moderation by its members, 'whilst the League of Arab States and the Council of Europe have had less success' (Butterworth 1978: ch. 8). This seems to give some credence to the idea that states can be socialized into a particular pattern of behaviour by membership of an international organization.

### Rule-making

The function of rule-making in international organizations is more obvious than that of socialization. Unlike the domestic political system, the international system has no central formal rule-making institution such as a government or a parliament. It should be noted that even in the domestic system there are often a number of subsidiary rule-making institutions apart from the most obvious governmental ones. Local or regional governments often have such powers delegated to them, and a number of bodies ranging from the civil services to trade unions and private associations make rules for the internal running of their organizations. It is not surprising that the sources of rules are more diverse in the international field with the absence of world government: they may be based on the acceptance of past practice or on ad hoc arrangements or they may be founded in bilateral legal agreements between states or they may emanate from international organizations.

Paul Tharp (1971: 5) lists the traditional 'confederal' principles on which most international organizations have based their rule-making:

1   The rules are formulated by unanimous or near-unanimous consensus of members.
2   Members have the practical option of leaving an organization and ending their assent to the existing rules.
3   Even within the bounds of membership, a state can assert the right to interpret unilaterally the rules to which it has consented.
4   The 'executive-bureaucratic' structure of the organization has little or no power to formulate (and implement) rules.
5   Delegates to the organizations' rule-making bodies are instructed by their governments and do not act as independent representatives.

6    The international organization 'has no direct relationship with private citizens of
     the member states'.

This leaves the formulation of rules – and their acceptance – in the hands of an
organization's member states and downgrades any possible autonomous role of the
institutions of the organization itself. Even so, the function of providing a focus for
the setting of rules is an important one, regardless of the technical process used by the
organization. Some are almost exclusively dedicated to rule-making (or, in some cases,
rule changing) whether they be the specialist organization such as the World
International Property Organization or the wide-ranging Third United Nations
Conference on the Law of the Sea. Other institutions have an element of rule-making
in their work: the UN General Assembly sometimes performs this task by adopting
resolutions or conventions on questions such as diplomatic practice, hijacking, or
relations with North Korea. Few organizations, including INGOs, have no rule-making
capacity for the simple reason that the membership has to agree on rules for the
running of the organization itself. Indeed, sometimes it is just these rules that can
cause greatest trouble: this was the case in 1965 when the French government boycotted
meetings of the Council of Ministers of the EEC, ostensibly over the new regulations
for the Common Agricultural Policy but in fact over the questions of majority decisions
in the Council and the role of the Commission of the Community.

   The European Union provides the most advanced model of another type of institution
when judged on the criteria of rule-making: that which has advanced beyond the
'confederal' model mentioned by Tharp and which can make its own rules independent
of the wishes of the member states. This represents a move towards what many see as
a more 'federal' model, with a central rule-making institution which the various parts
(member states) are obliged to obey. As yet the Union has not advanced so far and
only certain of its institutions can be called supranational (that is, existing above rather
than between states). The European Court of Justice clearly makes rules by its
judgements that are applicable throughout the EU and the European Commission pours
out administrative rules. Furthermore, both these bodies can have direct dealings with
private citizens, interest groups and firms in each of the member states. However, the
major rule-setting institution is still the Council of Ministers, which is dominated by
member states' representation and leans towards Tharp's 'confederal' description.

## Rule application

What has been said here about the formulation of rules in such organizations as the
European Union touches also on the function of rule application. In the domestic
political system, rule application is undertaken mostly by government agencies and,
*in extremis,* by the police, militia or armed forces. In the international political system,
rule application is left mainly to sovereign states, as there is no central world authority
with agents to undertake the task.

   Under certain circumstances, international organizations take on aspects of applying
generally accepted rules. Their supervision has been the task of organizations such as

•    the now-defunct Trusteeship Council (www.un.org/en/mainbodies/trusteeship/),
     which concerned itself with the keeping of the conditions of the International
     Trusteeship System (Chapter XII of the UN Charter).

- the Committee on Information of Non-Self-Governing Territories, which attempted a similar monitoring task for colonial areas under Article 73e of the UN Charter, and was succeeded in 1963 by the Special Committee on Decolonization (www.un.org/en/decolonization/specialcommittee.shtml). This Special Committee attempted a more vigorous implementation of the anti-colonial Declaration on the Granting of Independence to Colonial Countries and Peoples (Resolution 1514 (XV)). As this committee received little co-operation from colonizing states such as the United Kingdom, France, Portugal and Spain, its effectiveness was somewhat curtailed.
- the European Central Bank, from 2014, is to supervise the soundness of banks and credit institutions in the Eurozone states of the EU (www.ecb.europa.eu/ssm/html/index.en.html).
- the Department of Safeguards of the International Atomic Energy Agency (IAEA) assists in the application of safeguards for nuclear material and activities (www.iaea.org/safeguards/what.html). The IAEA has wide powers to keep track of the spread and use of fissionable materials, a task it attempted to fulfil with North Korea until it withdrew its membership in 1994 and with UN assistance in Iraq from the summer of 1991 until the 2003 invasion of that country (www.iaea.org/newscenter/statements/2003/ebsp2003n006.shtml).

INGOs have participated in the monitoring of international rule application by governments. The International Committee of the Red Cross – 'a private organisation governed by Swiss law' whose governing Committee consists of Swiss citizens (www.icrc.org/eng/who-we-are/overview-who-we-are.htm) – supervises the application of the rules of war and conflict in many parts of the world. It is assisted by national Red Cross and Red Crescent societies and the International Federation of Red Cross and Red Crescent Societies (which together make the International Red Cross and Red Crescent Movement). Amnesty International and the various international pressure groups of indigenous peoples, aboriginal rights and human rights participate in the implementation of the UN Universal Declaration of Human Rights. Again their most telling means of 'enforcement' is publicity and moral pressures – methods which are, after all, used in rule application in domestic society.

What seems to be lacking in international rule application is a means of enforcement when pleading, persuasion and pressure fail. Chapter VII of the UN Charter contains the instrumental potential for enforcing decisions in the case of 'any threat to the peace, breach of the peace, or act of aggression' but, as mentioned previously (pp. 125–6) this section was rarely used in the period of Superpower conflict. Only when the two Superpowers agreed that a certain settlement should be 'enforced', could the UN act either as the instrument for this policy or at least as a forum within which a bargain might be struck.

The Security Council agreed from 1966 to 1979 that economic sanctions against the illegal white minority regime in Rhodesia (now Zimbabwe) should be enforced. This task was partly delegated to the British navy whose 'Beira run' off the coast of Mozambique checked sanction-breaking imports of petroleum headed for Rhodesia until 1975. After the Yom Kippur War between Israel and Egypt plus Syria in October 1973, the two Superpowers agreed on a particular ceasefire and were prepared to see the United Nations re-establish UNEF under Security Council control (and with some NATO and Warsaw Treaty Organization contribution) for the purpose of ensuring the disengagement around the Suez Canal. Since 1989 there has been greater agreement within the Security Council about the imposition of Chapter VII: against Iraq in 1990 and then, among others, in the cases of Somalia, Rwanda, Haiti, Bosnia and Herzegovina, Albania, Liberia, Chad, Ivory Coast and South Sudan (United Nations Department of Political Affairs 2009). Nevertheless when the strategic interest of a Great Power is involved, as with the Russian takeover of Crimea from Ukraine in March 2014, a veto can be wielded in the Security Council and the UN has to be satisfied with visits to the parties by the Secretary-General rather than applying generally accepted norms.

International organizations as instruments or forums for rule application fit into the more traditional 'confederal' principles outlined by Tharp. As with rule-making, the European Union has been seen to lean towards the 'federal' model compared with most international organizations. It is part of the task of the European Commission to make sure that the laws of the Union are applied within the member countries and the European Commission may take a law-breaker to the European Court of Justice if necessary. To a great extent the actual enforcement of EU law is undertaken by the agents of the member governments – the local authorities, the ministries, the board and agencies – as if it were purely domestic law. Indeed the member states have incorporated EU law into their own domestic legal framework and have accepted the authority of the European Court of Justice. The EU has mobilized its member states to perform the task of rule application for it. Problems arise, however, when the deliberate policy of a member state is contrary to EU policy and when that state insists on applying *its* policy; for example, a subsidy to agriculture not agreed by the EU. Here enforcement of EU policy rests either on the final sanction of the state, realizing that it will lose other benefits if it insists on breaking the rule and alienating the other EU members, or on the state's government bowing to the judgement of the Court or on a political agreement to change the rules so that they become more acceptable to the renegade state. The latter can happen within sovereign states (governments change legislation which has been openly broken by powerful groups such as trade unions or multinational corporations) but for a government or for the European Union to do this too often weakens both confidence in its political system and its credibility as an applier of rules.

### Rule adjudication

Within the state, rule adjudication is normally carried out by the judiciary – law courts, arbitration panels, tribunals and so forth. The process is closely associated with that of rule-making, as courts can by their judgements develop or interpret the law in such a way that new standards are set. However, the prime aim is to pronounce on existing law; the judicial institutions are normally not involved in the political process of law making. The process of rule adjudication at the international level lacks the extensive institutions and compulsory nature of that at nation-state level. As with rule-making, there is a great deal of rule adjudication that arises from the existence of international organizations – that associated with their internal running – but a more important function is played by certain institutions whose task it is to adjudicate between the competing claims of states.

The most notable of these institutions are the International Court of Justice (ICJ) – the Permanent Court of International Justice (PCIJ) in the interwar period – and the Permanent Court of Arbitration. Using Tharp's criteria mentioned above, these organizations exhibit a 'confederal' nature meaning that, on the whole, states have to consent to disputes being heard by them. Some of the more geographically confined judicial institutions, such as the European Court of Justice or that of the Council of Europe's European Court of Human Rights, are less permissive by nature. The International Criminal Court, which 160 states decided to establish in July 1998, can, however, prosecute those from a country not party to the agreement, and under certain cases, the Security Council can compel co-operation with the court (www.un.org/law/icc/index.html).

Because international law is not always accepted by all parties, neither is it comprehensive and because of the permissive nature of enforcement of any laws, the process of rule adjudication at the international level is more difficult than at the national level. There is more frequent resort to political settlement to get rules accepted. In the past the politically open, industrialized Western democracies have tended to make greatest use of the PCIJ and ICJ (Rochester 1974: 31–6) probably because the sort of established international law on which those courts depended was that formulated by the trading nations of Western Europe and North America. However, the Court has developed a more global appeal. By 2014 the ICJ consisted of five judges from Europe (including one from Russia which also stretches into Asia), three from the Americas, three from Asia, three from Africa and one from Oceania. Of the ten cases pending, two involved two European states, two Oceanic states (with one against Japan) and six were between two Global South states (www.icj-cij.org/homepage/index.php).

## Information

International organizations also perform certain activities within the international political system which are useful but not directly involved in the conversion function of the system or in its maintenance and adaptation. They are invaluable in communication and information. The more traditional approach towards transmitting ideas and messages in the system was through national governments with the help of their diplomatic services. The growth in international organizations together with the increased and easier use of the media of communications has meant that sovereign states can no longer pretend to be dominant in the exchange of international information. The creation of global organizations such as the UN and its associated agencies has produced a forum for governments – the marketplace where they can issue and receive information. The UN and its agencies act as providers of information, as attested by the vast amount of printed and online material they produce – in particular statistical data. The World Weather Watch of the World Meteorological Organization (http://worldweather.wmo.int/) provides valuable information, as do the scientific services of the World Health Organization and the Food and Agriculture Organization. Some INGOs perform similar roles of providing a particular public with the knowledge it seeks, whether it be the specialist work of the International League of Associations for Rheumatology (www.ilar.org/) or the more widespread work of the World Organization of the Scout Movement (www.scout.org/worldscouting). Such organizations perform these functions in a dual role of forums within which members may meet and exchange ideas and actors that present their own output of information. The rise of information technology (IT) has allowed both INGOs and IGOs to reach individuals with

*Table 4.4* Websites of six IGOs and six INGOs

| | |
|---|---|
| Council of Baltic Sea States | www.cbss.org |
| European Union | europa.eu |
| Organization for Security and Cooperation in Europe | www.osce.org |
| North Atlantic Treaty Organization | www.nato.int |
| United Nations | www.un.org |
| World Health Organization | www.who.int |
| Greenpeace International | www.greenpeace.org |
| Human Rights Watch | www.hrw.org |
| International Federation of University Women | www.ifuw.org |
| Rotary International | www.rotary.org |
| Salvation Army International | www.salvationarmy.org |
| International Trade Union Confederation | www.ituc-csi.org |

information with less opportunity for censorship. Websites by international organizations have proliferated and provide a source of information for the student as well as for the citizen (see Table 4.4).

### *Operations*

Finally, international organizations undertake a number of operational functions, much in the same way as governments. These may be banking (International Bank for Reconstruction and Development, the Bank for International Settlements and the European Bank for Reconstruction and Development), providing aid (UN agencies and humanitarian INGOs), helping refugees (UN High Commission for Refugees), dealing with commodities (the European Union in its Common Agricultural and Common External Tariff policies) and running technical services (European Space Agency). These activities are ones not covered by other headings such as role application and may include the UN peace observation corps. The INGOs also make a contribution, especially in the aid area, with well-known names such as the International Committee of the Red Cross, Caritas and Oxfam prominent. Many of the operations undertaken by international organizations are associated with global governance, which will now be briefly examined.

## Global governance

If international organizations assist the process of the functioning of the international political system, to what extent does this help in the creation of a form of global governance? Global governance is basically the total effort of managing global affair. The Commission on Global Governance, established in 1995, provided the following definition:

> Governance is the sum of the many ways individuals and institutions, public and private, manage their common affairs. It is a continuing process through which conflicting or diverse interests may be accommodated and co-operative action may be taken. It includes formal institutions and regimes empowered to enforce compliance, as well as informal arrangements that people and institutions either have agreed to or perceive to be in their interest. . . .

At the global level, governance has been viewed primarily as intergovernmental relationships, but it must now be understood as also involving non-governmental organizations (NGOs), citizens' movements, multinational corporations, and the global capital market. Interacting with these are global mass media of dramatically enlarged influence.

(Commission on Global Governance 1995: 1)

This view of global governance 'does not imply, however, world government or world federalism' (Commission on Global Governance 1995: 1). It does mean some form of control and management of activities across frontiers, but not just by governments. Clearly there is an important role for both IGOs and INGOs in the process of global governance.

What does global governance cover? Clearly it is aimed at activities that cross frontiers and are normally outside the control of individual governments. World trade and commerce are classic examples. There is an increasing list for the world of the twenty-first century: international crime, drug smuggling, cross-border environmental problems, the internet, tourism, migration of peoples and the spread of diseases are just some of the more well-known. For each of these the mixture of instruments available for management differs.

The system available for the management of a particular set of issues internationally is referred to as an *international regime*. A favoured definition of an international regime is that it is 'sets of implicit or explicit principles, norms, rules and decision-making procedures around which actors' expectations converge in a given area of international relations' (Krasner 1983: 2). If global governance is the sum of ways that individuals and institutions manage their common affairs across the world, then international regimes are the toolkits for this activity. A glance at what is included in the box – norms, rules, decision-making procedures – shows that international regimes can be closely tied to the activities of international organizations, the functions of which have been examined above under just such headings. Of course, global governance can – and does – include the workings of the world economic market which can be undertaken on the basis of implicit understandings, private agreements and with little input from international organizations. The internet functions worldwide without recourse to any controlling international organization and, indeed, often beyond governmental control, though this status is claimed to be under threat (Global Commission on Internet Governance 2014).

Nevertheless, international organizations have found their place among the tools needed in international regimes to underpin global governance. Oran Young (1994: 164) has defined the role of international organizations in international regimes as being twofold. First, they can be instruments of regime formation that energize 'the institutional bargaining processes that produce constitutional contracts' giving rise to regimes. Then they can 'implement and administer the provisions of the governance systems they create' (Young 1994: 164). Another American author, Duncan Snidal (1990), points out the varied importance of international organizations in particular issue-areas. For example, that covered by Young – the environment – is one that is well served by international organizations in its global governance (see Gosovic 1992; Princen and Finger 1994; Young 1994; Pease 2007: ch. 9; Karns and Mingst 2010: ch. 11). The picture for regional security governance is varied. While the strongest elements have been seen in Europe, the 'normative concerns and security conceptualization is very different' in the regions of the Global South (Kirchner and Dominguez 2011: 327).

The existence of global governance, however strong or weak and in whatever form, also allows for action by global civil society. Civil society in the domestic context refers to the social action not organized by governments and its agents but by non-governmental movements, associations and organizations. These may be religious groups, trade unions, commercial companies or citizens' initiatives. Within the last twenty years the increased ease of travel and improved electronic communications have helped foster a growing civil society on a global scale. Not only do pressure and interest groups shadow – and sometimes disrupt – international gatherings such as the World Trade Organization's meeting in Seattle in late 1999 and the EU's European Council at Nice in December 2000, but there is now also a wider presence of civil society in most IGOs from the UN to the EU and the World Bank. Indeed, these organizations recognize the value of the agents of civil society. In the words of the former Secretary General of the UN, Kofi Annan: 'The United Nations once dealt only with Governments. By now we know that peace and prosperity cannot be achieved without partnerships involving governments, international organizations, the business community and civil society. In today's world, we depend on each other' (United Nations Office at Vienna 2014). Pressures from civil society can 'increase transparency and accountability in the governance of globalisation' but can also be exclusive, represent business rather than civic groups and be self-selecting (Scholte 2000: 173–201). Nevertheless, the role of states should not be ignored and Diehl (2005: 6) reminds us that 'lack of political will by members inhibits the long-term prospects of those [international] organizations for creating effective structures of global governance'.

## Conclusion

It can be seen that international organizations – IGOs and INGOs – play important roles and undertake particular functions in the world marketplace. It is difficult to imagine the contemporary world without them. In such a case, sovereign states would contact one another by the traditional means of diplomacy, at most conference diplomacy. National groupings and individuals might well have contact with those sharing common interests in other parts of the world but this relationship would not be formalized into a continuous structure with members from several states. Forums for discussion and exchange would be less frequent and would be one-off occasions with no certainty of any continuity. Governments and groupings trying to further their own ends internationally would have fewer instruments to use. Those tools available would be national ones, thereby avoiding the pressure for compromise, and the socialization process that comes with membership of an organization which one does not totally control. There would be no international organization acting in an independent role, no bodies willing to take up the tasks refused by sovereign states and national groups.

The international political system and global governance would still function, but less effectively. Demand by national groupings would be articulated and aggregated on a more ad hoc basis and the resources of the system would be less visible and probably more unevenly distributed. More than now, they would tend to be the resources – the norms, values, the proteges – of dominant regional powers or of a prevailing superpower. The outputs of the system would be more irregular while rule-making, application and adjudication would be more dependent on national decision than at the moment. Information, communication and operational activities would also be in national or private hands.

The number of international organizations has grown precisely because they have functions which cannot be fulfilled by national states and groupings. In their roles as instruments, forums and actors, they perform functions that help to keep the international political system working. The extent to which they may be able to help it adapt to new circumstances will be discussed in Chapter 5.

# 5 International organizations
## The future

At the end of the historical account in Chapter 1, the dynamic element in international organizations was introduced. These institutions form part of the present international system built up since the end of the Napoleonic Wars. A world with a different configuration of states – or indeed with no sovereign states as we know them – would present a different prospect than the present-day polity.

Some of the works cited in Chapter 3 give an indication of how future developments may affect international organizations. The approach of the realist school confines international organizations to a very restricted future with the only developments being those allowed for by the member states in pursuit of their national interests. The functionalist view of the future stresses international organizations serving humankind across state frontiers. The aspiration is to make the old nation state redundant. The neo-functionalists have attenuated this view of the future by accepting regional-based functional organizations and by emphasizing the importance of their having a political authority that can actively sap away the strength of sovereign state government. Economic structuralists would give intergovernmental organizations less import. After all, Marxist writers see a progressive advancement towards a communist world in which there are no oppressors and no oppressed, no want, no war, no divisions into classes or state. By definition, interstate organizations would also have withered away, though it is conceivable that worldwide interest organizations would continue, linking together those who play chess, football or even baseball in the free time provided by the communist millennium. Global South writers who stand outside the Marxist mainstream have either recommended that international organizations should develop symbiotic North–South relations to create a fairer, more secure world or suggested that they should act as instruments against imperialist exploitation and for co-operation between Global South states. 'One-world' globalists hope for the development of institutions that will serve the needs of the planet rather than the demands of a small elite of a minority species – mankind.

These viewpoints tend to prescribe how international organizations should develop in the sort of world the authors hope to see in the future. These prescriptions, dependent on change in the international political system, have consequences for the types of international organizations that might exist (if any) and their roles and functions. Should this book be rewritten after the triumph of functionalism or the achievement of world communist society, then Chapter 3 would have a completely different content. In the case of the arrival of communism (unlikely as that may seem after events in Eastern Europe 1989–90), such an effort would be considered superfluous, a mere rummaging in the dustbin of history.

Those with a set of beliefs – Marxism, freemarket competition, Islam, Christianity – tend to accept the inevitability of its complete triumph. Indeed one of these viewpoints (or one of the many others) may eventually prevail, sweeping all before it or mankind may first destroy itself and the planet. Until that time, we seem to face a future with a variety of systems, each with significant support, co-existing in this world. This plurality is reflected in the international political system. However, the present balance of forces within this system may change, as may the nature of the system itself. This chapter extrapolates the present trends in the position of international organizations and evaluates an alternative development.

## The probable future

It has been stated above that the growth in the number of IGOs is likely to decline with their number remaining at about 250, while the number of INGOs (at present about 27,000, according to Turner (2010: 83) or 8,000 using the more restrictive definition of Tallberg *et al.* (2013: 6)) could well grow modestly into the twenty-first century. Such an extension of present trends does not allow for the demise of IGOs and INGOs, and sheer numbers alone offer little information about the aims and activities of these organizations or about their continued role and function in the international system For the sake of clarity, this overview will divide international governmental organizations into those dealing with questions of international peace and security, and those covering economic, social and environmental questions.

### *IGOs dealing with peace and security*

The major IGO at present concerned with international peace and security is the UN, in particular the Security Council. Current threats to world peace are manifold and enduring: the continued presence of nuclear weapons in countries with political instability; the proliferation of weapons of mass destruction; terrorism; intra-state and transborder conflict; and ecological threats to security.

In the post-1945 period, the UN has developed its activities in peace and security. During the Cold War, it helped to freeze a number of Third World disputes and tried to prevent the Superpowers from being drawn into post-colonial conflict in Palestine, Kashmir, Suez, Cyprus, Congo, Yemen, Western Iran, Laos and Lebanon. The Superpowers dealt directly with each other over strategic matters and, during the 1970s and early 1980s, became increasingly directly involved in Third World conflicts. After the mid-1980s, the Soviet Union disengaged itself militarily from almost all of its Third World commitments, thereby leaving a vacuum that the UN and other international agencies helped to fill with observation teams in Angola and Afghanistan and humanitarian assistance to Mozambique and Ethiopia. Likewise, in the early 1990s, the United States was prepared to see regional efforts and UN involvement aimed at dampening conflict in Central America. However, the United States (together with its allies) was still willing to take on a 'world policeman's' role when basic interests were threatened, as in the case of the August 1990 Iraqi invasion of Kuwait. The increased propensity by other countries to ignore the resolutions of the United Nations – Israel over Jerusalem, the West Bank, the Golan Heights and Lebanon; Iran in the case of US embassy hostages in 1979–81; Iraq and Iran in their Gulf War; and Argentina's invasion of the Falklands – culminated in this Iraqi invasion.

Hopes that the end of the Cold War and the expulsion of Iraqi forces from Kuwait would bring a New World Order with the UN fulfilling its peace and security Charter obligations were not totally fulfilled. Threats to international peace and security did not conveniently mirror the Gulf War with a dictator from a large state invading a small one. However, the full panoply of international organizations – the UN, OSCE, WEU, NATO and EU – were used to solve the problems of former Yugoslavia and they were all involved in the international management of a continuing crisis. Despite this, the aspirations of the UN's Agenda for Peace at the start of the 1990s and the Brahimi report at the start of the 2000s have not been fulfilled. As mentioned in Chapter 4, UN activities in crisis management, conflict prevention, conflict management, peacekeeping and peacebuilding paid off with a reduction of world conflict by the 2000s, but the relentless nature of some conflicts and the addition of the 'War on Terror' led to a rise in the number of conflicts by the end of that decade. In particular, conflicts in Africa and the Middle East have seemed resistant to solution. Though international intervention in Liberia, and Sierra Leone brought an end to the worst conflict there, turmoil continues in the Congo and progress in bringing stability to Somalia always seems on a knife-edge. The conflict between Israel and the Palestinians endures and the hostility between Israel and Iran only heightened into the 2010s. Another notable factor was the reluctance of some Security Council members to sanction what they regarded as a too robust UN involvement in the internal affairs of states. This was seen with the Russian and Chinese prevention of UN action against the al-Assad government in Damascus.

Projecting this sort of activity into the future, it seems likely that the UN and regional security organizations will continue to be involved in international conflicts. However, if they are to follow the post-1990s trend, their involvement will often be too little, too late and they may be absent from significant disputes. The latter will be those taking place internally within a country (such as the Russian conflict with its own Chechen republic), or involving a power with a veto in the Security Council (as with the case of Russia and Crimea in 2014), or where there is a sudden and widespread attack by one sector of a population against another (as in Rwanda and Myanmar/Burma). The UN may end up trying to administer disaster areas such as East Timor and Kosovo, mainly because the international community – and the former occupying state – cannot agree on a more permanent political solution. The fracturing of any large state – Indonesia, India or China – could produce a number of such orphan states left outside the UN's door.

The UN Security Council may still offer the most suitable place for conflict to be taken. Potential warfare between India and Pakistan, Middle Eastern countries and African states should still end up on the agenda. However, it is more likely that either the United States, or a dominant regional power (such as South Africa in southern Africa, Nigeria in West Africa and Egypt in the Middle East) will first be called to assist with a diplomatic solution. The UN will only be able to make a minimum contribution to conflicts arising within the Commonwealth of Independent States, where Russia protects its interest closely, and the seas around China where the People's Republic of China has a distinct view of which islands are under its jurisdiction and of its own sphere of influence. In other regions, active maintenance of peace and security may also be subcontracted to regional organizations such as the AU, ECOWAS and the Arab League. The positive trend in international relations is that

[t]he deadliness of warfare has seen a marked decline over the last 50 to 60 years, and there are now significantly fewer armed conflicts around the world than during the peak of the early 1990s. Plus, contrary to popular notions, we find no evidence that non-state conflicts and one-sided violence have increased over the past two decades, the period covered by the datasets.

(Human Security Report Project 2012: 149)

Projecting this trend forward, interstate conflict would continue to become a rare event. The belief that civil wars are now more common is also challenged as is the notion that they are taking longer to end (Human Security Report Project 2012: 149). It would seem that the end of the Cold War has given international organizations a better opportunity to be involved in a wide variety of conflicts and that the peace efforts of these institutions have paid off. Projected forward, this could mean a less war-torn world.

The other side of this trend is that these improvements have been earned. Reduced involvement by international organizations in peace maintenance – or their exclusion from certain conflicts – could reverse the process. In other words, the pacification process is not automatic, it is one that has to have the right conditions, effective institutions available and continual hard diplomatic work.

In short, a projection forward of present trends in peace and security would show a less conflictual world with an array of international institution, including international organizations, to provide for solution for conflicts. Whether their services are taken up will depend on the area involved and on the willingness of relevant states to allow international organizations to be involved.

## IGOs on economic, social and environmental questions

The present IGOs dealing with economic, social and environmental questions, broadly defined, are currently faced with an uphill task. The size of economic and social problems has grown purely because the Earth's population has mushroomed since the Second World War, increasing by about a billion from 1945 to 3.4 billion in 1965, then by another billion up to 1980, over six billion people by 2000 and 7.17 billion by March 2014 (United States Census Bureau 2014). This in itself has created a problem of feeding, housing and educating an extra 4.6 billion people since 1945 on the same basis as the original 2.5 billion. However, the situation is not so simple. The growth in world population has taken place in those areas with the least utilized resources – the world has seemingly just been adding to its numbers of poor, underfed, diseased, unhoused and illiterate. At the same time, a shift of population from the land to the city has taken place, adding to urban congestion, most noticeably in the Global South. Too often resources have been misused, maldistributed or eroded away, thus adversely affecting the global environment.

The post-war institutions to deal with social and economic problems – the UN and its specialized agencies, the Bretton Woods system, and regional agencies – have found increasing difficulties in carrying out their tasks, as have newcomers such as the World Trade Organization. Growing challenges have often been met by reduced budgets, inefficient bureaucracies and greater national interference. Another phenomenon has been the series of mega-conferences and joint organizations established by the UN to deal with certain social and economic problems: the UN World Population Conferences followed by the UN Fund for Population Activities; the 1972 UN Conference on the Human Environment leading to the Environment Programme Secretariat being established in Nairobi; the Rio Conference on the Environment and Development in 1992 and the Rio+20 Conference on Sustainable Development in 2012; the UN Climate Change Conference in Bali, 2007; the UN Conferences on Desertification; the World Food Programme; the Beijing Fourth World Conference on Women of 1995; the 1982 Vienna meeting on Ageing; the 1990 World Summit on Children; the 1993 World Conference on Human Rights; the Copenhagen World Conference on Human Development in 1995; the Social Good Summit in 2012; and the longest running one of all – the Third UN Conference on the Law of the Sea, which resulted in the Montego Bay Convention of 1982. In some cases the number of IGOs dealing with a particular subject has grown surprisingly: by 1972 eight specialized agencies and regional UN agencies, as well as the EC, NATO, OECD and the Council of Europe, were dealing with environmental questions in Europe (Johnson 1972: 255–301). The Organization for Security and Co-operation in Europe and regional organizations such as the Council of Baltic Sea States can now be added to this list. Organizations dealing with a limited topic such as whaling have multiplied as the number of whales has declined.

A continuation of present trends in economic, social and environmental IGOs seems to point to larger bureaucracies, more politicized and less effective organizations, and meetings that define problems and set rules but are without the means to enforce decisions. On the economic side, dealing with the consequences of the post-2008 recession will continue to be in the hands of the central banks, the institutions of the EU for Europe and the IMF more generally. These will tend to act together, re-enforcing each other's decisions. Their main problem is that they are caught between wider economic and social forces. On the one hand, they will need to continue with policies of financial restraint to gain acceptance from the money markets and the ratings agencies. The latter not only rate the strength of sovereign states' finances and commercial banks but also that of multilateral financial institutions (http://video.standardandpoors.com/?video=MgAFFOAKWmRdxQQ2xAegtX8qbH#). On the other hand, the various financial institutions will have to be aware of public response to increasingly strict public policies required as part of loan or support deals. While the political and economic elite will be pressing ahead to 'complete' economic and monetary union within the Eurozone of the EU (see, for example, the address by Vito Constancio, a Vice-President of the ECB, at www.ecb.int/press/key/date/2012/html/sp121126.en.html), the public seem to be alienated from the process. Already by late 2013, only 22 per cent of respondents to an EU opinion poll felt that the EU was best able to take effective action against the effects of the economic and financial crisis, a result only ameliorated by the figures for the nation states (22%), the IMF (13%) and the G20 (12%) as being the best (http://ec.europa.eu/public_opinion/archives/eb/eb80/eb80_first_en.pdf, p.29). This mismatch between the wishes and hopes of peoples and their perception of international organizations to deliver, if it is to continue for any length of time, will place a strain on the legitimacy of such institutions and, eventually, their capabilities.

A continuation forward of action through international organizations against global illnesses could show a continuation of the positive results experienced so far. A mixture of governmental, NGO and WHO activity has helped to slow the spread of HIV/AIDS and has increased the number of those receiving treatment with anti-viral drugs (www.who.int/hiv/pub/drugresistance/drug_resistance_strategy/en/index.html). However, as with international action against TB, this could be put at risk by growing resistance to drugs. The area of food security is also a mixed one when present trends are rolled forward. Though the causes of lack of access to secure food supplies are manifold and include climate change, population growth, increased fuel costs and over-consumption by some, there has been some success by the World Food Programme in dealing with the hunger and its causes (www.wfp.org/), while after decades of internal dissension, the Food and Agriculture Organization seems to have returned to the task of helping to reduce world hunger with some success (www.fao.org/publications/sofi/en/).

A progression forward of current environmental trends suggests a difficult time for the planet and existing international organizations seem unable to change this, mostly because of resistance from certain member states and from commercial interests. The issue of climate change has been well publicized, not least by work sponsored by international organizations such as that of the Intergovernmental Panel on Climate Change (IPCC, www.ipcc.ch/) established by the UN, WMO and UNEP. However, the current indicators are that there will be little change in the human-driven impact of climate change, despite the efforts of international organizations and international agreements to restrain such developments (IPCC 2013: 13).

## Other futures

Although the future outlined for international organizations above has few surprises, it is one very much based on a continuation of events seen since the 1990s. However, there are other trends that may be considered in mapping out the future of international organizations.

The first involves general strategic developments. While the end of the Cold War left the United States as the only genuine world power (though the nuclear might of Russia would still entitle it to the name 'Superpower'), this has brought neither world peace nor a new world order any closer. Both Republican and Democrat administrations in the United States have been wary of increasing their use of international organizations and have often preferred bilateral links and ad hoc coalitions, though the post-2008 financial crisis obliged the United States to take full use of the international financial institutions. A more nationalistic Russian foreign and defence policy under President Putin and a more assertive policy by China could lead to a return to balance of power international politics with the favours of the EU and of Japan being sought by America, Russia and China. Added to this would be a new nuclear stand-off between India and Pakistan and possible similar ones between Israel and Iran or one or more Arab state in the Middle East.

What do international organizations have to offer in this situation? If the main players – the United States, Russia and China – do not wish to seek assistance outside their national frontiers, except to arrange alliances, there is little that the UN or others can do. However, if nothing else, the Secretariat of the UN and other IGOs such as the AU, as well as a range of INGOs, should be able to remind the powers of the costs of seeking security without concern for wider consequences, what was christened the 'security dilemma' over sixty years ago (Herz 1950). Increased arming of a state brings greater fear to possible adversaries and these in turn arm further, leading the original state to respond by another round of armaments. It seems that this is a process, the uselessness and cost of which new generations have to learn. After the lesson has been realized, there is the possibility of a return to the table and, given the need for at least three nuclear powers to discuss matters, there could well be a security conference that eventually becomes institutionalized, as in the case of the OSCE.

Second, this overall strategic situation may be complemented by a continuation of low-level conflicts, civil wars and mixed civil and international wars. The UN may not have the support, either financial or political, with which to engage itself in these. Is there an alternative to a 'pick-and-mix' approach whereby some conflicts are addressed because of great power interest, whereas others are left to fester? One answer is to share the task between the UN and regional agencies. This does not guarantee that conflicts are dealt with in either a fair or effective manner (Adibe 1998; Alagappa 1998) but learning of the lessons so far could lead to a more effective set of conflict avoidance and management instruments at regional levels, as well as more politically acceptable peacekeeping and peacemaking operations. This matter was addressed by a UN high-level panel (United Nations 2004) but many of its 101 recommendations have not been or are only partly implemented. The effects of the revolution in military affairs has moved on from the United States to affect medium-range powers such as the United Kingdom and France as well as smaller states as those in Scandinavia – all of which make strong contributions to peacekeeping and peacemaking efforts. Using the latest technologies, this has allowed military involvement in a conflict – such as that in Libya in 2011 – at a distance, decreasing the cost in human lives for the state with such technology and increasing its range and ability to aim at specific targets (Metz 2000). This may increase the willingness of states with such capability to become involved in military operations either under the UN banner or in a regional context. It does not solve the problem when troops on the ground are needed, as is the case for most peacekeeping operations. However, agreed ceasefires will be easier to monitor by technical means and lessons from the operations of the 1990s and 2000s need to be studied and applied to make future operations more effective.

Economic forecasts and those involving social and environmental developments may paint a bleak future for large parts of the world. The list of UN conferences on a range of world problems suggests that there has been plenty of talk but little action. While extreme poverty has been reduced since 1990, still over 2.4 billion people lived on less than two dollars a day in 2010 (World Bank 2014). It may seem that the most developed part of the planet will continue to reserve the lion's share of resources for itself and will consume them in a profligate manner adversely affecting the population. Even an economic recession merely slows the pace of the advance of the developed world. Even the modest aims of the 1997 Kyoto Convention on limiting greenhouse gases will be missed not just by automobile-addicted America but by environment-conscious Norway. This suggests that the process of globalization is one that is bringing the areas of the Global South increasingly into the consumerist world, regardless of adverse externalities.

What can international organizations do to encourage a fairer and ecologically greener world? Though the World Trade Organization may originally have been seen as a reflection of US economic hegemony, it now allows for the input and concerns of other states, and has included NGOs in its deliberations. Some 346 NGOs attended the Bali WTO meeting in 2013 (www.wto.org/english/thewto_e/minist_e/mc9_e/ngo_e. htm). It is up to the membership of the WTO to include environmental considerations more fully in the WTO rules and to IGOs and INGOs to campaign for such changes.

Furthermore UN agencies have had successes in advancing sustainable human development, including the strengthening of democratic governance (www.undp.org/content/undp/en/home/ourwork/democraticgovernance/overview.html). The World Bank Group has its own programme for improving governance and a public accountability section for recipient states (www.worldbank.org/html/extdr/thematic.htm), and the UN has established a panel to examine relations between the UN and civil society (United Nations General Assembly 2004). Modern technology has increased the opportunity for the involvement of civil society, including NGOs, in the UN's work. It would seem that as part of the 'privatising of world politics and the emergence of a global civil society, bilateral and multinational organizations are increasingly relying upon NGOs' (Gordenker and Weiss 1998: 30; see also Willetts 1996; Weiss and Gordenker 1996). A development of these activities could go some way to bringing a social concern about development to the global agenda.

The information age brings new challenges for international organizations. The internet forms a web that has emerged in an anarchic form, with governments finding it difficult to police because of its global nature and international organizations being involved only marginally with its development. Its use as a tool by NGOs has been noted. New technologies such as the internet, the social media and video-links offer new forums for groups to communicate, which was seen to affect the progress of the 'Arab Spring' of 2011–12 when large numbers came out on to the streets in Tunisia, Libya, Egypt, the Gulf states and Syria, not least in response to electronic communication. The emergence of protest and pressure coalitions that take full advantage of new modes of communication suggest that the international non-governmental organizations of the future will be more global than international and more networks and forums than formal organizations.

In a future where global governance takes on an importance of its own, there is likely to be a richer mix of institutions involved in the management of human activities across frontiers. The sovereign state will not disappear, but it will have to share the stable increasingly with IGOs, INGOs, transnational entities such as large firms, and new networks. The increased pressure on world resources and continued insecurity across the world will only stress the need for international organizations. Whether they find the resources to function effectively is another matter.

# Bibliography

Adibe, C. (1998) 'The Liberian Conflict and the ECOWAS-UN Partnership', in T. Weiss (ed.) *Beyond UN Subcontracting: Task-sharing with Regional Security Arrangements and Service-providing NGOs*, Basingstoke and New York: Macmillan and St Martin's Press, 67–90.

Adler, E. and Barnett, M. (eds) (1998) *Security Communities*, Cambridge: Cambridge University Press.

African Union (2014) *African Union. Peace and Security*, www.peaceau.org/en/ (18 January 2014).

Ahlenius, I.-B. (2010) 'Note to the Secretary General. End-of-assignment-report', *Washington Post*, 20 July, www.washingtonpost.com/wp-srv/hp/ssi/wpc/nations2.pdf?sid=ST2010071904739 (6 March 2014).

Alagappa, M. (1998) 'Regional arrangements, the UN and international security', in T. Weiss (ed.) *Beyond UN Subcontracting: Task-sharing with Regional Security Arrangements and Service-providing NGOs*, Basingstoke and New York: Macmillan and St Martin's Press, 3–29.

Alger, C.F. (1990) 'Grass-roots perspectives on global policies for development', *Journal of Peace Research* 27(2): 155–68.

Allen R. (1980) *How to Save the World: Strategy for World Conservation*, London: Kogan Page.

Almond, G. and Powell, G.B. (1966) *Comparative Politics. A Developmental Approach*, Boston: Little, Brown.

Alston, P. (1998) 'The UN's human rights record', in C. Ku and P. Diehl (eds) *International Law. Classic and Contemporary Readings*, Boulder, CO: Lynne Rienner, 355–68.

Alvarez, J.E. (2006) 'International organizations then and now', *American Journal of International Law* 100: 324–47.

Amin, S. (1977) 'Self reliance and the New International Economic Order', *Monthly Review* 29(3): 1–21.

Andersen, B. (1983) *Imagined Communities: The Origins and Spread of Nationalism*, London: Verso.

Angell, R. (1965) 'An analysis of trends in international organizations', *Peace Research Society International Papers* 3: 185–95.

Archer, C. (2008) *The European Union*, London and New York: Routledge.

Armstrong, D., Lloyd, L. and Redmond, J. (2004) *International Organisation in World Politics*, Basingstoke and New York: Palgrave Macmillan.

Ashley, R.K. (1984) 'The poverty of realism', *International Organization* 38(2): 22–6.

—— (1986) 'The poverty of neorealism', in R.O. Keohane (ed.) *Neorealism and its Critics*, New York: Columbia University Press, 255–300.

Atherton, A.L. (1976) *International Organizations: A Guide to Information Sources*, Detroit: Gale Research.

Baldwin, D.A. (1980) 'International interdependence: the evolution of a concept', mimeographed paper for British International Studies Association, Lancaster University, December 1980.

—— (ed.) (1993) *Neorealism and Neoliberalism: The Contemporary Debate*, New York: Columbia University Press.

Barnet, R.J. and Muller, R.E. (1975) *Global Reach: The Power of the Multinational Corporations*, London: Cape.

Barnett, M. and Adler, E. (1998) 'Studying security communities in theory, comparison, and history', in E. Adler and M. Barnett (eds) *Security Communities,* Cambridge: Cambridge University Press.

Barnett, M. and Finnemore, M. (2004) *Rules for the World: International Organizations in Global Politics,* Ithaca, NY: Cornell University Press.

Barros, J. (1979) *Office without Power: Secretary-General Sir Eric Drummond 1919–1933,* Oxford: Clarendon Press.

Beigbeder, Y. (1992) *Le role international des organisations non gouvernementales,* Brussels and Paris: Bruyland & L.G.D.J.

Bennett, A. Le R. (1977) *International Organizations: Principles and Issues,* Englewood Cliffs, NJ: Prentice-Hall.

Berdal, M. (2009) *Building Peace after War,* Abingdon: Routledge.

Berki, R.N. (1971) 'On Marxian thought and the problem of international relations', *World Politics* 24(1): 80–105.

Berkovitch, N. (1999) *From Motherhood to Citizenship: Women's Rights and International Organizations,* Baltimore: Johns Hopkins University Press.

Berridge, G.R. (2002) *Diplomacy. Theory and Practice,* Houndmills: Palgrave.

Best, G. (1999) 'Peace conferences and the century of total war: the 1899 Hague Conference and what came after', *International Affairs* 75(3): 619–34.

Bianchi, A. (1997) 'Globalization of Human Rights: the role of non-state actors' in G. Teubner (ed.) *Global Law without a State,* Aldershot: Dartmouth, 179–212.

Bieler, A. and Morton, A.D. (2004) 'A critical theory route to hegemony, world order and historical change: neo-Gramscian perspectives in International Relations', *Capital & Class* 82: 85–113.

Black, C.E. and Falk, R.A. (eds) (1969) *The Future of the International Legal Order, Vol. 1 Trends and Patterns,* Princeton: Princeton University Press.

—— (1972) *The Future of the International Legal Order, Vol. IV The Structure of the International Environment,* Princeton: Princeton University Press.

Boardman, R. (1981) *International Organization and the Conservation of Nature,* London: Macmillan.

Bodenheimer, S. (1971) 'Dependency and imperialism', *Politics and Society* 1(3): 327–57.

Boli, J. (2006) 'International non-governmental organizations', in W.W. Powell and R. Steinberg (eds) *The Nonprofit Sector,* New Haven, CT: Yale University Press, 333–46.

Boutros-Ghali, B. (1992) *An Agenda for Peace,* New York: United Nations, A/47/277-S/24111.

Bowett, D.W. (1970) *The Law of International Institutions,* 2nd edn, London: Stevens & Sons.

Bozeman, A. (1960) *Politics and Culture in International History,* Princeton, NJ: Princeton University Press.

Brierly, J.L. (1946) 'The covenant and the charter', *British Yearbook of International Law* 23: 83–94.

Brown, J.S. (1909) *The Hague Peace Conference of 1899 and 1907: Vol. 2,* Baltimore: Johns Hopkins University Press.

Brucan, S. (1977) 'Power and conflict', *International Social Science Journal* 29(1): 94–114.

Bull, H. (1966) 'The Grotian conception of international society', in H. Butterfield and M. Wight (eds) *Diplomatic Investigations,* London: Allen & Unwin.

—— (1972) 'The theory of international politics 1919–69', in B. Porter (ed.) *The Aberystwyth Papers: International Politics 1919–1969,* Oxford: Oxford University Press.

—— (1977) *The Anarchical Society. A Study of Order in World Politics,* Basingstoke: Macmillan.

Burgess, M. (2000) *Federalism and European Union. The Building of Europe 1950–2000,* London: Routledge.

Burton, J. (1972) *World Society,* Cambridge: Cambridge University Press.

Butler, W.E. (1988/89) 'International law, foreign policy, and the Gorbachev Style', *Journal of International Affairs (Columbia)* 42(2): 363–75.

Butterfield, H. and Wight, M. (eds) (1966) *Diplomatic Investigations,* London: Allen & Unwin.

Butterworth, R. L. (1978) *Moderation from Management: International Organizations and Peace,* Pittsburgh: University Center for International Studies.

Buzan, B. (1991) *People, State and Fear. A Study of Order in World Politics*, 2nd edn, Boulder, CO: Lynne Rienner.

Campbell, David (1998) 'Why fight: humanitarianism, principles and post-structuralism', *Millennium. Journal of International Studies* 27(3): 497–521.

Cantori, L.J. and Spiegel, S.L. (1970) *The International Politics of Regions: A Comparative Approach*, Englewood Cliffs, NJ: Prentice-Hall.

Cardosa, F.H. (1974) 'Notas sobre el estado actual de los estudios sobre dependencia' in J. Sierra (ed.) *Desarrollo Latinoamericano: Ensayos Criticos*, Mexico City: Fondo de Cultura Economica, 325–56.

Carr, E.H. (1939) *The Twenty Years Crisis 1919–1939*, London: Macmillan.

—— (1945) *Nationalism and After*, London: Macmillan.

—— (1946) *The Twenty Years Crisis 1919–1939*, 2nd edn, London: Macmillan.

Cassan, H. (1974) 'Le consensus dans la pratique des Nations Unies', *Annuaire Français de Droit International* 20: 456–85.

Cecil, Viscount (1941) *A Great Experiment*, London: Cape.

Chamberlain, J.P. (1955) 'International organization' in P.C. Jessup, A. Lande, O.J. Lissitzyn and J.P. Chamberlain (eds) *International Organizations*, New York: Carnegie Endowment for International Peace.

Chase-Dunn, C. and Inoue, H. (2012) 'Accelerating democratic global state formation', *Co-operation and Conflict* 47(2): 157–75.

Chen, K.C. (ed.) (1979) *China and the Three Worlds*, London: Macmillan.

Childers, E.B. (1990) 'The future of the United Nations', *Bulletin of Peace Proposals* 21(2): 143–52.

Chossudovsky, E.M. (1988) *'East-West' Diplomacy for Environment in the United Nations: The High-Level Meeting within the Framework of the ECE on the Protection of the Environment, A Case Study*, New York: UNITAR.

Chryssochoou, D.N. (1994) 'Democracy and symbiosis in the European Union: towards a confederal association?', *West European Politics* 17(4): 1–14.

Church, J. and McCaffrey, M. (2013) 'International organizations: available information and Documentation', in B. Reinalda (ed.) *Routledge Handbook of International Organization*, London and New York: Routledge, 27–40.

Clarke, G. (1998) 'Non-governmental organizations and politics in the developing world', *Political Studies* 46(1): 36–52.

Claude, I.L. (1964) *Swords into Plowshares*, 3rd edn, London: University of London Press.

—— (1968) 'International organization: the process and the institutions', in D. Sills (ed.) *International Encyclopedia of the Social Sciences*, vol. 8, New York: Macmillan and Free Press, 33–40.

—— (1971) *Swords into Plowshares*, 4th edn, New York: Random House.

Coate, R.A. and Puchala, D.J. (1990) 'Global policies and the United Nations System: A current assessment', *Journal of Peace Research* 27(2): 127–40.

Cocks, P. (1980) 'Towards a Marxist theory of European integration', *International Organization* 34(1): 1–40.

Commission on Global Governance (1995) *Our Global Neighborhood. The Report of the Commission on Global Governance*, New York and Oxford: Oxford University Press.

Constancio, Vitor (2012) *Completing and repairing EMU*, www.ecb.int/press/key/date/2012/html/sp121126.en.html (30 November 2012).

Cordier, A.W. and Foote, W. (eds) (1972) *Public Papers of the Secretaries-General of the United Nations, Vol. 2: Dag Hammarskjold 1953–1956*, London and New York: Columbia University Press.

Cox, R. (1980) 'The crisis of world order and the problem of international organization in the 1980s', *International Journal* 35(2): 370–95.

—— (1981) 'Social forces, states and world orders: beyond international relations theory', *Millennium: Journal of International Studies* 10(2): 126–55.

—— (1993) 'Gramsci, hegemony and international relations; an essay in method', in S. Gill (ed.) *Gramsci, Historical Materialism and International Relations*, Cambridge: Cambridge University Press, Cambridge Studies in International Relations 26.

—— (1994) 'The crisis in world order and the challenge to international organization', *Cooperation and Conflict* 29(2): 99–113.

Cox, R. with Sinclair, T. (1996) *Approaches to World Order*, Cambridge: Cambridge University Press.

Davies, N. (1997) *Europe: A History*, London: Pimlico.

Davies, T.R. (2008) *The Rise and Fall of Transnational Civil Society: The Evolution of International Non-governmental Organizations since 1839*, working paper CUTP/003, www.staff.city.ac.uk/tom.davies/CUWPTP003.pdf (4 April 2011).

de Cuellar, J.P. (1989) 'The role of the UN Secretary-General', in A. Roberts and B. Kingsbury (eds) *United Nations, Divided World*, Oxford: Clarendon Press.

Deen, T. (2012) 'Senior Management Heads Roll at World Body', *Global Policy Forum*, 25 January, www.globalpolicy.org/un-reform/un-reform-topics/management-reform/51224-senior-management-heads-roll-at-world-body.html?itemid=id#228 (16 March 2014).

Deutsch, K. Burrell, S., Kann, R., Lee, M., Lichterman, M., Lindgren, F., Loudenheim, F., and Wagener, R., (1957) *Political Community and the North Atlantic Area*, Princeton: Princeton University Press.

—— (1966) 'External influences in the internal behavior of states', in R.B. Farrell (ed.) *Approaches to Comparative and International Politics*, New York: Free Press.

Diehl, P.F. (2005) *The Politics of Global Governance: International Organizations in an Interdependent World*, 3rd edn, Boulder, CO: Lynne Rienner.

Dixon, W.J. (1981) 'The emerging image of UN politics', *World Politics* 34(1): 47–61.

Dolman, A. (1979) 'The like-minded countries and the New International Order: past, present and future prospects', *Cooperation and Conflict* 14(2–3): 57–85.

Donnelly, J. (1990) 'Global policy studies: a skeptical view', *Journal of Peace Research* 27(2): 221–30.

Duverger, M. (1972) *The Study of Politics*, London: Nelson.

Eagleton, C. (1948) *International Government*, New York: Ronald.

Etzioni, A. (1964) 'Atlantic Union, the southern continents, and the United Nations', in R. Fisher (ed.) *International Conflict and Behavioural Science*, New York: Basic Books.

Europa summaries of EU legislation (2010) 'Enhanced cooperation', http://europa.eu/legislation_summaries/institutional_affairs/treaties/lisbon_treaty/ai0018_en.htm (13 February 2014).

European Commission Competition (2012) *Microsoft Case. The Commission's Investigation*, http://ec.europa.eu/competition/sectors/ICT/microsoft/investigation.html (27 September 2012).

European Commission Standard Eurobarometer (2013) *Public Opinion in the European Union*, http://ec.europa.eu/public_opinion/archives/eb/eb80/eb80_first_en.pdf (15 February 2014).

European Court of Human Rights (2014) 'The Court', www.echr.coe.int/Pages/home.aspx?p=home (7 February 2014).

Fabian, L.L. (1971) 'International administration of peace-keeping operations', in R.S. Jordan (ed.) *International Administration: Its Evolution and Contemporary Applications*, New York: Oxford University Press.

Falk, R.A. (1969) 'The interplay of Westphalia and charter conceptions of international legal order', in C.E. Black and R.A. Falk (eds) *The Future of the International Legal Order*, Princeton: Princeton University Press.

Feld, W. (1971) 'Non-governmental entities and the international system: a preliminary quantitative overview', *Orbis* 15: 879–922.

Feld, W., Jordan, R.S. with Hurwitz, L. (1994) *International Organizations. A Comparative Approach*, 3rd edn, Westport, CT: Praeger.

Feuer, L.S. (ed.) (1969) *Marx and Engels. Basic Writings on Politics and Philosophy*, London: Fontana.

Finkelstein, L.S. (1995) 'What is global governance', *Global Governance* 1: 367–72.

Fisher, R. (ed.) (1964) *International Conflict and Behavioural Science*, New York: Basic Books.

Franck, T.M. (1989) 'The good offices function of the UN Secretary-General', in A. Roberts and B. Kingsbur (eds) *United Nations, Divided World*, Oxford: Clarendon Press.

Freedman, L. (1991) 'The Gulf War and the new world order', *Survival* 33(2): 195–209.

G20 (2010) *About G20*, www.g20.org/about_what_is_g20.aspx (4 April 2011).

—— (2011) *Cannes Summit Final Declaration*, www.g20.org/Documents2011/11/Cannes%20 Declaration%204%20November%202011.pdf (7 November 2011).

—— (2012) *The VII Leaders' Summit Concludes*, www.g20mexico.org/index.php/en/press-releases/460-concluye-la-vii-cumbre-de-lideres-del-g20 (26 September 2012).

—— (2013) *Infographics about G20 member countries*, http://en.g20russia.ru/infographics/20121201/780989503.html (6 February 2014).

Gerbet, P. (1977) 'Rise and development', *International Social Science Journal* 29(1): 7–27.

Ghebali, V.-Y. (1986) 'The politicization of the UN specialized agencies: The UNESCO syndrome', in D. Pitt and T.G. Weiss (eds), *The Nature of United Nations Bureaucracies*, London: Croom Helm, 118–36.

Gill, S. (1992) 'The emerging world order and european change: the political economy of the European Union', in R. Miliband, and L. Panitch (eds), *The Socialist Register. New World Order?* London: Merlin Press, 157–96.

Gilpin, R. (1975) *U.S. Power and the Multinational Corporation: the Political Economy of Foreign Direct Investment*, New York: Basic Books.

—— (1981) *War and Change in World Politics*, New York: Cambridge University Press.

—— (1984) 'The richness of the tradition of political realism', *International Organization* 38(2): 287–304.

Gladwyn, Lord (Sir Gladwyn Jebb) (1953) 'The free world and the United Nations', *Foreign Affairs* 31(3): 382–91.

—— (1966) 'World order and the nation state – a regional approach', *Daedalus* 95(2): 694–703.

Global Commission on Internet Governance (2014) *Frequently Asked Questions*, www.ourinternet.org/#faq (20 March 2014).

Goodrich, L.M., Hambro, E. and Simmons, A. (1969) *Charter of the United Nations: Commentary and Documents*, 3rd edn, New York: Columbia University Press.

Gordenker, L. and Weiss, T. (1998) 'Devolving responsibilities: a framework for analysing NGOs and services', in T. Weiss (ed.) *Beyond UN Subcontracting: Task-sharing with Regional Security Arrangements and Service-providing NGOs*, Basingstoke and New York: Macmillan and St Martin's Press, 30–45.

Gosovic, B. (1992) *The Quest for World Environmental Cooperation*, London: Routledge.

Gosovic, B. and Ruggie, J.G. (1976) 'On the creation of a new international economic order', *International Organization* 30(2): 309–45.

Gregg, R.W. (1981) 'Negotiating a New International Economic Order: the issue of venue', in R. Jütte and A. Gross-Jütte (eds), *The Future of International Organization*, London: Frances Pinter.

Grieco, J. (1993) 'Understanding the problem of international cooperation: the limits of neoliberal institutionalism and the future of realist theory', in D.A. Baldwin (ed.), *Neorealism and Neoliberalism: The Contemporary Debate*, New York: Columbia University Press, 301–38.

Griffiths, M. (1992) 'Order and international security: the real Realism?', *Review of International Studies* 18(2): 217–40.

Haas, E.B. (1958) *The Uniting of Europe: Political, Social and Economic Forces, 1950–1957*, 1st edn, Stanford, CA: Stanford University Press.

—— (1961) 'International integration: the European and the universal process', *International Organization* 25: 336–92.

—— (1964) *Beyond the Nation State*, Stanford, CA: Stanford University Press.

—— (1968) *The Uniting of Europe: Political, Social and Economic Forces, 1950–1957*, 2nd edn, Stanford, CA: Stanford University Press.

—— (1970) 'The study of regional integration: reflections on the joy and anguish of pretheorizing', *International Organization* 24(2): 607–46.

—— (1975) *The Obsolescence of Regional Integration Theory*, Berkeley, CA: Institute of International Studies.

—— (1976) 'Turbulent fields and the theory of regional integration', *International Organization* 30(2): 173–212.

Haas, E.B. and Rowe, E.T. (1973) 'Regional organizations in the United Nations: is there externalization?', *International Studies Quarterly* 17(1): 3–54.

Haas, E.B. and Schmitter, P.C. (1964) 'Economic and differential patterns of political integration', *International Organization* 18(4): 705–37.

Haas, M. (1971) *International Organization: An Interdisciplinary Bibliography*, Stanford, CA: Hoover Institute.

Haas, P., Keohane, R. and Levy, M. (eds) (1995) *Institutions for the Earth: Sources of Effective International Environmental Protection*, Cambridge, MA: MIT Press.

Hankey, Lord (1946) *Diplomacy by Conference. Studies in Public Affairs 1920–1946*, London: Ernest Benn.

Hansen, H.E., McLaughlin Mitchell, S. and Nemeth, S.C. (2008) 'IO mediation of interstate conflicts: moving beyond the global versus regional dichotomy', *Journal of Conflict Resolution* 52(2): 295–324.

Henig, R.B. (ed.) (1973) *The League of Nations*, Edinburgh: Oliver & Boyd.

Herren, M. (2009) *Internationale Organisationen seit 1865. Eine Globalgeschichte der internationalen Ordnung*, Darmstadt: Wissenschaftliche Buchgesellschaft.

Herz, J. (1950) 'Idealist internationalism and the security dilemma', *World Politics* 2(2): 157–80.

Hettne, B. and Söderbaum, F. (2006) 'The UN and regional organizations in global security: competing or complementary logics?' *Global Governance* 12(3): 227–32.

Hew, D. (2007) *Brick by Brick: The Building of an ASEAN Economic Community*, Singapore: Singapore Institute of Southeast Asian Studies.

Higgins, C. (2014) '11 reasons to be optimistic in 2014', *Impatient Optimists. Bill & Melinda Gates Foundation*, www.impatientoptimists.org/Posts/2014/01/11-Reasons-to-Be-Optimistic-in-2014 (1 February 2014).

Higgins, R. (1969) *United Nations Peacekeeping 1946–1967: Documents and Commentary, Vol.1 – The Middle East*, London: Oxford University Press.

—— (1980) *United Nations Peacekeeping 1946–1967: Documents and Commentary, Vol. 3 – Africa*, London: Oxford University Press.

Hinsley, F.H. (1967) *Power and the Pursuit of Peace*, Cambridge: Cambridge University Press.

Hoffmann, Lord (2009) 'The universality of human rights' *Judicial Studies Board Annual Lecture* 19 March, www.judiciary.gov.uk/Resources/JCO/Documents/Speeches/Hoffmann_2009_JSB_Annual_Lecture_Universality_of_Human_Rights.pdf (8 February 2014)

Hoffmann, S. (1970) 'International organization and the international system', *International Organization* 24: 389–413.

Holland, M. (1993) *European Community Integration*, London: Pinter.

Horn, H. (2011) 'Has Europe reached its Articles of Confederation moment?', *The Atlantic*, 8 December, www.theatlantic.com/international/archive/2011/12/has-europe-reached-its-articles-of-confederation-moment/249616/ (27 March 2014).

Hudson, M.O. (1944) *International Tribunals, Past and Future*, Washington, DC: Carnegie Endowment for International Peace and Brookings Institution.

Human Rights Watch (1992) *War Crimes in Bosnia-Herzegovina. A Helsinki Watch Report*, New York, NY: Human Rights Watch.

—— (2013) *World Report 2014*, New York, NY: Human Rights Watch.

Human Security Report Project (2010) *Human Security Report 2009/2010*, Vancouver: Simon Fraser University.

—— (2012) *Human Security Report 2012*, Vancouver: Simon Fraser University.

Hunter, D.B. (2014) 'International environmental law. Sources, principles and innovations' in P.G. Harris (ed.) *Routledge Handbook of Global Environmental Politics*, London and New York: Routledge, 124–37.

Imber, M.F. (1989) *The USA, ILO, UNESCO and IAEA. Politicization and Withdrawal in the Specialized Agencies*, London: Macmillan.

Independent Commission on Disarmament and Security Issues (1982) *Common Security. A Programme for Disarmament*, Palme Report, London: Pan.

Independent Commission on International Development Issues (1980) *North-South: A Programme for Survival*, Brandt Report, London: Pan.

International Council of Scientific Unions (2014) 'Our Members', www.icsu.org/about-icsu/our-members (28 February 2014).

International Monetary Fund (2012) 'IMF's response to the global economic crisis', www.imf.org/external/np/exr/facts/changing.htm (26 September 2012).

International Organization for Standardization (2014) 'ISO membership manual', www.iso.org/iso/iso_membership_manual_2013.pdf (28 February 2014).

IPCC (Intergovernmental Panel on Climate Change) (2013) 'Summary for policymakers', in T.F. Stocker, D. Qin, G.-K. Plattner, M. Tignor, S.K. Allen, J. Boschung, A. Nauels, Y. Xia, V. Bex and P.M. Midgley (eds), *Climate Change 2013: The Physical Science Basis. Contribution of Working Group I to the Fifth Assessment Report of the Intergovernmental Panel on Climate Change*, Cambridge and New York: Cambridge University Press, www.climatechange2013.org/images/report/WG1AR5_SPM_FINAL.pdf (20 March 2014).

Jackson, J. (1997) *The World Trading System. Law and Policy of International Economic Relations*, 2nd edn, Cambridge, MA: MIT Press.

Jackson, R. and Sørensen, G. (1999) *Introduction to International Relations*, Oxford: Oxford University Press.

Jacobsen, H.K. (1979) *Networks of Interdependence: International Organizations and the Global Political System*, New York and Westminster, MD: Alfred A. Knopf/Random House.

James, A. (1990) *Peacekeeping in International Politics*, London: Macmillan.

James, R.R. (1971) 'The evolving concept of the international civil service', in R.S. Jordan (ed.), *International Administration: Its Evolution and Contemporary Applications*, New York: Oxford University Press.

Jenkins, R. (1971) *Exploitation*, London: Paladin.

Jenks, C.W. (1945a) 'Some constitutional problems of international organizations', *British Yearbook of International Law* 22: 11–72.

—— (1945b) *The Headquarters of International Institutions. A Study of their Location and Status*, London: Royal Institute of International Affairs.

—— (1962a) 'The significance for international law of the tripartite character of the International Labour Organization', *Transactions of the Grotius Society* 22: 45–81.

—— (1962b) 'Some legal aspects of the financing of international institutions', *Transactions of the Grotius Society* 28: 87–132.

Johnson, B. (1972) 'The United Nations institutional response to Stockholm: a case study in the international politics of institutional change', *International Organization* 26(2): 255–301.

Jordan, R.S. (ed.) (1971) *International Administration: Its Evolution and Contemporary Applications*, New York: Oxford University Press.

Jorgensen, K-E. (2009) *The European Union and International Organizations*, London: Routledge.

Joyner, C. and Martell, E. (1998) 'Looking back to see ahead.: UNCLOS III and lessons for global commons law', in C. Ku and P. Diehl (eds) *International Law. Classic and Contemporary Readings*, Boulder, CO: Lynne Rienner, 445–72.

Judge, A.J.N. (1978) 'International institutions: diversity, borderline cases, functional substitute and possible alternatives', in P. Taylor and A.J.R. Groom (eds) *International Organizations: A Conceptual Approach*, London: Frances Pinter.

Kaiser, K. (1968) 'The interaction of regional subsystems. Some preliminary notes on recurrent patterns and the role of superpowers', *World Politics* 21(1): 84–107.

Karns, M.P. and Mingst, K.A. (2010) *International Organizations: The Politics and Process of Global Governance* 2nd edn, Boulder, CO: Lynne Rienner.

Katzenstein, P., Keohane, R.O. and Krasner, S.D. (1998) 'International Organization and the Study of World Politics', *International Organization* 52(4): 645–85.

Kegley, C. (ed.) (1995) *Controversies in International Relations Theory. Realism and the Neoliberal Challenge*, New York: St Martin's Press.

Kelsen, H. (1950) *The Law of the United Nations*, London: Stevens & Sons.

Kent, A (2007) *Beyond Compliance. China, International Organizations, and Global Security*, Stanford: Stanford University Press.

Keohane, R. (1984) *After Hegemony, Cooperation and Discord in the World Political Economy*, Princeton: Princeton University Press.

—— (ed.) (1986a) *Neorealism and Its Critics*, New York: Columbia University Press.

—— (1986b) 'Theory of world politics: structural realism and beyond', in R. Keohane (ed.) *Neorealism and Its Critics*, New York: Columbia University Press, 158–203.

—— (1993) 'Institutional theory and realist challenge after the Cold War', in D.A. Baldwin (ed.) *Neorealism and Neoliberalism: The Contemporary Debate*, New York: Columbia University Press, 269–300.

—— (1998) 'International institutions: can interdependence work?' *Foreign Policy* Spring: 82–96.

—— (2009) 'The old IPE and the new', *Review of International Political Economy* 16(1): 34–46.

Keohane, R. and Hoffmann, S. (1990) 'Conclusions: community politics and institutional change', in W. Wallace (ed.) *The Dynamics of European Integration*, London: Pinter for the Royal Institute of International Affairs, 276–300.

Keohane, R. and Nye, J.S. (1971) *Transnational Relations and World Politics*, Cambridge, MA: Harvard University Press.

—— (1977) *Power and Interdependence: World Politics in Transition*, Boston, MA: Little Brown.

Keohane, R., Haas, P. and Levy, M. (1995) 'The effectiveness of international environmental institutions', in P. Haas, R. Keohane, and M. Levy (eds) *Institutions for the Earth: Sources of Effective International Environmental Protection*, Cambridge, MA: MIT Press, 3–24.

Keynes, J.M. (1919) *The Economic Consequences of the Peace*, London: Macmillan.

Kindleberger, C.P. (ed.) (1970) *The International Corporation*, Cambridge, MA: MIT Press.

Kirchner, E. and Dominguez, R. (2011) *The Security Governance of Regional Organizations*, Abingdon and New York: Routledge.

Kiss, A. (1998) 'The international protection of the environment', in C. Ku and P. Diehl (eds) *International Law. Classic and Contemporary Readings*, Boulder, CO: Lynne Rienner, 391–414.

Kiss, A. and Shelton, D. (1991) *International Environmental Law*, New York: Transnational Publishers Inc.

Klepacki, Z.L. (1973) *The Organs of International Organizations*, Alphen aan den Rijn: Sijthoff and Nordhoff.

Knutsen, T. (1992) *A History of International Relations Theory*, Manchester and New York: Manchester University Press.

Kozyrev, A. (1990) 'The USSR: new approach to the UN', *International Affairs* (Moscow), July: 12–19.

Krasner, S. (1983) 'Structural causes and regime consequences: regimes as intervening variables', in S. Krasner (ed.) *International Regimes*, Ithaca and London: Cornell University Press, 1–21.

—— (1991) 'Global communications and national power: life on the Pareto frontier', *World Politics* 43(3): 336–66.

Kratochwil, F. (1989) *Rules, Norms and Decisions*, Cambridge Studies in International Relations 2, Cambridge: Cambridge University Press.

Kratochwil, F. and Mansfield, E. (eds) (1994) *International Organization. A Reader*, New York: HarperCollins.

Kratochwil, F. and Ruggie, J. (1994) 'International organization: a state of the art on the art of the state', in F. Kratochwil and E. Mansfield (eds) *International Organization. A Reader*, New York: HarperCollins, 4–19.

Ku, C. and Diehl, P. (eds) (1998a) *International Law. Classic and Contemporary Readings*, Boulder, CO: Lynne Rienner.

—— (1998b) 'International law as operating and normative systems', in C. Ku and P. Diehl (eds) *International Law. Classic and Contemporary Readings,* Boulder, CO: Lynne Rienner, 3–15.

Kubalkova, V. and Cruickshank, A.A. (1980) *Marxism-Leninism and Theory of International Relations,* London: Routledge & Kegan Paul.

Lauterpacht, E. (ed.) (1970) *International Law, Being the Collected Papers of Hersch Lauterpacht, Vol. 1,* Cambridge: Cambridge University Press.

Lauterpacht, Sir H. (1934) *The Development of International Law by the Permanent Court of International Justice,* London: Longman.

Lawson, S. (2012) *International Relations,* 2nd edn, Cambridge: Polity Press.

Light, M. (1988) *The Soviet Theory of International Relations,* Brighton: Wheatsheaf Books.

Lindberg, L.N. (1963) *The Political Dynamics of European Economic Integration,* Stanford, CA: Stanford University Press.

—— (1966) 'Integration as a source of stress on the European Community system', *International Organization* 20: 223–65.

Lindberg, L.N. and Scheingold, S.A. (1970) *Europe's Would-Be Polity,* Englewood Cliffs, NJ: Prentice-Hall.

Lisbonne-de Vergeron, K. (2007) *Contemporary Chinese Views of Europe,* Chatham House Report, London: Royal Institute of International Affairs.

Little, R. and McKinlay, R.D. (1978) 'Linkage-responsiveness and the modern state: an alternative view of interdependence', *British Journal of International Studies* 4(3): 209–25.

Lorimer, J. (1890) *Studies National and International,* Edinburgh: William Green and Sons.

Luard, E. (1977) *International Agencies: The Emerging Framework of Interdependence,* London: Macmillan.

—— (1990) *International Society,* Basingstoke: Macmillan.

McCormick, J.M. and Kihl, Y.W. (1979) 'Intergovernmental organizations and foreign policy behavior: some empirical findings', *American Political Science Review* 73(2): 494–504.

MacKenzie, D. (2010) *A World Beyond Borders: An Introduction to the History of International Organizations,* Toronto: University of Toronto Press.

McLaren, R.I. (1985) 'Mitranian functionalism: possible or impossible?', *Review of International Studies* 11(2): 139–52.

Majone, G. (1994) 'Ideas, interests and institutions: explaining the revival of policy analysis in the 1980s', paper presented at the XVIth World Congress of the IPSA, 21–5 August, Berlin.

Mansbach, R.W., Ferguson, Y.H. and Lambert, D.E. (1976) *The Web of World Politics,* Englewood Cliffs, NJ: Prentice-Hall.

Marks, G., Hooghe, L. and Blank, K. (1996) 'European integration from the 1980s: state-centric v. multi-level governance', *Journal of Common Market Studies* 34(3): 341–78.

Marx, K. and Engels, F. (1965) *Manifesto of the Communist Party,* Moscow: Progress Publishers.

Mazower, M. (2012) *Governing the World: The History of an Idea,* London: Allen Lane.

Mazrui, A. (1967) *Towards a Pax Africana: A Study of Ideology and Ambition,* London: Weidenfeld & Nicolson.

Mearsheimer, J. (1990) 'Back to the future: instability in Europe after the Cold War', *International Security* 15(1): 5–56.

Metz, S. (2000) *Armed Conflict in the 21st Century: The Information Revolution and Post-modern Warfare,* Carlisle, PA: Strategic Studies Institute.

Michalek, S.J. (1971) 'The League of Nations and the United Nations in world politics: a plea for comparative research and universal international organizations', *International Studies Quarterly* 15: 387–441.

Miles, L. (2011) *Fusing with Europe? Sweden in the European Union,* Aldershot, and Burlington, VT: Ashgate.

Mingst, K. and Karns, M. (eds) (2000) *The United Nations in the Post-Cold War Era,* Boulder, CO: Westview Press.

Mitrany, D. (1965) 'The prospect of integration: federal and functional', *Journal of Common Market Studies* 4(2): 119–49.

—— (1966) *A Working Peace System*, Chicago: Quadrangle Books.

—— (1975a) *The Functional Theory of Politics*, London: Martin Robertson.

—— (1975b) 'The prospect of integration: federal or functional', in A.J.R. Groom and P. Taylor (eds) *Functionalism: Theory and Practice in International Relations*, London: University of London Press, 25–37.

Moore, H. and Selchow, S. (2012) 'Global civil society and the internet', in M. Kaldor, H. Moore and S. Selchow (eds) *Global Civil Society 2012*, Houndmills: Palgrave Macmillan.

Moravcsik, A. (1993) 'Preferences and power in the European Community: a liberal intergovernmentalist approach', *Journal of Common Market Studies* 31(4): 473–524.

—— (1998) *The Choice for Europe: Social Purpose and State Power from Messina to Maastricht*, Ithaca, NY: Cornell University Press.

Morgenthau, H.J. (1960) *Politics Among Nations. The Struggle for Power and Peace*, New York: Alfred A. Knopf.

—— (1970) *Truth and Power: Essays of a Decade 1960–70*, London: Pall Mall Press.

Morozov, G. (1977) 'The socialist conception', *International Social Science Journal* 29(1): 28–45.

Moynihan, D. (1979) *Dangerous Place*, London: Secker & Warburg.

Murphy, C.N. (1994) *International Organization and Industrial Change. Global Governance since 1850*, London: Polity Press.

Myrdal, G. (1955) 'Realities and illusions in regard to intergovernmental organisations', in *Hobhouse Memorial Lecture 1955*, London: Oxford University Press, 3–28.

Neumann, I.B. (1994) 'A region-building approach to Northern Europe', *Review of International Studies* 20(1): 53–74.

Nicolson, Sir H. (1969) *Diplomacy*, 3rd edn, London: Oxford University Press.

Niebuhr, R. (1936) *Moral Man and Immoral Society. A Study in Ethics and Politics*, New York: Charles Scribner's Sons.

—— (1948) 'The illusion of world government', *Foreign Affairs* 27: 379–88.

Nørgaard, A.S. (1994) 'Institutions and Post-Modernity in IR: the "New" EC', *Cooperation and Conflict* 29(3): 245–87.

Northedge, F.S. (1976) *The International Political System*, London: Faber.

Nye, J. (1970) 'Comparing common markets: a revised neo-functionalist model', *International Organization* 24(4): 796–835.

—— (1972) 'Regional institutions', in C.E. Black and R.A. Falk (eds) *The Future of the International Legal Order. Vol. IV: The Structure of the International Environment*, Princeton: Princeton University Press.

—— (1995) 'Foreword', in P. Haas, R. Keohane and M. Levy (eds) *Institutions for the Earth: Sources of Effective International Environmental Protection*, Cambridge, MA: MIT Press, ix–xi.

—— (2002) 'Globalism versus globalization', *The Globalist*, www.theglobalist.com/globalism-versus-globalization/ (31 January 2014).

O'Brien, C.C. (1962) *To Katanga and Back*, London: Hutchinson.

O'Brien, C.C. and Topolski, F. (1968) *The UN Sacred Drama*, London: Hutchinson.

OECD (2011) *The Crisis and Beyond*, http://stats.oecd.org/Index.aspx?DatasetCode=SNA_TABLE1 (7 November 2011).

Osakwe, C. (1972) *Participation of the Soviet Union in Universal International Organizations*, Leiden: A.W. Sijthoff.

Ó Tuathail, G. (1996) *Critical Geopolitics. The Politics of Writing Global Space*, London: Routledge.

Padelford, N.J. (1954) 'Regional organization and the United Nations', *International Organization* 8(1): 203–16.

—— (1955) 'Recent developments in regional organizations', *Proceedings of the American Society of International Law*.

Pease, K.-K.S. (2007) *International Organizations: Perspectives on Governance in the Twenty-first Century*, 3rd edn, Upper Saddle River, NJ: Pearson Education Inc.

Peaslee, A.J. (1975) *International Governmental Organizations – Constitutional Documents, Part 2*, 3rd edn, The Hague: Martinus Nijhoff.

Pentland, C. (1976) 'International organizations', in J.N. Rosenau *et al.* (eds) *World Politics – An Introduction*, New York: The Free Press.

Peterson, V.S. and Runyan, A.S. (1993) *Global Gender Issues*, Boulder, CO: Westview Press.

Pevehouse, J. and Russett, B. (2006) 'Democratic international governments promote peace', *International Organization* 60(4): 969–1000.

Phelan, E.T. (1949) *Yes and Albert Thomas*, London: Cresset Press.

Pinder, J. (1991) *European Community*, Oxford: Oxford University Press.

Pinker, S. (2011) *The Better Angels of our Nature*, London: Allen Lane.

Pitt, D. and Weiss, T.G. (eds) (1986) *The Nature of United Nations Bureaucracies*, London: Croom Helm.

Plano, J.C. and Riggs, R.E. (1967) *Forging World Order*, London: Collier/Macmillan.

Porter, B. (ed.) (1972) *The Aberystwyth Papers: International Politics 1919–1969*, Oxford: Oxford University Press.

Princen, T. and Finger, M. (1994) *Environmental NGOs in World Politics. Linking the Local and the Global*, London and New York: Routledge.

Prügl, E. (2004) 'International institutions and feminist politics', *The Brown Journal of World Affairs* X(2): 69–84.

Putin, V. (2014) 'President Putin's address to parliament over Crimea', *RT*, http://rt.com/politics/official-word/vladimir-putin-crimea-address-658/ (24 March 2014).

Raghaven, C. (1990) *Recolonization, GATT, the Uruguay Round and the Third World*, London and New Jersey: Zed Books.

Reinalda, B. (2009) *Routledge History of International Organizations*, London and New York: Routledge.

—— (ed.) (2013) *Routledge Handbook of International Organization*, London and New York: Routledge.

Reuter, P. (1958) *International Institutions*, London: Allen & Unwin.

Richards, J. (1999) 'Toward a positive theory of international institutions: regulating international aviation markets', *International Organization* 53(1): 1–37.

Rittberger, V. and Zangl, B. (2006) *International Organization. Polity, Politics and Policies*, Houndmills and New York: Palgrave and Macmillan.

Roberts, A. and Kingsbury, B. (1989) *United Nations, Divided World. The UN's Roles in International Relations*, Oxford: Clarendon Press.

Rochester, J.M. (1974) *International Institutions and World Order: The International System as a Prismatic Polity*, Beverly Hills and London: Sage Professional Papers in International Studies.

—— (1990) 'Global policy and the future of the United Nations', *Journal of Peace Research* 27(2): 141–5.

Roginko, A.Y. (1989) 'Arctic environmental cooperation: incentives and obstacles', *Current Research in Peace and Violence* 12(3): 133–43.

Rosecrance, R., Alexander, A., Koehler, W., Kroll, J., Laqueuer, S. and Stoeker, J. (1977) 'Whither interdependence?', *International Organization* 31: 425–72.

Rosenau, J. and Czempiel, E-O. (1992) *Governance without Government: Order and Change in World Government*, Cambridge Studies in International Relations 20, Cambridge: Cambridge University Press.

Rosenau, J.N., Thompson, K.W. and Boyd, G. (eds) (1976) *World Politics – An Introduction*, New York: The Free Press.

Royal Institute of International Affairs (RIIA) (1946) *United Nations Documents 1941–1945*, London: Royal Institute of International Affairs.

Russell, R. and Muther, J.E. (1958) *A History of the United Nations Charter. The Role of the United States 1940–1945*, Washington, DC: The Brookings Institution.

Russett, B.M. (1967) *International Regions and the International System: A Study in Political Ecology*, Chicago: Rand McNally.

Russett, B.M. and Starr, H. (1992) *World Politics: The Menu for Choice*, 4th edn, San Francisco: W.H. Freeman.

Saarikoski, V. (1995) 'Regional alternatives: the breaking of the Europe between?', in C. Archer and O-P. Jalonen (eds) *Changing European Security Landscape*, Tampere: University of Tampere, 228–56.

Saeter, M. (1991) 'Föderalismus und Konföderalismus als Strukturelemente europäischer Zussamenarbeit Zur Vergangheit und Zukunft von EG und KSZE', in W. Link, E.Schütt-Wetschky and G.Schwan (eds) *Jahrbuch Für Politik/Yearbook of Politics*, Berlin: Nomos.

Sandholz, W. and Stone Sweet, A. (2010) *Neo-functionalism and Supranational Governance*, http://scienze politiche.unical.it/bacheca/archivio/materiale/1821/OPE%202010-2011/neofunctionalim%20and%20suprnational%20governance.pdf (8 June 2014).

Scharf, M. (2007) *The Law of International Organizations. Problems and Materials*, 2nd edn, Durham, NC: Carolina Academic Press.

Schermers, H.G. (1972) *International Institutional Law. Vol. 1: Structure*, Leiden: A.W. Sijthoff.

Schiavone, G. (2008) *International Organizations. A Dictionary and Directory*, 7th edn, Basingstoke and New York: Palgrave Macmillan.

Scholte, J.A. (1993) 'From power politics to social change: an alternative focus for international studies', *Review of International Studies* 54(Spring): 281–301.

—— (2000) 'Global civil society', in N. Woods (ed.) *The Political Economy of Globalization*, Basingstoke: Macmillan, 173–201.

Schwarzenberger, G. (1941) *Power Politics*, London: Cape.

Selznick, P. (1957) *Leadership in Administration*, New York: Harper & Row.

Sheets, T. and Maarer, C. (eds) (2000) *The European Directory of International Organization 2000*, London: Europa.

Shevardnadze, E. (1990) 'Foreign policy and science', *International Affairs* (Moscow), March: 23ff.

Sieberson, S.C. (2008) *Dividing Lines between the European Union and its Member States: The Impact of the Treaty of Lisbon*, The Hague: Asser Press.

Sierra, J. (ed.) (1974) *Desarrollo Latinoamericano: Ensayos Criticos*, Mexico City: Fondo de Cultura Economica.

Sills, D. (ed.) (1968) *International Encyclopedia of the Social Sciences*, vol. 8, New York: Macmillan and Free Press.

Singer, D. and Wallace, M. (1970) 'Intergovernmental organization and the preservation of peace, 1918–64', *International Organization* 24(3): 520–47.

Skjelsbaek, K. (1971) 'The growth of international non-governmental organisation in the twentieth century', *International Organization* 25(3): 420–42.

Smith, S. (1997) 'New approaches to international theory', in J. Baylis and S. Smith (eds) *The Globalization of World Politics*, Oxford: Oxford University Press.

Snidal, D. (1990) 'IGOs, regimes, and cooperation: challenges for international relations theory', in M. Karns and K. Mingst (eds) *The United States and Multilateral Institutions*, London and New York: Routledge.

Society for Anglo-Chinese Understanding (SACU) (1979) *China's World View*, London: Anglo–Chinese Cultural Institute.

Soroos, M. (1986) *Beyond Sovereignty: The Challenge of Global Policy*, Columbia: University of South Carolina Press.

Southern African Customs Union (2014) *Welcome to the SACU website*, www.sacu.int/ (7 February 2014).

Speeckaert, G.P. (1957) 'The 1,978 international organizations founded since the Congress of Vienna: a chronological list', *Documents for the Study of International Nongovernmental Relations*, no. 7, Brussels: Union of International Associations.

Spillius, A. and Waterfield, B. (2010) 'Wikileaks: UN angrily hits back at US "interference"', *Daily Telegraph*, 29 November, www.telegraph.co.uk/news/worldnews/northamerica/usa/8168966/Wikileaks-UN-angrily-hits-back-at-US-interference.html (16 March 2014).

Sterling, R.W. (1974) *Macropolitics: International Relations in a Global Society*, New York: Alfred A. Knopf.

Strong, M. (1990) 'What place will the environment have in the next century – and at what price?', *International Environmental Affairs* 2(3): 211–12.

Sullivan, M.P. (1978) 'Competing frameworks and the study of contemporary international politics', *Millennium: Journal of International Studies* 7(2): 93–110.

Sylvester, C. (1994) *Feminist Theory and International Relations in a Postmodern Era*, Cambridge: Cambridge University Press.

Symonds, R. (1971) 'Functional agencies and international administration', in R.S. Jordan (ed.) *International Administration: Its Evolution and Contemporary Applications*, New York: Oxford University Press.

Szasz, P.C. (1981) 'Thomas Jefferson conceives an international organization', *American Journal of International Law* 75: 138–40.

Tallberg, J., Sommerer, T., Squatrito, T. and Jönsson, C. (2013) *The Opening Up of International Organizations. Transnational Access in Global Governance*, Cambridge and New York: Cambridge University Press.

Tandon, Y. (1978) 'The integration of international institutions from a Third World Perspective', in P. Taylor and A.J.R. Groom (eds) *International Organisation: A Conceptual Approach*, London: Frances Pinter, 365–77.

Teubner, G. (ed.) (1997) *Global Law without a State*, Aldershot: Dartmouth.

Thakur, R. and Weiss, T.G. (2006) *The UN and Global Governance*, Bloomington, IN: Indiana University Press.

Tharp, P.A. (ed.) (1971) *Regional International Organisations: Structures and Functions*, London: St Martin's Press.

Thatcher, M. (1993) *The Downing Street Years*, London: HarperCollins.

Thomas, J. and Meyer, M. (1997) *The New Rules of Global Trade. A Guide to the World Trade Organization*, Ontario: Carswell.

Tranholm-Mikkelsen, J. (1991) 'Neofunctionalism: obsolete or obstinate? A reappraisal in the light of the new dynamism of the EC', *Millennium: Journal of International Studies* 20(1): 1–22.

Turner, E.A.L. (2010) 'Why has the number of international non-governmental organizations exploded since 1960?', *Cliodynamics: the Journal of Theoretical and Mathematical History* 1: 81–91.

Union of International Associations (1974) *Yearbook of International Organizations,* 15th edn, Brussels: Union of International Associations.

—— (1999) *Statistics: International Organizations by Year and Type 1909–1999,* www.uia.be/fr/statistics-international-organizations-year-and-type-1909–1999 (12 February 2012).

—— (2014) *Yearbook of International Organizations, 2014/2015 – Vol. 1: Organization Descriptions and Cross-References*, Brill: Leiden.

United Nations (2000) 'Report of the Secretary-General on the work of the organization', *General Assembly Official Records*. Fifty-fifth series, supplement No. 1, New York: United Nations.

—— (2004) *A More Secured World. Our Shared Responsibility.Report of the High-Level Panel on Threats, Challenges and Change*, www.un.org/en/peacebuilding/pdf/historical/hlp_more_secure_world.pdf (20 March 2014).

—— (2011) *Promoting Peaceful, Political Solutions to Conflict*, www.un.org/wcm/content/site/undpa/ (25 September 2013).

—— (2013a) *United Nations Current Peacekeeping Operations*, www.un.org/en/peacekeeping/documents/operationslist.pdf (25 September 2013).

—— (2013b) 'United Nations mission to investigate allegations of the use of chemical weapons in the Syrian Arab Republic Report on the alleged use of chemical weapons in the Ghouta area of Damascus on 21 August 2013', www.un.org/disarmament/content/slideshow/Secretary_General_Report_of_CW_Investigation.pdf (25 September 2013).

—— (2014) *OPCW-UN Joint Mission*, http://opcw.unmissions.org/Default.aspx?tabid=6576& language=en-US (2 March 2014).

United Nations Department of Economic and Social Affairs NGO Branch (2009) *Introduction to ECOSOC Consultative Status*, http://esango.un.org/paperless/Web?page=static&content=intro (15 February 2014).

United Nations Department of Peacekeeping Operations (2003) *Handbook on United Nations Multidimensional Peacekeeping Operations*, www.peacekeepingbestpractices.unlb.org/Pbps/library/Handbook%20on%20UN%20PKOs.pdf (20 March 2014).

United Nations Department of Political Affairs (2009) *Repertoire of the Practice of the Security Council 16th Supplement 2008–2009*, www.un.org/en/sc/repertoire/2008–9/Part%20VII/08–09_Part%20VII.pdf#page = 168 (10 February 2014).

United Nations General Assembly (2004) 'Fifty-eighth session. Agenda item 59. Strengthening the United Nations System', http://daccess-dds-ny.un.org/doc/UNDOC/GEN/N04/376/41/PDF/N0437641.pdf?OpenElement (4 April 2011).

—— (2011) 'United Nations Programme of Assistance in the Teaching, Study, Dissemination and Wider Appreciation of International Law (Agenda item 80)', www.un.org/en/ga/sixth/66/PoA.shtml (6 June 2014).

United Nations Office at Vienna (2014) *NGO Liaison Service*, www.unvienna.org/unov/en/ngo_liaison_service.html (17 February 2014).

United Nations Office of the Special Advisor on the Prevention of Genocide (2012) *Responsibility to Protect*, www.un.org/en/preventgenocide/adviser/responsibility.shtml (27 March 2014).

United Nations Peacebuilding Commission (2012) 'The Peacebuilding Commission (PBC)', www.un.org/en/peacebuilding/ (25 September 2013).

United Nations Peacekeeping (2013) 'Peacekeeping Fact Sheet', www.un.org/en/peacekeeping/resources/statistics/factsheet.shtml (11 February 2014).

United States Census Bureau (2012) *U.S. and World Population Clock*, www.census.gov/popclock/ (31 March 2014).

—— (2014) *Population Clock*, www.census.gov/ (10 June 2014).

Urquhart, B. (1990) 'Beyond the "sheriff's posse"', *Survival* 32(3): 195–205.

Vasquez, J.A. (1979) 'Colouring it Morgenthau: new evidence for an old thesis on quantitative international politics', *British Journal of International Studies* 5(3): 21–8.

Verrier, A. (1981) *International Peacekeeping*, Harmondsworth: Penguin.

Viotti, P. and Kaupi, M. (1999) *International Relations Theory. Realism, Pluralism, Globalism, and Beyond*, 3rd edn, Boston, MA: Allyn and Bacon.

Virally, M. (1977) 'Definition and classification: a legal approach', *International Social Science Journal* 29(1): 58–72.

Vitali, S., Glattfelder, J.B. and Battiston, S. (2011) 'The network of global corporate control', *arXiv:1107.5728v2 {q-fin.GN}* 19 Sep: 1–36, http://arxiv.org/pdf/1107.5728.pdf (28 September 2013).

Volgy, T.J., Fausett, E., Grant, K.A. and Rodgers, S. (2008) 'Indentifying formal intergovernmental organizations', *Journal of Peace Research* 45(6) 837–50.

Waever, O., Buzan, B., Kelstrup, M. and Lemaitre, P. (1993) *Identity, Migration and the New Security Agenda in Europe*, London: Pinter.

Wagner, R.H. (1974) 'Dissolving the state: three recent perspectives on international relations', *International Organization* 28(2): 435–66.

Wallace, M. and Singer, D. (1970) 'Intergovernmental organization in the global system 1815–1964', *International Organization* 24(2): 239–87.

Waltz, K. (1970) 'The myth of national interdependence', in C.P. Kindleberger (ed.) *The International Corporation*, Cambridge, MA: MIT, 205–23.

—— (1979) *Theories of International Relations*, Cambridge, MA: Addison-Wesley.

—— (1986) 'Political structures', in R. Keohane (ed.), *Neorealism and Its Critics*, New York: Columbia University Press, 70–97.

Ward, B. and Dubos, R. (1972) *Only One Earth. The Care and Maintenance of a Small Planet*, Harmondsworth: Penguin.

Warleigh, A. (1998) 'Better the devil you know? Synthetic and confederal understandings of European integration', *West European Politics* 21(3): 1–18.

Webber, D. (2006) 'Regional integration in Europe and Asia: a historical perspective', in B. Fort and D. Webber (eds) *Regional Integration in East Asia and Europe: Convergence or Divergence?* Abingdon: Routledge, 289–311.

Weintraub, S. (1977) 'The role of the United Nations in economic negotiations', in D.A. Kay (ed.) *The Changing United Nations*, New York: Academy of Political Science.

Weiss, T. (1982) 'International bureaucracy: myth and reality of the international civil service', *International Affairs* 58(2): 286–306.

—— (ed.) (1998) *Beyond UN Subcontracting: Task-sharing with Regional Security Arrangements and Service-providing NGOs*, Basingstoke and New York: Macmillan and St Martin's Press.

—— (2009) 'The UN's Role in Global Governance', *UN Intellectual Briefing Project. Briefing Note* Number 15, www.unhistory.org/briefing/15GlobalGov.pdf (13 February 2014).

Weiss, T. and Gordenker, L. (eds) (1996) *NGOs, the UN and Global Governance*, Boulder, CO: Lynne Rienner.

Wells, L.J. (1971) 'The multinational business enterprise: what kind of international organization?', in R.O. Keohane and J.S. Nye (eds) *Transnational Relations and World Politics*, Cambridge, MA: Harvard University Press, 97–114.

Wessels, W. (2001) 'Nice results: the millennium IGC in the EU's evolution', *Journal of Common Market Studies* 39: 197–219.

—— (2005) 'The constitutional treaty-three readings from a fusion perspective', *Journal of Common Market Studies, Annual Review 2004/2005*: 11–36.

Whitworth, S. (1997) *Feminism and International Relations: Towards a Political Economy of Gender in Interstate and Non-Governmental Institutions*, Basingstoke: Macmillan Press.

Wight, M. (1968) 'Why is there no international relations theory?', in Butterfield, H. and Wight, M. (eds) *Diplomatic Investigations*, Cambridge, MA: Harvard University Press, 17–35.

—— (1991) *International Theory: The Three Traditions*, Leicester: Leicester University Press.

Willetts, P. (1990) 'Transactions, networks and systems', in A.J.R. Groom and P. Taylor (eds) *Framework for International Co-operation*, London: Frances Pinter, 255–84.

—— (ed.) (1996) *The Conscience of the World: The Influence of Non-Governmental Organizations in the UN System*, London: Hurst.

—— (2010) *Non-Governmental Organizations in World Politics*, London and New York: Routledge.

Wohlforth, W. (2008) 'Realism', in C. Reus-Smit and D. Snidal (eds) *The Oxford Handbook of International Relations*, Oxford: Oxford University Press, 131–49.

Wolfers, A. (1962) 'The actors in international politics', in A. Wolfers (ed.) *Discord and Collaboration*, Baltimore: Johns Hopkins University Press.

Woolf, L. (1916) *International Government*, 2nd edn, London: Allen & Unwin.

World Bank (2012) *The Little Data Book on Information and Communication Technology*, www.itu.int/ITU-D/ict/publications/material/LDB_ICT_2012.pdf (26 September 2012).

—— (2013) *Governance & Public Sector Management*, http://go.worldbank.org/SGO4LFRSS0 (14 February 2014).

—— (2014) *Poverty Overview*, www.worldbank.org/en/topic/poverty/overview (20 March 2014).

World Commission on Environment and Development (1987) *Our Common Future*, Brundtland report, Oxford: Oxford University Press.

World Council of Churches (2014) *Public Statements, Speeches, Sermons, Letters and Other Official Texts by the General Secretary*, www.oikoumene.org/en/resources/documents/general-secretary (12 February 2014).

Wright, Q. (1965) *A Study of War*, 2nd edn, Chicago: University of Chicago Press.

Wright, S. (1993) 'Human rights and women's rights: an analysis of the United Nations Convention on the Elimination of All Forms of Discrimination Against Women', in K.E. Mahoney and P. Mahoney (eds) *Human Rights in the Twenty-first Century. A Global Challenge*, Dordrecht, Boston and London: Martinus Nijhoff, Kluwer Law, 75–88.

Yalem, R. (1965) *Regionalism and World Order*, Washington, DC: Public Affairs Press.
—— (1966) 'The study of international organization, 1920–65; a study of the literature', *Background* 10(1): 1–56.
Yeselson, A. and Gaglione, A. (1974) *A Dangerous Place – The United Nations as a Weapon in World Politics*, New York: Grossman.
Young, O. (1989) *International Cooperation. Building Regimes for Natural Resources and the Environment*, Ithaca and London: Cornell University Press.
—— (1994) *International Governance. Protecting the Environment in a Stateless Society*, Ithaca and London: Cornell University Press.
Zacher, M. with Sutton, B. (1996) *Governing Global Networks. International Regimes for Transportation and Communications*, New York: Cornell University Press.
Zimmern, Sir A. (1939) *The League of Nations and the Rule of Law*, 2nd edn, London: Macmillan.

## Websites

Anti-Slavery International, www.antislavery.org (25 September 2013)
Council of the Baltic Sea States, www.cbss.org (26 March 2014)
European Central Bank, www.ecb.int (30 November 2012)
European Union, http://europa.eu (26 March 2014)
European Union, Eurobarometer, http://ec.europa.eu/public_opinion/index_en.htm (26 March 2014)
Elizabethtown College *The WWW Virtual Library: International Affairs Resources*, www2.etown.edu/vl/ (25 March 2014)
Global Governance A Review of Multilateralism and International Organizations, http://journals.rienner.com/loi/ggov (26 March 2014)
Global Policy Forum, www.globalpolicy.org/ (26 March 2014)
Global Policy Forum NGOs, www.globalpolicy.org/ngos.html (26 March 2014)
Greenpeace International, www.greenpeace.org (26 March 2014)
Human Rights Watch, www.hrw.org (26 March 2014)
International Court of Justice, www.icj-cij.org (26 March 2014)
International Criminal Court, www.icc-cpi.int/en_menus/icc/Pages/default.aspx (26 March 2014)
International Federation of University Women, www.ifuw.org (26 March 2014)
International Organization, http://journals.cambridge.org/action/displayJournal?jid=INO (26 March 2014)
International Studies Association International Organization section, www.isanet.org/ISA/Sections/IO.aspx (26 March 2014)
North Atlantic Treaty Organization, www.nato.int (26 March 2014)
Organization for Security and Cooperation in Europe, www.osce.org (26 March 2014)
Organization for the Prohibition of Chemical Weapons, www.opcw.org/ (15 January 2014)
Rotary International, www.rotary.org (26 March 2014)
Salvation Army International, www.salvationarmy.org (26 March 2014)
South African-Botswana-Lesotho-Swaziland Customs Union, www.sacu.int/about.php?id=396 (28 March 2014)
Union of International Associations, www.uia.org (26 March 2014)
United Nations, www.un.org (26 March 2014)
United Nations *An Agenda for Peace. Preventive diplomacy, peacemaking and peacekeeping*, www.un.org/en/ga/search/view_doc.asp?symbol = A/47/277 (26 March 2014)
United Nations *Report of the Panel on UN Peace Operations*. Brahimi Report, www.un.org/en/ga/search/view_doc.asp?symbol = A/55/305 (26 March 2014)
United Nations *Current Peacekeeping Operations*, www.un.org/en/peacekeeping/operations/current.shtml (26 March 2014)
United Nations *United Nations and Civil Society*, www.un.org/en/civilsociety/index.shtml (26 March 2014)

United Nations *United Nations Peacekeeping*, www.un.org/en/peacekeeping (26 March 2014)

United Nations "We the Peoples": Press Release GA/9704, www.un.org/News/Press/docs/2000/20000403.ga9704.doc.html (26 March 2014)

United Nations *Promoting Peaceful, Political Solutions to Conflict*, www.un.org/wcm/content/site/undpa/ (2 April 2011).

United Nations (2012) List of Peacekeeping Operations 1948–2013, www.un.org/en/peacekeeping/documents/operationslist.pdf (26 March 2014)

United Nations Department of Political Affairs *Peacemaking and conflict prevention.* www.un.org/wcm/content/site/undpa/main/issues/peacemaking (26 March 2014)

United Nations Development Programme *Democratic Governance*, www.undp.org/content/undp/en/home/ourwork/democraticgovernance/overview.html (29 November 2012)

United Nations General Assembly *Resolution adopted by the General Assembly 60/1. 2005 World Summit Outcome.* www.un.org/en/preventgenocide/adviser/pdf/World%20Summit%20Outcome%20Document.pdf#page=30 (26 September 2012)

United Nations Peacebuilding Commission *United Nations Peacebuilding Commission.* www.un.org/en/peacebuilding/ (26 September 2012)

United Nations Trusteeship Council, www.un.org/en/mainbodies/trusteeship/ (26 March 2014)

World Bank Group *Governance & Public Sector Management* http://go.worldbank.org/SGO4LFRSS0 (25 March 2014)

World Health Organization, www.who.int (26 March 2014)

World Organization of the Scout Movement, www.scout.org/worldscouting (15 February 2014)

World Trade Organization, http://wto.org (29 November 2012)

Yahoo's Government, International Organizations site, http:// dir.yahoo.com/Government/international_organizations/ (26 January 2001)

*The Yearbook of International Organizations*, www.uia.org/yearbook (26 March 2014)

# Index

Made in the USA
Las Vegas, NV
07 February 2023

67075491R00111